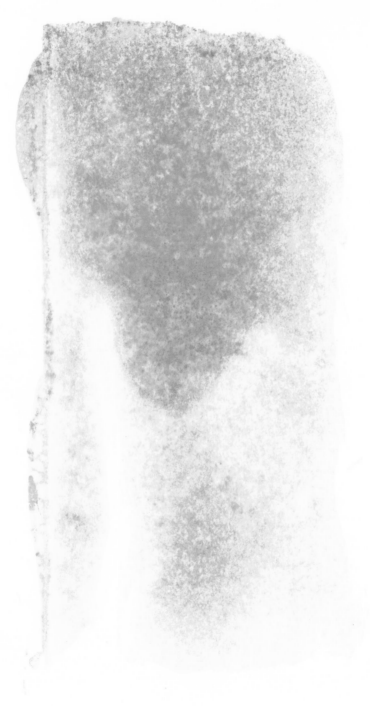

*State Building
and
Conflict Resolution
in
Colombia,
1986–1994*

State Building
and
Conflict Resolution
in
Colombia,
1986–1994

Harvey F. Kline

The University of Alabama Press

Tuscaloosa and London

1 2 3 4 5 6 7 8 9 10 / 07 06 05 04 03 02 01 00 99 98

∞

The paper on which this book is printed meets the minimum requirements of
American National Standard for Information Science-Permanence of Paper for
Printed Library Materials, ANSI Z39.48-1984.

Library of Congress Cataloging-in-Publication Data

Kline, Harvey F.
State building and conflict resolution in Colombia, 1986–1994 /
Harvey F. Kline.
p. cm.
Includes bibliographical references and index.
ISBN 0-8173-0943-8 (alk. paper)
1. Colombia—Politics and government—1974– 2. Conflict
managment—Colombia. 3. Barco, Virgilio. 4. Gaviria Trujillo,
Cesar. 5. Guerrillas—Colombia. 6. Paramilitary forces—Colombia.
7. Narcotics dealers—Colombia. 8. Human rights—Colombia. I. Title.
F2279 .K54 1999
320.9861'09'048—ddc21
98-25405
CIP

British Library Cataloguing-in-Publication data available

Dedicated with Love to the Memory of

Ray Martin Kline

1897–1966

and

David Atwell Rendleman, Jr.

1919–1997

Neither ever visited Colombia nor wrote a book. Both planted trees—but more important, both guaranteed their immortalities by having children.

Contents

Tables

Preface

This is the fifth book I have written about Colombia, including the one I coauthored with Gary Hoskin, Francisco Leal, Dora Rothlisberger, and Armando Borrero at the Universidad de los Andes in the early 1970s. Those books have come from research trips to Colombia in 1968–1970, 1974, 1980–1981, 1991, 1992, and 1994.

To collect data for this book, I made four trips to Bogotá. The dates of the trips were (1) June 15–August 1, 1991, (2) July 1–29, 1992, (3) May 17–June 1, 1994, and (4) July 25–August 2, 1995. The point of the first trip in 1991 was to study the constituent assembly, which was still meeting. In 1992 the negotiations with the *Coordinadora Guerrillera Simón Bolívar* were being emphasized; in 1994, the priority was on the drug and paramilitary groups. Although the 1995 trip was primarily to give some of the results of this research at the meeting of the *Asociación de Colombianistas,* I used the opportunity to collect recent publications related to the theme of this book and to reinterview several of the individuals who had already proved to be of great value.

My research techniques were different on each trip, and in these first pages I would like to answer questions about *why, how,* and *who* with regard to this book.

I remember very well that the *why* question first came from a friend in Washington, D.C., in early 1991, before I began this project. "Why take the risk," he asked, "of going to a country with so much violence since you are already a tenured, full professor?" There is no simple answer to this question, although it turned out that I was barely affected by the violence so rampant in Colombia, including in Bogotá. In part it was because I was eager to get back to research after a seven-year hiatus spent in university administration, and I had many contacts in Bogotá from previous trips. Also I had many good friends in Colombia who were always willing to share their time and affection.

Another part was that I had used secondary sources to follow closely the growth of Colombian turbulence in the Betancur and Barco years (1982–1990). I had read and written about the assassination of Luis Carlos Galán—a leading candidate for president in 1990 and a man my age whom I had interviewed in 1981. Also I was intrigued by the constituent assembly and by the plans of the new Colombian president to resolve the conflicts.

Because conflict resolution was one matter of concern to the United States Institute of Peace, I submitted a proposal and received a grant from the institute that made three trips to Bogotá possible; on those trips I collected information for this book. I am grateful to the Institute of Peace for that support, but of course they have no responsibility for the contents of this book. That is mine alone.

As for the *how* question, the answer to that changed dramatically during the course of this investigation. In writing the original proposal for the project, I had anticipated conducting many more interviews than, in the end, I conducted. As I explained to the helpful people at the institute, I had suspected during my 1980–1981 research trip—and a decade later confirmed—that a group of Colombian social scientists were already doing the research I had proposed to do for the Betancur period. They had also done most of the research I proposed for the Barco period, and even some for the Gaviria years. I decided that it was both redundant and imperialistic for the visiting *gringo* to redo what had been done so well by Colombians, many of whom had Ph.D.s from prestigious universities in the United States and Europe. As a result of that decision, I often quoted from the Colombians' publications when they supplied information that I would have had to conduct interviews to get. When the subject was the Gaviria government, and when the Colombian investigations had not yet been published, I interviewed the researchers, who gladly shared their information with me.

There are two sets of interviews in this book. The first set was conducted in 1991 by Colombian professors from the Departamento de Ciencia Política of the Universidad de los Andes; they interviewed seventeen members of the constituent assembly and one presidential adviser between July and December. The eighteen were selected using two criteria: (1) that at least one delegate from every political movement be interviewed and (2) that the most influential delegates in each movement be interviewed.

Because of my close association with the *departamento* (not only during this study but also during visits as professor and researcher in 1968–1970, 1974, and 1980–1981), I was allowed to add two questions to the interviews: "In the matter of peace in Colombia, what importance did the national constituent assembly have? Did it accomplish what you hoped?" The questions were posed in this way to see what the members of the assembly thought would be the specific characteristics of the new constitution that might lead to conflict resolution. I added this question to a questionnaire that included many other questions that were being used by a team in the Departamento de Ciencia Política to write a book on the assembly. I am particularly indebted to Gabriel Murillo, then director of the *departamento,* and John Dugas, head of the *Constituyente* project, for allowing me to add these questions. Analysis of them, however, is my responsibility.

In addition, I conducted seventeen interviews during the three trips to Bogotá. As will be noted, they included both Colombian government members and Colombian scholars. The former were chosen because of their positions dealing with the issues of peace that are covered in this book, whereas the scholars were chosen because of their known expertise on the issues.

In all interviews, the respondents were informed that the author was funded by the United States Institute of Peace but that, as an independent scholar, he would analyze the information himself. They were also given the right to refuse to be interviewed, even in light of a promise that their names would not be used and that they would not be described in a way that would allow knowledgeable people to identify them.

I used no recording devices during the interviews. Instead, I made extensive notes on the comments immediately after the interviews and reconstructed them as soon as possible by writing them out on a computer. In the book, where quotations are indicated as coming from interviews, the material between quotation marks is my paraphrase of comments.

Two other interviews are quoted in this book, having been carried out in Bogotá in relation to another book. A complete list of interviews, both by the Universidad de los Andes Constituyente Team and by the author, appears in the bibliography.

A final note about the *how* question includes the use of secondary sources. Even before I began making trips to Bogotá, I read, every week, *El Espectador, Semana,* and *Noticias de Colombia (NOTICOL)*—an Internet source based at the Universidad de los Andes in Bogotá that sent daily selections scanned from various Colombian newspapers— as well as the *New York Times;* I read scholarly literature as well. In Bogotá in 1991, I used two major sources of published information to find the new features that had been added to the constitution to resolve conflict: (1) articles in national newspapers from January 1990 through July 1991, as compiled in the data bank on the constituent assembly of the Departamento de Ciencia Política of the Universidad de los Andes, and (2) the *Gaceta Constitucional,* official publication of the assembly, collected in the same data bank. In both 1992 and 1994

I once again consulted the newspaper clippings of the Departamento de Ciencia Política of the Universidad de los Andes on the other themes of this book. (All sources are listed in the notes.)

I think the extensive use of those sources is justifiable for at least three reasons. First, many of the quotes from newspapers and magazines are from reporters' interviews with government officials, guerrilla and paramilitary leaders, and representatives of the drug groups. As such the information is primary rather than secondary, unless contradicted by the interviewee. Second, as this is a book about the governance struggle, much of the public debate is carried out in the mass media. Information from the media, whether factually correct or not, is often perceived to be so by many of the Colombian participants in the debates. Egregious errors also lead to public replies.

Third, those are the sources used by Colombian social scientists; interviewing the participants on one side of the debate—current guerrilla fighters, drug dealers, and members of paramilitary squads—is simply too dangerous. If Colombians cannot do it because of the risk involved, how can a North American social scientist think of trying?

Finally, the answer to the *who* question: In addition to the United States Institute of Peace, dozens of Colombians spent time with me. Many good friends at the Universidad de los Andes helped me by making suggestions, just as they had on the three previous research trips. This time they were joined by new friends in the *Instituto de Estudios Políticos y Relaciones Internacionales* of the Universidad Nacional. Second, five individuals (three from the Universidad de los Andes and two from Universidad Nacional)—experts on the constituent assembly, negotiations with the guerrilla groups, the drug trade, and paramilitary groups—read first drafts of chapters 6 through 9, making suggestions for corrections and additions.

My sincere thanks go to all of these individuals. I look forward to their appraisals of the final product. Even more I look forward to returning to a Colombia that has indeed resolved its conflicts.

My appreciation also goes to John Martz. As my first professor of Latin American politics, it was his enthusiasm about studying Latin America that led me to follow that career. In addition to being a role model and mentor, he was a friend. Our paths crossed in Bogotá while I was working on this book, and I was certain that our mutual interest in Latin America would bring us together many other times after that. Although his sudden death in Caracas in August 1998 means that I will not have that opportunity, he will always remain my intellectual inspiration.

Finally, let me say a few words about the dedication. One of the constant themes of this book is the loss of human life to the endemic violence in Colombia. As the process of publishing this research was nearing its end, my father-in-law, David Atwell Rendleman, Jr., died as a result of cardiovascular problems, not of violence. Years before, as I was finishing my undergraduate days, my father, Ray Martin Kline, died of a similar illness. And during my five years of living in Colombia, a former student of mine was kidnapped and killed, presumably by a guerrilla group. Luis Carlos Galán, whom I greatly admired and whom I interviewed, died from narco bullets.

I learned some time ago a saying in Colombia: An individual can do three things to guarantee immortality—plant a tree, write a book, or have a child. The most essential thing connecting the two men in whose memory this book is dedicated was their children. The key thing that distinguished them from citizens of Colombia, where the primary cause of death is homicide, is that they lived their God-given years without human intervention prematurely ending their years on earth.

¡Ojalá Colombia llegue a tal situación dentro de poco!

Acronyms

ACDEGAM	*Asociación Campesina de Agricultores y Ganaderos del Magdalena Medio* (Association of Ranchers and Peasants of the Magdalena Medio)
AD-M19	*Alianza Democrática M-19* (Democratic Alliance M-19)
ANAPO	*Alianza Nacional Popular* (National Popular Alliance)
ANDI	*Asociación Nacional de Industriales* (National Association of Industrialists)
ARENA	*Alianza Republicana Nacional* (Nationalist Republican Alliance)
CGSB	*Coordinadora Guerrillera Simón Bolívar* (Simón Bolívar Guerrilla Coordinator)
CNG	*Coordinadora Nacional Guerrillera* (National Guerrilla Coordinator)
CRS	*Corriente de Renovación Socialista* (Socialist Renovation Current)
CTC	*Confederación de Trabajadores Colombianos* (Confederation of Colombian Workers)
DAS	*Departamento Administrativo de Seguridad* (Administrative Department of Security)
ELN	*Ejército de Liberación Nacional* (Army of National Liberation)
EPL	*Ejército de Liberación Popular* (Army of Popular Liberation)
FARC	*Fuerzas Armadas de la Revolución Colombiana* (Armed Forces of the Colombian Revolution)

FEDECAFE   *Federación Nacional de Cafeteros* (National Federation of Coffee Growers)

M-19   *Movimiento 19 de Abril* (19th of April Movement)

MAS   *Muerte a Secuestradores* (Death to Kidnappers)

MORENA   *Movimiento de Restauración Nacional* (Movement of National Restoration)

MRN   *Movimiento Muerte a Revolucionarios del Nordeste Antioqueño* (Death to Revolutionaries of the Antioquian Northeast Movement)

MSN   *Movimiento de Salvación Nacional* (Movement of National Salvation)

PSC   *Partido Social Conservador* (Social Conservative Party)

SAC   *Sociedad de Agricultores Colombianos* (Society of Colombian Farmers)

UP   *Unión Patriótica* (Patriotic Union)

*State Building
and
Conflict Resolution
in
Colombia,
1986–1994*

1

Introduction

Attempts at Conflict Resolution in Colombia, 1986–1994

This book presents a study of two Colombian presidents' attempts to resolve the conflicts in their country. Both President Virgilio Barco Vargas (1986–1990) and President César Gaviria Trujillo (1990–1994) felt they had to do something to end the use of violence by leftist guerrillas, drug dealers, and paramilitary groups. Those groups were using violence against the government, as well as the people, and were thereby controlling vast areas of the country. In reaction, the government itself was at times violating the human rights of Colombians.

Previous chief executives had used force primarily to suppress law-breaking groups, with only limited results. For example, Barco's immediate predecessor, Belisario Betancur Cuartas (1982–1986), had negotiated cease-fires with guerrilla groups, but all efforts failed in the end. So, both President Barco and President Gaviria sought peaceful ways out of the conflicts. In so doing they were attempting to change patterns that had been established in more than 150 years of Colombian history.

All of the policies of the two presidents included some form of bargaining—either through formal negotiations, as with the guerrilla groups, or more indirectly, as with drug dealers and paramilitary groups. This study will show that the Barco and Gaviria administrations had some successes in these efforts but that they also had many failures. It will also show that human rights violations and common crime rose during the two presidencies.

State Building and the Colombian Background

The purpose of this chapter is to place the Colombian case within the framework of the general problem of state building. I analyze the activities of the two Colombian presidents as attempts to make their country's government more effective. Therefore, this is a study of an activity that is common in nations, particularly in their founding stages but throughout their histories as well. In this introductory section, I first look at the general phenomenon of state building.

No state—even the most economically developed state—can implement all of the decisions made in all of its territory. In his introduction to *The Formation of National States in Western Europe*, Charles Tilly discusses the variables in the process; he and his contributors decided to compare "the organization of armed forces, taxation, policing, the control of food supply, and the formation of technical personnel . . . activities which were difficult, costly, and often unwanted by large parts of the population. All were essential to the creation of strong states; all are therefore likely to tell us something important about the conditions under which strong or weak, centralized or decentralized, stable or unstable, states came into being."[1] Tilly also states that the chief regret of the group was having omitted the judicial system.

Elsewhere, Tilly suggests that conflict such as that seen in Colombia is common in state making; he argues as follows: "At least for the European experience of the past centuries, a portrait of war makers and state makers as coercive and self-seeking entrepreneurs bears a far greater resemblance to the facts than do its chief alternatives: the idea of a social contract, the idea of an open market in which operators of armies and states offer services to willing consumers, the idea of a society whose shared norms and expectations call forth a certain kind of government."[2] Indeed, he says that although third world countries in the twentieth century are not exactly like the Europe of the sixteenth and seventeenth centuries, a thoughtful exploration of the European case might serve us well.[3]

Although ineffectiveness in implementation is possible no matter how political leaders are chosen, a number of recent scholars have been particularly interested in those Latin American cases in which the leaders are elected. Philippe Schmitter and Terry Karl suggest that a country is not a democracy if popularly elected officials are unable to exercise their constitutional powers without being subjected to overriding opposition from unelected officials and if the polity is not self-governing, that is, able to act independently of constraints imposed by some other overarching political system.[4] It is clear that these criteria were added because of countries such as Guatemala, Nicaragua, and Chile, in which either the military or foreign governments prevented the implementation of decisions.

Samuel Huntington also expresses his concern about "front" democracies when he states that his "minimal definition" needs to consider certain other matters. He says that "conceivably a society could choose its political leaders through democratic means, but these political leaders might not exercise real power. They might be the fronts or puppets of some other group. To the extent that the most powerful collective decision makers are not chosen through elections, the political system is not democratic."[5]

Edward Banfield suggests another way that a regime might not be democratic when he forcefully argues as follows: "A regime is not a liberal democracy unless there are institutions—laws, courts, and police—capable of finding when rights have been violated and of putting a stop to their violation. Such institutions can exist and function only if public opinion permits and requires. In a liberal democracy one who contemplates violating the law must know in advance that if push comes to shove his effort must fail because public opinion will not stand for it."[6]

Banfield is arguing that a country is not a democracy if the rights of its people are not being observed, whether because of human rights violations by the government or personal injuries inflicted by third parties. Hence a government cannot be a democracy if the government kills citizens, or if private groups do so. Furthermore, a regime cannot be democratic if *rule adjudication*—the term used by the structural functionalist Gabriel Almond[7]—is done by private groups rather than by the government.

By focusing on the implementation dimension, this study incorporates something close to what thirty years ago some scholars of political development called state building. Theda Skocpol argued ten years ago that we should bring the state back in to its central place in explanations of social change and politics, and, when we do so, "we shall be forced to respect the inherent historicity of sociopolitical structures, as we shall necessarily attend to the inescapable intertwining of national-level developments with changing world historical contexts. We do not need a new or refurbished grand theory of 'The State.' Rather, we need solidly grounded and analytically sharp understandings of the causal regularities that underlie the histories of states, social structures, and transnational relations in the modern world."[8] I hope this study will have those characteristics.

However, the Western European version of state building is not the only one. For example, the Latin American countries have differed from the Europe of three and four centuries ago in the clientelistic nature of their politics. John D. Martz, in his excellent analysis of this kind of politics in Colombia, places the origin clearly in Spanish and Portuguese colonization when he states:

> The Mediterranean and Latin American regions became notable laboratories for the nurturing of clientelism under conditions of patrimonialism. The Spanish and Portuguese colonizers of the New World recognized the utility of the system in terms of an indentured and subservient labor force. On large plantations and landed properties, the costs of production were minimized. Catholicism, in preaching the helplessness of mankind and the needs for benefactors, provided otherworldly justification for the acceptance of traditional values and practices. This also seemingly excused, or at least explained, the practice of repression when employed by the patron. The coercive nature of the patron-client linkage was omnipresent, with the latter entrapped in a vicious circle of obedience, subservience, and impoverishment.[9]

Martz discusses how this "traditional clientelism" relationship became "patrimonial" and later "bureaucratic"[10]; he concludes by warning: "Agendas for action and national policies priorities would be worthy of the proudest and most unrepentant champion of Weberian legal-rational principles. As a practical matter, however, the experience has often given lie to such rosy expectations. Without for the moment engaging further in questions concerning the relative efficacy of governance this is merely to stress once more the clientelistic impulses of the modernizing bureaucratic state in Latin America."[11]

Barbara Geddes puts this question in the "rational choice" theoretical framework when she introduces the idea of the "politician's dilemma." In a clientelistic system, this dilemma is whether the leader will use government resources for political or for economic gain. Although this can be seen from the viewpoint of either the followers or the leader, in the end, Geddes says: "The president as well as his coalition partners faced a wrenching conflict between their need for immediate political survival and the longer-run collective interests in economic performance and regime stability. This is the politician's dilemma writ large. And this dilemma . . . creates many of the obstacles to improving state capacity."[12]

The insights of Martz and Geddes must be kept in mind while studying Colombian politics. Francisco Leal Buitrago and Andrés Dávila Ladrón de Guevara argue that political gain has been central in Colombian politics throughout its history. Most basically, they argue, for the Liberal and Conservative parties to monopolize power it was necessary that clientele relationships become the principal manner of articulation in the institutionalized political system or the norms that regulate politics.[13] Thus it might be more important that new government programs give patronage jobs to followers than that the programs solve the problem of violence.

Outline of this Study

In chapter 2 I will put the study of the two presidents, Barco and Gaviria, in historical perspective, thus beginning the process of "analytical induction" suggested by Evans, Rueschemeyer, and Skocpol.[14] I will show that Colombia had a weak state even before the emergence of the guerrilla groups, drug dealers, and paramilitary squads that would weaken it further. Conflict resolution became, as I will show, a complex matter because both governments were dealing with various kinds of violence, not with a single phenomenon. In short the Colombian government did not have effective control of much of the country. Although the power of the military in Guatemala and other countries prevented the establishment of a strong civilian state, in Colombia the blended power of guerrillas, narcos, and paramilitaries made the state nonexistent in some parts of the country and weak in others.

In the chapters that follow chapter 2, I describe four interrelated governmental activities. The first was political. For years the putative justification for guerrilla violence had been the closed political system. As a result, President Barco attempted to have the National Congress modify the national constitution, which was the constitutional way to make amendments. After his failure to do that, during the Gaviria government the people of Colombia elected a constituent assembly, which wrote a new magna carta. (Barco's activities are discussed in chapter 3; Gaviria's are described in chapter 6.)

The second activity was negotiation. Both presidents attempted to negotiate peace settlements with the leftist guerrilla groups within Colombia's boundaries. President Barco succeeded with the *Movimiento 19 de Abril* (19th of April Movement, M-19), whereas Gaviria succeeded with the *Ejército de Liberación Popular* (Army of Popular Liberation, EPL) at the beginning of his presidency and near the end with the *Corriente de Renovación Socialista* (Socialist Renovation Current, CRS), a part of the *Ejército de Liberación Nacional* (Army of National Liberation, ELN) and with an even smaller part of the *Fuerzas Armadas de la Revolución Colombiana* (Armed Forces of the Colombian Revolution, FARC). But Gaviria failed with the two largest guerrilla groups—the

FARC and the ELN. (Barco's negotiations are described in chapter 4; Gaviria's are discussed in chapter 6.)

The third activity was to try to solve the drug-related crime problems of the country. Both Barco and Gaviria used a combination of force and indirect bargaining, although they did so in different ways. Barco failed completely to end the drug terrorism, although some analysts later said that his tough policy made the Gaviria policy possible. Gaviria did end the drug terrorism, albeit not directly through plea bargaining as he had planned. (Barco's drug policy is described in chapter 4; Gaviria's is in chapter 7.)

The final activities of the two presidents that I analyze were related to indirect bargaining with paramilitary groups. In bargaining with these groups, one of the complications was that many times the groups had been set up with the blessing of the government and under the auspices of the armed forces. I will demonstrate that the Barco government made few attempts to control paramilitary groups, whereas the Gaviria government had a considerable degree of success by giving them the same opportunities to plea bargain that the drug dealers were given. (Barco's dealings with the groups are described in chapter 5; Gaviria's are discussed in chapter 8.)

Underlying Themes

Throughout this study I address the following questions, intentionally focusing on the criminal justice aspect of the problem of state building:

1. To what extent are human rights respected and protected by the government? Inversely, to what extent are they violated?
2. To what extent do official police forces exist that protect the property and personal security of citizens from lawbreakers? Inversely, to what extent is this police function performed by nongovernmental groups or not performed at all?
3. To what extent is the official court system able to realize the entire judicial process (evidence gathering, indictment, trial, verdict)? Inversely, to what extent is this judicial function performed by nongovernmental groups or not at all?

If there are difficulties in the "modern" nations of the world in having complete implementation of decisions, the case of underdeveloped countries is even more dramatic, given the poverty and the institutional weakness of their governments. Although precise measures are not proposed in this study, it is assumed that analysis can show when there are significant increases or decreases in the effectiveness of implementation.

My discussions in chapters 3 through 8 center around comparisons of the Barco and Gaviria policies that had the two primary goals of eliminating the lawless elements and ending the de facto government that controlled large parts of the country—a "government" made up of guerrilla groups, drug terrorists, and paramilitary squads.[15] The comparisons show that the Gaviria government operated in an international and domestic context that was different from that of Barco.

I begin each of these two sections by describing the context in which decisions were made, following with the specific policies, and concluding with an analysis of the causes of the various successes and failures. I recognize that this is an arbitrary scheme, but I make clear in the conclusion of chapter 2 that the context of bargaining with the three groups was different in the two administrations. I also make clear that the dividing lines among the three are ever-changing and ambiguous. Although guerrilla groups emerged first, they later made alliances with drug groups and then entered the drug trade directly. Paramilitary squads began under the auspices of farmers and ranchers whose activities were within the legitimate economy; later, the squads were primarily funded by drug dealers. In short, there was a constantly changing panorama in which the only "logic" could be captured by the phrase, "The enemy of my enemy is my friend."

In chapter 9 I turn to the changes in the constitution to make it more democratic and the reforms to the judicial system to make it more effective. The chapter includes the abortive Barco attempt to change the rules of the political game through a regular constitutional amendment and with the constituent assembly. In this analysis, I show that the two presidents were attempting to construct a system that would give more legitimacy to the process of Colombian democracy. I then turn to the changes in the legal system that the two presidents brought, including activities before and after the establishment of the constituent assembly, as well as the actions taken at that assembly meeting.

Chapter 10, the concluding chapter, shows that changes of governmental policies on paper are much easier to bring about than the more difficult and costly changes in implementation. The difficulties caused by institutional weakness and inertia are detailed. I show trends in crime statistics, including homicides, kidnapping, disappearances, and other human rights abuses. Although this is not a statistical study in a strict sense, these data permit a comparison of the amount of violence in Colombia *before* attempts to lessen it with the amount *during* the Barco government and the amount *during* the Gaviria years. In that way the effects of the policies described on the level of violence in Colombia can be discerned. Because the data show no important improvement in the lives of Colombians, the book concludes with an explanation of why the two governments did not have more success in ameliorating violence.[16]

Conclusion

I entered into this study having made no judgments about whether the Barco or Gaviria policies had been successes or failures. One might be optimistic and state, as Hakim and Lowenthal do: "As devastating as the violence has been, Colombia's political institutions continue to demonstrate resilience and flexibility. The country's political leaders and most citizens remain committed to democratic rule, and the constitutional reform process now underway may strengthen that commitment. But democratic politics is being severely tested in Colombia, and its survival cannot be guaranteed."[17]

Or, alternatively, one could be pessimistic and conclude, as one individual who was interviewed did: "Have you read Hobbes lately? If not you should, because we are back to the jungle."[18]

During the writing of this book, I found myself vacillating between optimism and pessimism. I admit to having felt euphoric on July 4, 1991, when the new constitution was signed, with members of a constituent assembly made up of different races and genders celebrating. But I was extremely pessimistic three years later when the morning news told of the capture of an urban bus, the occupants of which were robbed and raped, while they were held hostage for over three hours as the bus drove around Bogotá without lights. The following year I returned to Bogotá for a conference, enjoying the time with Colombians who had been friends for nearly three decades. But I conclude this book with little reason for optimism.

2

The Historical Context for Bargaining

The Weak Colombian State and the Emergence of Opposition

The purpose of this chapter is to place the bargaining conducted by the Barco and Gaviria administrations in historical context. To that end, I begin with a description of the Colombian state and follow with an accounting of the emergence of guerrilla groups, drug dealers, and paramilitary squads.

Colombian State Building before 1986

Scholars have long argued that the Spanish brought a nondemocratic culture to Latin America, unlike the Lockean liberal tradition the British brought to North America.[1] In that nondemocratic culture, political authority was centralized in the king and his viceroyalties; rules were also issued by the Council of the Indies and applied in the new world by viceroys, *audiencias* (courts), and *cabildos* (town councils), none of which were selected by democratic methods. However, the government was not efficient, even though in structure it appeared to be a centralized bureaucracy. In practice it functioned using the formula, "I obey, but do not comply."

The latter phrase, John Phelan argues, reflected a centralization of authority in the viceroys and governors that was more apparent than real. Phelan concludes:

> Geographic isolation of the colonies, wide divergence in regional conditions, and only partial awareness of these conditions on the part of the central authorities made some such institutional device desirable. The formula's origins go back to the Roman law concept that the prince can do no injustice. The "I obey" clause signifies the recogni-

tion of subordinates of the legitimacy of the sovereign power who, if properly informed of all circumstances, would will no wrong. The "I do not execute" clause is the subordinate's assumption of the responsibility of postponing the execution of an order until the sovereign is informed of the conditions of which he may be ignorant and without a knowledge of which an injustice may be committed.[2]

So the Spanish colonial administration incorporated, in practice, a balance between the principles of authority and flexibility, with the highly centralized decision making invested in the king and the Council of the Indies being counterbalanced by substantial decentralized decision making exercised by bureaucratic subordinates in the colonies.[3]

In a historical study of what today is Ecuador, Phelan found that the subjugation of the coastal areas was never as intensive as the conquest of the Sierra. In fact many coastal areas remained unconquered until the nineteenth and twentieth centuries.[4] Further, the imperial administration was not as centralized as had been assumed. A good many decisions were actually made in the Indies among several competing agencies, with local conditions and local interest groups playing a significant role.[5]

In addition, the Spanish failed to wipe out corruption because of "the inadequate salary scale on several levels. . . . The Spanish imperial bureaucracy was midway between a patrimonial bureaucracy in which officials were paid in kind, in tips, and in graft and a modern administration with regular, monetary salaries paid out of the state."[6]

Although there are no comparable studies of colonial Nueva Granada, certain inferences might be made by combining Phelan's work on Ecuador and David Bushnell's study of Colombia. In Bushnell's words, in Nueva Granada the system "though often marked by corruption, inefficiency, and abuse, was neither much worse nor much better than most systems of government in the world at that period."[7] Further, in Nueva Granada there were surely regional differences. Even though the Spanish crown might have had substantial authority in Bogotá (as it did in Quito), that surely did not mean that it had authority in Medellín, any more than it did in Esmeraldas. Indeed, Bushnell argues: "This political disunity was to some extent inevitable. Certainly no part of Spanish America had so many natural obstacles to unity—so many obstacles to transportation and communication per square kilometer—as New Granada, with a population scattered in isolated clusters in various Andean ranges, not to mention other settlements along the coast."[8]

In Nueva Granada the process of independence was regional, with Cartagena and Bogotá often going separate ways. And if the fall of the Spanish crown led to the lack of a legitimate political regime, it also led to a more decentralized or nonexistent state bureaucracy. And *patrias chicas* (vast territories dominated by a local family) were strengthened, as were large individual landholdings. Many times, large numbers of landowners held power within their territories—in effect, forming private governments.

National decision makers never decided to construct a large police force that would allow the national government to apply its decisions in all parts of the country. As former president Alfonso López Michelsen pointed out in 1991, private landowners in the nineteenth century made the rules for the areas of their landholdings, chose some of their employees to enforce them, and kept workers who misbehaved (according to the landowner's standards) in what amounted to private prisons.

López argues that the country had made a trade-off. Nueva Granada was different from other Latin American countries in that violence did not originate in the government: "On the contrary the root of the violence has been the lack of government, the absence of discipline, and the propensity to anarchy. . . . The rule has been impunity and, in exceptional cases, excessive punishment. From this, the reason has been the inverse of what is supposed, or that because of the weakness of the State, citizens began taking justice into their own hands."[9]

Among the reasons for this decision was the Colombian leaders' fear of the institutions of a strong state (especially the armed forces and the police). Too many other Latin American countries had seen such institutions end elective governments. Also, Colombian leaders, primarily from the upper economic groups, did not want to raise taxes that a strong military and national police would necessitate; those taxes would necessarily come from their own economic sector. Better to let those who needed a police force (the large landowners) do it themselves, paying a sort of "users' fee." Not constructing a national police force left effective power in local hands instead of delegating it to some far-off national government.

The Colombian situation was far from unique in this. Charles Tilly showed the similarity to earlier European cases when he argued, "Early in the state-making process, many parties shared the right to make violence, the practice of using it routinely to accomplish their ends, or both at once."[10]

The federalist period of nineteenth-century Colombia led to less centralized authority. During the regime with more centralized authority, the politicians in Bogotá, fearing militaries and police forces, never built an institutional structure to enforce laws. During federalism those rights reverted to the states.

Things did not change during the twentieth century. For the first fifty-eight years of the century, the political parties were in intense conflict, each fearing that it might lose any strong state it created to the other, hated party. Then there was a sixteen-year period of coalition government between the Liberals and Conservatives that was mandated by the constitution. Colombian sociologist Francisco Leal Buitrago argues that during the years of that National Front, Colombia lost another opportunity to build a strong state. With the National Front, Leal Buitrago writes, "Bureaucratization and clientelism substituted for sectarianism as the source of reproduction of the political parties. But in spite of the profundity of this change, the long-lasting political weakness of the State was not significantly altered. The bureaucratization of bipartyism and the transformation of clientelism into the axis of the political system prevented the widening and modernization of the State from significantly increasing the extent of the state."[11]

In the chapters to follow I discuss the policies of two presidents who, although powerful, were not the only governmental actors. With regard to those various actors in the weak Colombian state, Geddes points out: "Discussion of the state usually assumes that states behave as unitary actors. In reality, they often do not. The problem is not that there is 'no there there,' but that there are too many theres there—each having different capacities, intentions, and preferences. Some parts of the state may express independent preferences while others, often the larger parts, reflect societal interests."[12] Accordingly, I consider the president and his cabinet, the military, and the upper-level economic interest groups (gremios).

The President and His Cabinet

The Colombian constitution of 1886 gave impressive power to the president. However, he had to share that power with a cabinet named and removed without the need for congressional approval. Hence it appeared that a president, if he had the inclination, could at times personally (or along with a few ministers) make policy changes. Thus it is said that Carlos Lleras Restrepo was able to force a renegotiation of oil contracts in the Putumayo region, despite multinational corporation recalcitrance.[13] Today the president is likely to have his way with ministers; disagreements lead to removals. But at times ministers are allowed to go on their own, without the supervision of the president.

Ministers tend to change frequently. Some observers suggest that although "minor" ministers come and go with great rapidity, there are two "superministers"—the minister of the treasury *(hacienda)* and the minister of defense. Any action having to do with the allocation of financial resources would have to be approved by the relevant minor minister and the superminister of *hacienda*. Therefore, it is argued, rapid turnover in minor ministries is not so important as long as there is stability in the *hacienda* portfolio.[14]

Those two superministers are surely important in a president's policies that have to do with guerrilla groups, drug dealers, and paramilitary squads. However, the minister of interior must be added as another important actor, as well as the office of the presidency and the various individuals named to play more ad hoc roles in peace policy.

At times ministers (with or without presidential approval) apparently have considerable "initiative space," that is, the power to suggest changes without constraint.[15] How much of this initiative space is "decision space," however, depends on the strength of the affected interests.

But even if the president, the ministers, and the ad hoc actors agree on policy within an area, there are societal constraints to their power. The president and the ministers cannot unilaterally make public policy if the interests of organized economic interest groups are involved and if the policy changes must be made through laws that pass through the National Congress rather than through the executive implementation of previous laws.

The Gremios

A few economic interest groups have joined the traditional parties as the most powerful forces in Colombia since the beginning of the National Front. Today some even suggest that the economic groups are of greater importance than the parties. All economic sectors of the upper- and middle-income groups are organized. But the most powerful seem to be those "peak" organizations of economic activities—the National Federation of Coffee Growers and a few other producer associations.[16]

Although there is no peak organization that includes all producer associations, the National Association of Industrialists (ANDI, *Asociación Nacional de Industriales*) approximates one, as it includes not only the large industrialists but also firms from the agribusiness, insurance, financial, and commercial sectors. It is powerful for three reasons: (1) its wealth and social prestige, (2) the common overlapping of membership of the group with that of the government, and (3) the fact that industrialization has been a major goal of almost all Colombian presidents during the last half-century. ANDI tends to oppose anything that might negatively affect the private sector but historically has supported the government when there is opposition to the basic system of government.

One very special producer association is the National Federation of Coffee Growers (FEDECAFE, *Federación Nacional de Cafeteros*). This association is open to any person interested in developing the coffee industry but is dominated by the large coffee growers. The federation collects various taxes on coffee and has used its wealth to invest in banks and shipping. It has a close relationship with the government, given the importance of coffee to economic policy. One big difference between Colombia and other Latin American countries is the degree of privatization of certain key functions. Nowhere else would a legally private organization be allowed to do what FEDECAFE does; the governments would do it directly.

Other major producer associations come from the upper sector; all seek to maintain the status quo. The following generalizations about their political behavior can be made. First, most elements of the private sector have been antimilitary, and some of the organizations were important in the 1957 fall of Rojas Pinilla. Although they might sometimes disagree with the policy of a government, they have supported the political regime, whether it was the National Front or the system in place since the end of the Front. Second, the associations tend to react to governmental policy rather than initiate policy. With the growth of the executive branch—both in the ministries and the decentralized institutes—the associations have developed strong ties with that branch. This does not mean, however, that they will not use connections within the Congress if such is the preferable way to block governmental policy.

With the lack of differentiation of the political parties and their factions, interest articulation and aggregation increasingly have been done by the *gremios* (who have made efforts to be bipartisan) and by the church and the military. For example in April 1981, the *gremios* (not for the first time) stated the position that some held when the "Frente Gremial" published an analysis of Colombian problems. Composed of the presidents of ANDI, the Colombian Chamber of Construction (CAMACOL), the Colombian Federation of Metallurgical Industries (FEDEMETAL), the National Federation of Merchants (FENALCO), and the National Association of Financial Institutions (ANIF), the *Frente* did not limit itself to issues directly affecting the economic activities of the *gremios*. Rather, general issues such as inflation, lack of housing for the poor, and the minimum wage were considered; solutions were proposed. In so doing, the *Frente* was aggregating interests the way political parties presumably do.

The Military

In the early years of the National Front, the role of the military changed to one of primary responsibility for the planning and implementation of counterinsurgency, in this case, to end *La Violencia*. This change was reinforced when, in 1961, U.S. government policy instigated military assistance programs geared to internal security. By 1962 the Colombian military, with U.S. assistance, was involved in developing antiguerrilla operations, intelligence techniques, and military civic-action programs. At the same time, the size of the military grew from 23,000 (1961) to 53,500 (1966). By 1980 it had reached 64,000.

In the years since the end of the National Front, the role of the military has *increased* in Colombian politics. The resurgence of guerrilla activity in 1975 forced the military to increase counterinsurgency actions. But the most dramatic change came as a result of the Security Statute *(Estatuto de Seguridad)* of the government of Julio César Turbay (1978–1982). Within a month after Turbay's inauguration, Minister of Defense General Camacho Leyva announced an "unrestrained offensive" against guerilla activities. With the Security Statute, the military received power to try offenders. A vigorous campaign in 1979 led to the arrest of some one thousand people, including artists and intellectuals, many of whom have said that they were tortured. In 1980 and 1981 a "search and destroy" tactic was used in the El Pato–Guayabero region of Caquetá, displacing thousands of *campesinos* (country dwellers). In 1981 large numbers of troops were successful in defeating an M-19 invasion in southern Colombia.

The Colombian military was reluctant when it was brought into antidrug activities in the 1980s. It has had notable success. However, in some cases it has been shown that military officers were paid off by the drug leaders. The most recent infusion of U.S. aid to the military has been to fight drugs, including some US$65 million worth of equipment after the August 1989 assassination of Luis Carlos Galán. After it was alleged that the military was using these funds to fight guerrillas rather than drug dealers, the latter task was given back to the national police in 1991.

Since these changes, there have been tensions about the role the military is to play. Should it remain apolitical—true to Colombian tradition? Or should it speak up about the social and economic problems of the nation? On at least three occasions (the first in 1965 and the last in 1981), individual military leaders have found it necessary to talk about basic societal problems. In 1981 Commander of the Army General Landazábal Reyes wrote in *Army Review:* "We are convinced that the army can militarily destroy the guerrillas, but we are also convinced that even with this, subversion will continue as long as the objective and subjective conditions in the economic, social, and political areas, which daily impair and disrupt stability, are not modified."[17] The first two military leaders who made similar statements were relieved of their posts; Landazábal was later replaced.

As I will show later in this book, there was substantial military opposition to the Betancur national dialogue, and when the M-19 seized the Palacio de Justicia in 1985, some Bogotá pundits wondered if the president was really in control of the troops. The same sentiments came out in December 1990 when the army attacked the FARC headquarters. Yet those who thought that the president really did not control the generals had reason for second thoughts when, in August of 1991, President Gaviria named a civilian minister of defense—the first since the 1940s. The Colombian military simply accepted the decision, and some even argued that it was healthy for them.

All of these happenings, and others, have led to debates in Colombia about the military. During the Turbay years, on one side were the people who argued that the military ruled, with civilians serving only as figureheads. General Camacho, they argued, was more powerful than President Turbay. The military, they said, had plans that even the civilian leaders did not know about. Human rights were being violated; people were being tortured and killed; hundreds were held for long periods of time, without bail and without counsel, before being found innocent in courts-martial. There had, in short, been a "Uruguayanization" of Colombian politics.

The other side argued that the military was doing no more or no less than what the elected civilians had instructed them to do. Camacho met almost daily with President Turbay, but the latter was the one making policy. If individual military men used torture, they were operating against orders when they did so.

Conclusions are difficult in this area, especially as military officers are typically less open with inquiring social scientists than civilian leaders are. Several points might be made, however. First, the guerrillas in Colombia are not now as serious a threat to the status quo as the urban guerrilla *tupamaros* were in Uruguay. Further, the lower classes have not been mobilized as they were in Chile, either by political parties or by labor unions. For these reasons, as well as historical tradition, a "bureaucratic authoritarian" regime seems unlikely at the moment. However, if the guerrillas were to become more powerful or the lower classes more mobilized in antiregime parties or labor unions, a greater role for the military might be probable.[18]

Second, under the Security Statute the military did have a more active role than at any time since at least 1958. In addition to being used in judicial and counterinsurgency activities, military forces have been used in campaigns in drug-producing areas of the country.

Third, it seems certain that at least some military officers feel that the social and economic inequities of the society must be corrected. Their number is unknown, as is their propensity to do more than speak and write about their concerns.

Finally, the military has still not developed a corporate identity, nor does it have prestige with civilians. Major interest groups would look with caution at a military regime and would actively oppose it if it had visions of a strong state, to the detriment of individual capitalism. In short, a military coup would be received with mixed reactions in civilian life. In military circles, there would be great debate about what to do with power.

The New Problems of the Colombian State

In this environment, which was created by a weak and divided state, problems arose in Colombia. The guerrillas entered with the justification of ideology, the drug dealers with the millions of dollars that their illicit trade produced, and the paramilitary squads with the rationalization that they were doing no more than protecting the basic human rights of life and property.

The Guerrilla Groups

The first complication to this already complex political regime was the fact that some individuals chose to oppose the government through armed force rather than in elections. Leftist revolutionary groups in the countryside go back to the final years of *La Violencia* and have continued ever since. In the years since the National Front there have been four major guerrilla organizations in Colombia. They have been a constant nuisance to the government, although it seems improbable that, divided as they are, they will be able to take power. Estimates of the total number of insurgents have varied wildly, with one calculating between four and five thousand armed members in the early 1980s and another suggesting a high of seventeen thousand by 1984. In July 1992, officials in the executive branch of government estimated that the number was seventy-five hundred, with two-thirds belonging to the FARC and one-third to the ELN.[19]

The first such group to emerge, toward the end of *La Violencia* in 1962, was the pro-Castro ELN. The ELN story began with the arrival in Cuba of a group of Colombian scholarship students at the height of the Cuban missile crisis of 1962. Some in the group asked for and obtained military training and began a series of discussions about a "foco" strategy (as called for by Ché Guevara) for Colombia. The ELN was officially born on July 4, 1964, and was initially composed primarily of university students.[20]

In 1966 the Communist Party–dominated FARC was founded, although Communist-oriented peasant defense groups predated that by more than fifteen years. As early as 1949 the Communist Party had urged the proletariat and other people to defend themselves. In the same year Communists joined Liberals in "resistance committees" to oppose the Conservative government. The government violence begun in 1955 was directed against the areas where the Communists were strongest. The Alberto Lleras government initiated military actions against the Communist-influenced area, but it was in July 1964 that leaders from the east and south of Tolima held a meeting and began calling themselves the Southern Bloc. The FARC was founded two years later.[21]

After 1974 a pro-Chinese (Peking) People's Liberation Army *(Ejército Popular de Liberación)* adopted the "prolonged people's war" strategy and very soon was close to extinction.[22] Yet, as the discussion in chapter 6 will show, it did maintain a separate identity until 1991, when the majority part of it agreed to a cease-fire, while a dissident group continued fighting in the *departamento* (department) of Córdoba.

The best known of Colombian groups was the *Movimiento 19 de Abril,* named after the date on which the election was "stolen" from presidential candidate Gustavo Rojas Pinilla in 1970. The M-19, claiming to be the armed branch of Rojas's party, the National Popular Alliance (ANAPO, *Alianza Nacional Popular*), made its appearance in January 1974 when it stole a sword that belonged to Simón Bolívar.

The group arose from a sector that had been expelled from the Communist Party and the FARC, and a sector that came out of the socialist wing of ANAPO. Throughout its existence the M-19 had an undeniable connecting thread: the concept of the present struggle as a continuation of the crusade for freedom—as the "second independence." Also constant was the group's tendency to substitute audacious political-military feats for the patient work of building a political movement.[23]

The M-19 was not considered a serious urban-guerrilla threat until after it kidnapped and murdered the leader of the Confederation of Colombian Workers (CTC, *Confederación de Trabajadores Colombianos*) in the early 1976. It also received international publicity when it tunneled into a Bogotá arsenal and stole arms (1979), when it kidnapped all those (including the U.S. ambassador) attending a cocktail party at the Dominican Republic Embassy in Bogotá (1980), and when it kidnapped and executed a missionary from the United States (1981). Although originally an urban-guerrilla group, the M-19 also participated in rural activities in Chocó and in the Nariño-Putumayo areas in 1981.

The M-19 caused a reaction of amusement and admiration when it participated in such activities as distributing stolen food to the poor and robbing the homes of the rich, allegedly to give the take to the poor. However, before the elections for the constituent assembly in 1990 (see chapter 9) it was always impossible to verify just how much popular support M-19 had. Indeed, the amount of popular support for all the guerrilla movements is open to speculation. It is alleged that the Colombian Communist Party actively supports the FARC. Some student groups no doubt aid (and individual students join) the different movements.

Governments since the National Front have tried to find methods to end the guerrilla violence peacefully. During the presidency of Alfonso López Michelsen (1974–1978) the government tried, for the first time, to open negotiations with the groups. This effort was frustrated by the Colombian military's systematic blocking of any negotiations of the government with the ELN, which the armed forces thought they would soon annihilate.[24]

Julio César Turbay (1978–1982) also tried to bring a nonviolent solution to the problem. After intense negotiations with the Congress, an amnesty law was signed by the president in March 1981. Under it, guerrillas had four months to take advantage of the law, which applied to all except those who had participated in "atrocious crimes" such as kidnapping, extortion, non-combat-related homicide, arson, the poisoning of water, and "in general . . . acts of ferocity or barbarism."[25] In February 1982, President Turbay decreed another amnesty opportunity, basically along the same lines as the 1981 law.[26] The amnesty attempts of the Turbay presidency had very limited success, in part no doubt because of what Turbay's Security Statute had done to indicate that he was likely to make peace with the guerrillas.[27]

In the first six weeks of his presidency, Belisario Betancur (1982–1986) announced that he was going to name another Peace Commission. Also, Law 35 of 1982 granted amnesty to all those in armed conflict with the government before November 20, except those who had committed non-combat-related homicides, those who had committed homicides including "cruelty," and those whose victim had been in a position of "inferior strength." Guerrillas already in jail for the pardoned crimes, whether indicted or convicted, would be released. In the first three months some four hundred guerrillas accepted the amnesty.[28]

This boldest Betancur initiative as president was based on the assumption that guerrilla violence could be understood as the product of the objective circumstances of poverty, injustice, and the lack of opportunities for political participation. Agreements were reached with three guerrilla groups—the *Fuerzas Armadas Revolucionarias de Colombia*, the *Ejército Popular de Liberación*, and the *Movimiento 19 de Abril*. The truces were supposed to be accompanied by a National Dialogue—never very well defined but presumably having to do with government assistance to violence-affected areas.

The Betancur initiative, however, did not end there. After negotiations between the government and the largest guerrilla group, on April 1, 1984, the president announced an agreement with the FARC that included (1) a cease-fire for a period of one year, (2) the creation of a high-level commission to verify the carrying out of the agreement, (3) the granting of a series of juridical, political, and social guarantees in order to facilitate the transition of the guerrilla forces back into democratic life, and (4) a program of rehabilitation of the peasant areas affected by the violence. A similar truce was agreed to the following month with the M-19 and the EPL. Only the *fidelista* ELN had not signed a truce by the end of May 1984.[29]

By the end of 1985, however, two of the three truces had been broken. Leaders of the EPL and the M-19 accused the government of causing the rupture, whereas the government held the guerrilla groups responsible. The M-19 announced its decision to return to combat on June 20, 1985, with its leader Alvaro Fayad, proclaiming: "The problem is that the oligarchy does not want to give up anything because they think that the solution of this country comes from the submission and silencing, not only of the guerrilla movement, but also of the democratic sectors and of the new forces that want a different life."[30] Casualties increased over the following months. Then on the morning of November 6, 1985, the M-19 seized the Palacio de Justicia on the Parque Bolívar in downtown Bogotá. By the time the army reestablished control the following day, 100 people were dead, including 11 of the 24 Supreme Court justices, and the palace had been gutted by fire.

Although the FARC was still formally in truce at the end of the Betancur government, in fact hostilities had also resumed between that group and the government. Clearly, the new president had to deal with a guerrilla problem.

Drug Dealers

Another problem that arose for the Colombian government was powerful, drug-organized crime. The simple appearance of drug trafficking, and even the organized crime that accompanied it, at first was not considered a threat to Colombian democracy. However, it became so when drug groups became so powerful that any politician, judge, or journalist opposing them was either bought off or killed.

The country's role in the international drug market developed very rapidly. One reason for this was the major drive against drugs launched by Mexico in 1975, at the urging of the U.S. government. This led to Colombia becoming "the epicenter of marijuana production in the hemisphere." Colombia came to be the provider of 70 percent of U.S. marijuana imports.[31]

This provided start-up cash for drug entrepreneurs. Two of these—Carlos Lehder Rivas and Jorge Luis Ochoa—had an idea. Instead of using "mules" (individuals carrying small amounts of drugs) and trying to make money by selling cocaine in small quantities at high prices, they decided to go for lower prices and higher volume. In retrospect this seems like an obvious idea, but at the time it was revolutionary. They accomplished this by using airplanes, having their pilots fly in slowly at low altitudes, employing traffic lanes already used by others—for example, by oil-rig pilots. This caused a mushrooming of cocaine sales in the United States, which can be shown by the fact that in 1970, U.S. customs seized only one hundred kilos of cocaine, whereas by 1982 this figure was forty-five metric tons.[32]

It is estimated that, although in 1970 the country exported relatively small amounts of cocaine and marijuana, by 1979 it shipped some 37 metric tons (40.8 short tons) of cocaine and 15,000 tons (16,538 short tons) of marijuana. The Sierra Nevada region in Caribbean coastal Colombia, including parts of the *departamentos* of Guajira, César, and Magdalena, became the world's largest area of marijuana cultivation after the 1975 herbicide spraying in Mexico. This area had, by 1978, 19,000 hectares (46,914 acres) of marijuana cultivation, employing some 18,500 people.[33]

Estimates of the exact amounts of cultivation—and foreign earnings—are guesses at best. One study concluded that the total earnings of the "other economy" in 1979 were US$3.2 billion, and one might make similar estimates for the López years. Of this total, US$2.15 billion (about 70 percent) came from marijuana; US$460 million (11 percent) came from cocaine; and the remaining 11 percent came from "traditional" contraband in coffee (US$150 million), sugar, cattle, and cement (US$440 million). As in other parts of the Colombian economy, the small marijuana farmer received only about 7 percent of the total export value; the high concentrations of income from marijuana and cocaine were in the hands of a few people.

Summarizing his conclusions, one North American scholar in the early 1980s made several points about the illicit income earned by Colombians from drug sales. The sales (1) contributed approximately 6 percent to the nation's 30 percent annual inflation rate; (2) jeopardized Colombia's financial institutions and rendered precarious all forms of governmental economic planning; (3) diverted large sums of governmental funds to suppress growing and trafficking; (4) contributed substantially to Colombia's becoming a food-importing country; (5) shrank the pool of money available for legitimate lending, and raised credit rates to the point that borrowers turned to extralegal sources to secure financing; (6) contributed to increased tax evasion among a populace already noted for not paying taxes; (7) penetrated and/or gained control of legitimate private corporations; (8) became the largest source of dollars in the underground economy and added millions to the nation's foreign exchange surplus; and (9) grossly inflated the value of farm land, property, goods, services, and even art works, in trafficking areas.[34] All of these trends were to continue during the 1980s.

The emergence of the drug trade must be put into the context of other events in Colombian society. After the 1950s, peasants were being forced off the land. Many of them went to "misery belts" around the major cities; others colonized the more remote parts of the country. In the latter, as Colombian political scientists Luis Javier Orjuela and Cristina Barrera P. point out:

> There communities with very weak social cohesion were set up, in lo-
> cations with only a scarce presence of state institutions. Those areas
> were especially ideal for the flourishing of a parallel economy based
> on the cultivation and trafficking of cocaine and marijuana. There the
> drug dealers filled the space left by the state; they constituted for
> thousands of Colombians a social security system that provided the
> income through assuring transportation and the prices that no one
> guaranteed to the [other] small peasant producers.[35]

In one study of the impact of drug trafficking in Antioquia, Mario Arango Jaramillo studied twenty drug dealers; 70 percent came from *campesino* backgrounds; only two had university education, and eleven had only primary education.[36] Although there is no way to know whether this is representative of the country as a whole, it does raise an important possibility: drug trade not only filled the political space unoccupied by the government but gave economic opportunities that were unlikely in the legitimate economy.

The response of the Colombian government was tentative and experimental. The López administration reacted to the drug trade by opening a *ventanilla siniestra* ("left-handed" or "sinister" window) in the Banco de la República. At that window, anyone could exchange dollars for pesos—with no questions asked. Other dollars entered the economy through the long-flourishing black market for dollars. Many other dollars were simply not brought into the country but placed in banks and investments in other countries. At the beginning of the 1970s the dollars that entered through this window were equal to some 20 percent of the legal exports; at the beginning of the following decade they were 48 percent.[37]

A new economic group, whose importance is hard to estimate, grew up around the illicit drug industry. It is called the Mafia by Colombians and cartels[38] by foreigners. The assumption quite often is that foreign-organized crime, particularly from the United States, is also involved. Whether this is true or not, the Colombian drug industry did hold a national convention secretly in December of 1981, which 223 drug-gang bosses attended. One notable "accomplishment" of the meeting was the creation of a death squad called MAS (*Muerte a Secuestradores*, Death to Kidnappers). The *mafioso* pledged US$7.5 million to the squad, whose goal was to kill all kidnappers and to end the guerrilla practice of kidnapping people, including the "honest, hard working drug gang bosses," for ransom to finance their subversive activities.[39]

Before Belisario Betancur became president in 1982, Colombian leaders had largely paid no attention to the increasing drug trade in the country. During 1983 and early 1984, Justice Minister Rodrigo Lara Bonilla led the Betancur government in stepped-up attacks on the drug centers and on the *narcotraficantes* (drug dealers) Lara suspected that the drug money was being invested in legitimate enterprises, including professional soccer and bicycle racing. Further, he accused several members of Congress of having received drug money for their campaigns.

The Betancur antidrug campaign intensified when, on April 30, 1984, thugs hired by the *narcotraficantes* assassinated Minister Lara. The Betancur government reacted immediately. It decreed a state of siege for the entire country; it directed raids against the property of suspected drug dealers, including eighty in the city of Medellín alone; it began a program of aerial spraying of marijuana for the first time; and it enforced an extradition treaty with the United States. The results of the campaign were impressive. By the end of 1984 they had seized 2,851,000 kilograms of marijuana and 23,931 kilograms of cocaine, destroyed 268 cocaine-processing laboratories, and arrested 2,773 individuals.[40]

Nevertheless, by the beginning of the Virgilio Barco government, years of near-laissez-faire policies had led to the strong position of drug dealers (called narcos here as a manner of shorthand) within Colombian society. They had used their wealth to enter every facet of it. It was clear that many of the elite, without direct connections to this illicit commerce, did not oppose it because of the needed hard currency it brought to the country. At the very least, even if after the consensus had been reached that something had to be done, it would have taken decades of active government intervention to remove the drug traffickers from their positions of strength. Past Colombian inability to apply the law against less-organized crime made it unrealistic to expect the government to have much success against the drug trade.

From time to time the leaders of the drug trade tried to meet with the government to find a solution to the conflict. The narcos had their first contact concerning a negotiation with the national procurator, Carlos Jiménez Gómez, in September of 1983. Medellín drug leader Pablo Escobar sent a message to the procurator to ask if he was amenable to meet with spokespersons of the narcos to discuss the possibility of a national solution to the problem of narcotrafficking through negotiation with the government. The meeting was held in Bogotá in the office of the procurator, with the attendance of Escobar, José Gonzalo Rodríguez Gacha, the Ochoa brothers, and Carlos Lehder. The narcos said that they could not live with their families and that they had the same right to amnesty as the guerrillas. The procurator listened to them and talked to some of them two more times about the same subject.[41]

In June 1984 former president Alfonso López, after informing Betancur, met with Pablo Escobar and Jorge Luis Ochoa in Panama. The drug leaders contended that the Lara assassination had been carried out by the Drug Enforcement Agency to create problems for them in Colombia. Bernardo Ramírez, minister of communications, asked Procurator Jiménez Gómez to travel to Panama to continue the conversations. Jiménez said that he would, only if Betancur asked him to. Betancur did, and in June of 1984 the procurator also met with Pablo Escobar, Rodríguez Gacha, and the Ochoa brothers. The dialogue was very similar to that with López, but this time there was also a formal, written document: "The Memorandum of the Mafia."

After his Panama meeting with the narcos, Alfonso López had an interview with *El Tiempo* in which he said that the government should have accepted the narco proposal because "the drug trade must be ended using whatever means and for that reason if these gentlemen want to turn over their laboratories, runways and crops and sell their airplanes, then I believe that probably the best manner to end this problem is the quickest one to arrive at the objective." Later in the same interview he stated, "They maintained that the people they represented had more or less good relations with the army" and that they had been "alongside [the armed forces] against the guerrillas."[42]

When he got back to Bogotá, after talking to Betancur, Jiménez Gómez passed the memorandum on to a friend in the U.S. Embassy. In Bogotá there was general opposition to the negotiations; the idea died for lack of support. The narcos with whom the conversations took place in 1984 had no pending cases in the justice system and hence no need of amnesty. The size of the drug trade increased, and the nature of the violence in Colombia changed for the worse in the ensuing five years.

As Orjuela and Barrera P. concluded, during the presidency of Belisario Betancur the policy of the Colombian government in relation to the narcos was "ambiguous and full of dilemmas: total war or negotiation; application of the Treaty of Extradition or its revision. The interviews of members of the government with the drug dealers and the fact that the president was informed ahead of time about those contacts, [all this] did not give the official proceedings a clear and satisfactory explanation to the public."[43]

Paramilitary Groups

Colombian history has been replete with examples of paramilitary groups; the most notable of the twentieth century is usually considered to be *La Violencia* of the 1946–1966 period. The first self-defense groups to organize themselves were the "peasant self-defense groups" in Chaparral (Tolima), with a concentration of one thousand families. In the 1950s similar groups appeared in other places, including Meta, Caquetá, and Huila. Ironically, the *Fuerzas Armadas de la Revolución Colombiana* originated in one such group.

National Procurator Horacio Serpa later defined "self-defense groups" as people who "are rooted in determined areas where they reside with their families, dedicated to productive work, always respecting the authorities and the law, without ever exceeding the purpose of their responsibility and never participating in criminal activities."[44] Henry Pérez, leader of the paramilitary group in Magdalena Medio, using different semantics, said, "A self-defense group is a group of people who are within a political and military organization, who try to defend the interests of a community in face of any kind of aggression."[45] And a member of the office of the presidency, in a confidential interview in July 1992, with a smile stated that for the Colombian military, a self-defense group was one that they themselves had armed, while a paramilitary group was one armed by someone else.[46]

In writing this book, I have not worried about these questions of semantics. Rather, I describe the origin and development of private defense groups, concluding with a discussion of the policies of the Barco and Gaviria governments toward these vigilante organizations that at times brought the drug dealers and members of the armed forces together. Without judgment implied, I shall use the term *paramilitary groups*.

The legal basis of the paramilitary groups was Decree 3398 of President Guillermo León Valencia (1965) and Law 48 of 1968 (during the presidency of Carlos Lleras Restrepo). The basic clause said that any citizen could be used by the government in activities to reestablish normality. In the 1970s, with the growth of the FARC and the progressive hostility of it toward the civilian population, the peasants of traditional political affiliation, especially in areas like Magdalena Medio and Urabá (see map), adopted the "self-defense" structure to repel the guerrilla aggression.

Many of the self-defense groups of the 1980s arose basically as a phenomenon of spontaneous generation. It was the response of those who had lost their toleration in the face of the constant demands of the guerrillas and who knew that the government could not guarantee the protection of honor, life, and property in all the national territory.[47] Although later both the drug dealers and the guerrillas were involved, this was not so at the origin of the paramilitary groups.

The nature of the problems that caused the formation of the early paramilitary groups is shown in a statement by a medium-sized farmer in Urabá. "Here the communists and the guerrillas want to throw us out. But we're not going to let them screw us. Journalist, everything I'm saying is true. But don't print my name."[48] Off the record the banana growers affirmed that the government had never worried about the zone. Before the formation of the paramilitary groups, the work inspectors and the judges of the region could not work because the machine guns of the FARC and the EPL would not let them. Also there were armed unions. According to the banana growers they might as well have declared independence from Colombia.[49]

Although some Colombians argue that the country has a history of "permanent and enduring warfare,"[50] it is clear that the intensity had increased by the 1980s. After a low point in 1973 and 1974, with "only" 16.8 murders per 100,000 people (twice as high a rate as in the United States and three times that in Western Europe), by 1987 the murder rate would reach 52.8 per 100,000—the fourth highest ever recorded in the world. Homicide had become the leading cause of death for males between eighteen and forty-five and the second leading cause overall. In 1987 alone there were some 16,200 homicides—a 15 percent increase over 1986—and the Colombian government estimated that the murder rate was higher than even in the worst years of *La Violencia*.[51]

One "special" paramilitary group was MAS, which, as mentioned earlier, was formed by drug leaders in 1981. Some Colombian experts see the emergence of MAS as more than just a narco way to protect themselves from kidnapping by guerrilleros. Orjuela and Barrera P. argue as follows: "The appearance of MAS marks the beginning of a new strategy of a dominant sector within narcotrafficking activities, in virtue of which the emerging elite would face militarily those who tried to hurt any of their interests; in this way the entry doors of paramilitarism were being opened in Colombia." Even more, they continue, MAS became converted into the "expression of a violent mentality," making the 1980s the decade of "death to everyone."

The two political scientists continue: "In this way the drug trade became the catalyst of violence in Colombia, by stimulating "the proliferation of armed groups that irrigate violence and terror in the cities, with the recourse of death as a form of just, settling of accounts, of a simple means of intimidation."[52]

So the rule of law in Colombia was lacking not only because of guerrillas and drug dealers but also because of paramilitary groups, at times set up by the armed forces to assist them in their struggle against guerrillas. These paramilitary groups, as chapters 5 and 8 will show, quite often became de facto governments in certain parts of the country, just as the guerrillas and the narcos had in others.

Conclusion

The preceding discussion makes it clear why any individual becoming president of Colombia in 1986 would have faced a difficult situation. When Virgilio Barco became president on August 7, 1986, he inherited the problem that Gustavo Gorriti argues all countries with guerrilla challenges have:

> The authorities in the threatened countries must confront the nightmarish realities that any Third World democracy faces when battling a determined group of ruthless insurgents. A well-planned insurgency can severely test the basic assumptions of the democratic process. While they provoke and dare the elected regime to overstep its own laws in response to their aggression, the insurgents strive to paint the very process they are trying to destroy as a sham. If ensnared in such perverse dynamics, most Third World democracies will find their legitimacy eroding, and may eventually cease to be democracies altogether.[53]

Barco also encountered other effects of guerrilla wars, as noted by Peter Hakim and Abraham Lowenthal (although apparently El Salvador no longer fits, while Mexico perhaps does):

> In four countries—Colombia, Peru, Guatemala, and El Salvador—governments face insurgent threats to their effective control of national territory. Each of them confronts a vicious cycle of violence and counterviolence that, to varying degrees and in different ways, is undermining the institutions, procedures, and values essential to democracy. As long as the violence continues, democratic practice will

remain truncated and precarious. The armed forces will intrude in political decisions, the authority of civilian leaders and institutions will be compromised, economic progress will be blocked, policies will remain polarized, and human rights abuses will persist at levels that destroy confidence in the democratic process.[54]

But the Colombian president would face not only the guerrilla problem but also the drug dealers and the paramilitary squads. Clearly, he would have to make decisions about which group violating the law was the highest priority to deal with; likewise, he would have to decide which branch of the armed forces (army or national police) to use. And he would have to make sure that all members of his executive branch were following his instructions. Finally, there was always a lack of good information about temporary coalitions, both within and among the various lawbreakers.

At a certain level of generality, I would suggest the following distinctions among guerrilla groups, drug dealers, and paramilitary squads in Colombia, based on their goals, the locations of their violence, and the victims of that savagery. The goals of the guerrilla groups were political—to change the economic, social, and political systems. The goals of the drug dealers were economic—simply to be left alone so that they could make money. The paramilitary squads always had the goal of protecting economic groups from guerrilla bands, although those economic groups changed from ranchers and farmers producing legal goods to drug dealers. The place of conflict for the drug dealers was the larger cities; that of the paramilitary squads and guerrillas was the countryside. The victims of the drug dealers were anyone who had the bad luck to be near when a bomb was exploded, whereas the guerrilla groups affected farmers and the soldiers who tried to stop them. In their first stage, the paramilitary groups targeted guerrillas and their suspected sympathizers, whereas in the second stage soldiers became victims as well. Clearly, the situation was not a two- or even a four-person game situation.

The Virgilio Barco Government, 1986–1990

The highest priority for Virgilio Barco was to have a government formed entirely from his own Liberal Party, with the minority Conservatives relegated to the position of "loyal opposition." During the 1986 presidential campaign Barco had called for a "program-government," although it was far from clear how he could have a government consisting of only his party because Article 120 of the constitution required that the president give "adequate and equitable" participation to the party that came in second in the election. After the election he promised to follow that article, "paying attention to the political realities of the circumstances." At the same time, the leader of the Conservative Party, Misael Pastrana Borrero, proposed that his party enter into "thoughtful opposition." However, there would be bipartisan agreements on "themes of national interest" such as the guerrilla war, the drug traffic, the election of mayors, and a "statute of opposition."[1] Barco later followed the letter of Article 120, offering three cabinet positions to the Conservatives. The positions were declined and a one-party government existed for the first time since that of Laureano Gómez (1950–1953).

By erasing the final bit of constitutionally mandated coalition government from the National Front, Barco attempted to open up the government so groups like the guerrillas would enter politics instead of combat. Mario Latorre, member of the circle around Barco popularly called *El Sanedrín* (the Sanhedrin) suggested that the moment of truth had arrived: "When did Colombia get so screwed up? If the country does not take advantage of the opportunity that it has, if the Liberal party or the Conservatives, or those of the UP *[Unión Patriótica]*, do not take advantage of this opportunity, this country is going to hell."[2] If this new regime were a success, its architects (like Latorre) argued, the voters would be able to judge the policy of a president and his party and vote in the next election accordingly.

Yet the years were to show that Colombian politicians and Virgilio Barco would not be able to carry out this idea. The following three chapters will demonstrate how public order degenerated during the Barco years, due slightly less to guerrilla groups than to drug dealers and paramilitary squads.

3

Barco's Guerrilla Policy

The focus of this chapter is on the policies of the Virgilio Barco government for ending conflict with the guerrilla groups. I will demonstrate that the government took a more active role in its last two years, with some notable successes.

It was surprising that President Barco announced no new initiative for dealing with the guerrilla problem at his inauguration on August 7, 1986, because at the time, although there were approximately five thousand guerrillas of the FARC in a truce with the government, there were still another two thousand not observing a truce. The latter came from the Ricardo Franco Group and the CNG (*Coordinadora Nacional Guerrillera*, National Guerrilla Coordinator) made up of the M-19, EPL, ELN, and *Quintín Lame.*[1] Further, a report of the minister of defense had given the following figures for guerrilla-related deaths from May 1985 through May 1986: guerrillas, 764; military, 384; and civilians, 670. Leaders of the *Unión Patriótica* (UP [Patriotic Union], the legal political party formed by the FARC during the Betancur democratic opening) added that about three hundred of its militants had been killed by death squads during the same period.[2]

This situation was surely less serious than that faced by the Betancur government four years previously, even with all of those deaths. At that time there had perhaps been as many as seventeen thousand individuals in fifty-five guerrilla fronts in the country. John Agudelo Ríos, president of Betancur's Peace Commission, concluded that the policies of the Betancur government led to the end of 95 percent of the guerrilla activities. This was done despite the problems he had faced as president of the Peace Commission, including the lack of support of the government, the pessimism of the Colombian people, and the poor economic conditions being suffered by the country. Agudelo concluded, "I believe personally that, if it hadn't been for our actions, today there would be a civil war in Colombia."[3]

Guerrilla Policy during Barco's First Year

During its first year, the Barco government faced three basic issues having to do with the guerrilla groups: the continuing battles between them and the forces of the government; the continuation of dialogue between the government and the FARC; and the investigations of the incident involving the Palacio de Justicia.

The Continuing Violence

The early months of the Barco presidency saw an intensification of the violence. One pundit suggested that more shots were fired in the first one hundred days of the Barco government than in the entire Betancur period. Newspaper editorialists started considering the possibilities of either an "Argentinization," suggesting a "dirty war" of the military, police, and death squads against suspected guerrillas and drug-dealers, or a "Central Americanization," meaning a full-blown civil war.

With the exception of the FARC, guerrilla groups had formed the CNG, whose combatants continued their activities in various parts of the country. Evidence suggested that the M-19 was on the decline within the group, its numbers reduced by previous conflicts and its leadership divided between those who favored a long, protracted war and those who thought that a single, dramatic confrontation was the solution. Within the CNG it appeared that the leadership was increasingly taken over by leaders of the ELN. The most notable single action of the M-19 during the time period was the June 1986 attempt to assassinate the minister of government when he was on his way to the presidential palace.

The FARC did stay in truce for the entire first Barco year, although there were battles between FARC fronts and the government. Further, as mentioned earlier, the militants of the FARC-organized UP were being killed. Carlos Ossa Escobar, the Barco-appointed peace adviser, opined that the attacks against UP members came from both right- and left-wing groups that wished to push FARC out of its truce. A UP congressman, Braulio Herrera, agreed with Ossa on the motivation but suggested that it was the "high-level military commanders interested in definitively ending the peace process" who were mostly responsible.[4]

By November 1986, however, a FARC communiqué warned that the country was on the verge of civil war. Seven of its twenty-seven fronts were fighting with government troops, not because they had broken the truce, they said, but because they had to defend themselves when attacked. This was the reason that the level of violence was increasing, and, to combat that trend, the FARC leadership called for a "civic strike against fascism and for the right to life."[5] It should be remembered that, under the Betancur peace plan, there were cease-fires without demobilizations.

Continuing Negotiation

In October 1986, Braulio Herrera outlined FARC conditions for a demobilization of their fronts. In effect he called for more democracy in the country when he said two things: (1) that the state of siege would have to be lifted and the constitutional article (121) allowing for such a state revised and (2) that the controversial Article 120 (which required the president to give "adequate and equitable" participation to the second-largest party in his government) would have to be abolished for there to be true democracy. Also he said that the death squads would have to be disbanded before the FARC would "initiate the process of the demobilization of its fronts."[6] The guerrillas would raise the same issue during the Gaviria years (see chapter 6).

President Barco called for a reorganization of the peace process in August of 1986. The numerous commissions would be replaced with a kind of "superminister." That one person would be Carlos Ossa Escobar, until then the president of the *Sociedad de Agricultores Colombianos* (Society of Colombian Farmers, SAC), a powerful *gremio* of large landowners. Ossa would be under the direct orders of the president and would be the coordinator of all of the activities having to do with reconciliation and rehabilitation.

As 1987 began, the Barco government denied that the FARC had broken its truce agreement. FARC leaders, on their part, restated that the peace process was experiencing difficulties because of "the offensive of militarism against it" and proposed that the Barco government reestablish the Peace Commission.[7]

The next development in government-guerrilla relationships came in February 1987 when the *Unión Patriótica* declared itself independent of the FARC. Jaime Pardo Leal, presidential candidate of the UP in the previous year, stated that his organization was not a political mouth-

piece of the guerrilla group and that it would continue its political activities, even if the FARC broke its truce with the government. Some
pundits saw this action as a first step toward such a breaking of the
truce.

Investigation of the Palacio de Justicia Incident

The final issue Barco faced consisted of the various reports on the
November 1985 takeover of the Palacio de Justicia by the M-19. Because
many considered that incident to be representative of the Betancur failure with the guerrillas, how the Barco government reacted to the reports was of utmost importance. The first report came from the national procurator; others followed from a special commission, from
some of the participants, and from President Betancur.

National Procurator Carlos Jiménez Gómez condemned both sides—
government and guerrillas—in his analysis. The action of the M-19
was a "typical act of war," and the government reaction was a "battle
of war." No one could justify the act of the M-19 in taking the palace.
It was a continuation of the harshest guerrilla activities in the country
coming from the most messianic group, as the M-19 had been showing
in other ways since it left its truce in May 1985. As Jiménez Gómez
stated, "If there is in national public opinion a universally accepted
opinion, it is the absolute lack of justification for that guerrilla operation as a reply to the government that had most profoundly in history
faced and discussed the objective and subjective causes of the socioeconomic and political conflict begun by the guerrillas."[8]

However, the decision of the government not to negotiate, not to
dialogue—to use a "strong hand"—was to be denounced before the
National Congress because "with a better handling of the situation the
hostages could have been saved without the necessity that the State negotiate or cede any of its prerogatives." The decision was made almost
immediately, as the arrival of the tanks at the palace, as well as other
events, demonstrated. The members of the president's cabinet were in
the dark about what was going on, although "it was happening at a
distance close, very close to their meeting room." In that context President Betancur had to take the responsibility for the decisions.[9]

The procurator concluded:

Can the State cover with the same repressive action some citizens outside of the law and some innocent citizens, before having attempted
all of the means in its power to try to rescue the latter safely? Is this

decision legitimate, to apply immediately to them, for whatever reason, the same treatment? ... The Procurator can only reply to those questions negatively. ... The conclusion is simple: before beginning the final battle, the arms of the state should wait until every effort has been made to maintain the rights of innocent civilians.[10]

On the basis of these conclusions, the procurator resolved to denounce President Betancur and Minister of Defense General Miguel Vega Uribe in the lower house of Congress.

At about the same, time a second report appeared, this one from the Special Tribunal of Criminal Instruction. This analysis of the takeover concluded that the M-19 and its leader Alvaro Fayad had planned the action six months before it happened. In addition to a detailed military plan, documents revealed by the tribunal included a procedure for the trial of Belisario Betancur by the Supreme Court. Ironically, the M-19 was using a violent means (the takeover of the Supreme Court) in order to then use a democratic method (impeachment trial by the court) to remove Betancur from office.

In testimony before the tribunal, Betancur's predecessor, Liberal Julio César Turbay, stated that he would have followed the same strategy Betancur did. Testimony from some of the cabinet officials in the presidential palace that day was that they had suggested conversations with the M-19, as well as a cease-fire during the talks. That the president himself had made the important decisions was affirmed by Minister of Government Jaime Castro, when he testified: "For me it was clear that he [Betancur] always exercised, without any limits, his position as commander in chief of the military and of the police. ... This condition was shown especially when the president ordered that the public forces act to achieve the reestablishment of public order, the liberation of the hostages, and recovery of the Palace and when he decided not to accept the suggestion that some made to suspend or cancel the on-going operations."[11]

The Continuing Violence in Barco's Second Year

Virgilio Barco's second year was one of active combat with the four major groups who kept their separate identities and to a degree worked on their own. However, in October 1987, along with the smaller *Quintín Lame* group, the four published a joint declaration as the *Coordinadora Guerrillera Simón Bolívar* (CGSB, Simón Bolívar

Guerrilla Coordinator),[12] which replaced the previous CNG coordinating group. And by November 1987 it was apparent that even the most stable cease-fire—that with the FARC—had ended.

The guerrilla warfare had three general tactics: to damage the economy, to kidnap, and to fight. Guerrilla groups took action—perhaps more than in previous years—against economic targets. Most notable were the actions of the ELN in bombing petroleum pipelines, especially the Caño Limón–Covenas pipeline taking Occidental Petroleum crude from the eastern plains to port. In addition, actions by both ELN and FARC groups in the Magdalena Medio petroleum fields (making it especially difficult for foodstuffs to get to isolated areas) led to the abandonment of oil wells. As petroleum had become an important export once again for Colombia, the guerrilla groups clearly were hurting the economy. The military (with loans of helicopters from Occidental) began patrolling the pipeline more than before, but with mixed success.

Nevertheless for nearly two years, the Barco government made no new initiative in attempting to negotiate with the guerrilla groups. The government did take actions to increase the size of and support for the Colombian military.

The Alvardo Gomez Kidnapping

The turning point of Barco guerrilla policy came with the most news-generating action of 1988, which began on May 29 when Alvaro Gómez Hurtado—Conservative leader and presidential candidate in 1986—was kidnapped by the M-19 as he left mass in Bogotá. This is the first case of many to be seen in this study in which actions against a well-known political or economic leader have much greater importance than many kidnappings or deaths of ordinary, poor people. Further, there was a certain irony in this kidnapping, as was pointed out by Antonio Caballero in *El Espectador:* "The kidnapping of Alvaro Gómez is a personal and family tragedy, one more among the thousands that deny ordinary life in Colombia. . . . A 'normal' tragedy, then: an everyday occurrence of the normalcy of violence within which we live in this country. Nevertheless, it is also a valuable example. Because Alvaro Gómez has always represented, during his long and influential political career, that intellectual and spiritual tendency . . . that resulted in using violence as a natural solution to problems."[13] Caballero was referring to the early activities of Alvaro Gómez during *La Violencia.*

Although it was apparent from the beginning that some urban terrorist group had carried out the act, it was not clear which one because, as explained by one official of the Administrative Department of Security (DAS, *Departamento Administrativo de Seguridad*), "The number of groups who carry out such actions has proliferated so much."[14] The first ransom statement came from a group called Colombians for Peace. The Barco government announced immediately that it would not negotiate with terrorists, including the kidnappers of Alvaro Gómez, but also set up a special group to deal with the case.

By mid-July it was known that Gómez was being held by the M-19. Two conversations took place in Panama, without the direct participation of the Colombian government, given its position on negotiation with terrorists. The first was attended by Monseñor Darío Castrillón (who would become the leader of the group), two Conservative senators, and a representative of Conservative daily, *El Siglo*. The second meeting included representatives of both political parties, economic interest groups, and human rights groups. The eventual agreement was that Gómez would be released by the time of a meeting of the National Dialogue on July 29. He was liberated on July 20—National Independence Day—after fifty-four days of captivity.

After the Agreement of Panama, the process of National Dialogue agreed to therein followed a rapid chronology. Beginning on July 26 the Preparatory Committee, coordinated by Monseñor Castrillón, started work leading to the national "summit"; on July 29 the meetings started, without the participation of the government. The summit made many recommendations, including that of constituting a Commission for Democratic Coexistence *(Comisión de Convivencia Democrática)* that should start on August 22.

The Barco government did not attend the National Dialogue meeting, held in the Institute of Pastoral Orientation of Usaquén (in the northern part of Bogotá), although many—including Liberal leaders and Alvaro Gómez—encouraged that participation. Neither did guerrilla leaders attend because the government refused to grant them safe conduct to do so. Some fifty individuals, including Alvaro Gómez, did attend, and the M-19 sent a declaration indicating its willingness to enter peace talks.

The meeting concluded with the agreement that a so-called Preparatory Commission would receive recommendations until August 15 to establish the "framework for action" to be taken at the Commission of Democratic Coexistence that would begin in Bogotá within three weeks. This commission was to explore solutions for "the crises in which the country is living." Cardinal Alfonso López Trujillo, a participant at the Usaquén meeting, summarized it as follows: "The people participating in this meeting at the top, that we have brought together to combine aspirations and energies for the good of the Fatherland, convinced of the urgency of pursuing a systematic dialogue that might lead to concrete proposals, commit ourselves to a great national convocation. We will take part in it with all our energy, and we invite other parts of the country to unite [with it] with patriotic goals and with the positive desire to find the remedies that the Fatherland needs."[15]

Meanwhile a follow-up committee (Comité de Seguimiento) began its work hindered by various difficulties, including the lack of safe-conduct passes and guarantees for the guerrillas. On August 17 the committee met with President Barco. On the following two days the committee went to La Uribe (the FARC headquarters in the mountains of Meta) to receive the peace proposal of the guerrilla groups. As stated by CGSB, their proposal included five major points:

1. The groups of the CGSB thought that the armed conflict in the country required a political solution because therein lay its causes.
2. They promised to respect human rights and the Geneva Convention and to "humanize" the conflict; at the same time they called for the government to do the same.
3. They stated the willingness of the ELN to suspend bombings of pipelines, as a gesture directed to the solution of the petroleum and energy problems. The government should negotiate on these matters.
4. They proposed that debate about a new constitution take place with the people so that it could be the "maximum expression of their political rights."
5. They supported the petitions of the Central Unitaria de Trabajadores (CUT, Unified Central of Labor Unions) and its call for a general strike.[16]

Despite this proposal, the following week, on the morning of August 26, 1988, army and police forces were ambushed by more than three hundred FARC and ELN guerrillas in the departamento of Córdoba. Ten members of the army and four policemen died, as well as twenty-five guerrillas.[17]

Guerrilla violence increased over the following weeks, and October began with the "definitive" end of the cease-fire with the FARC. The Unión Patriótica called for a new cease-fire so that there could be a direct dialogue between the government and the guerrillas. And President Barco promised that his new Initiative for Peace would continue, although "no one believes the empty words of the subversive groups." He also said that those who really wanted peace should demonstrate it with acts.[18]

The Barco initiative would require guerrilla groups to turn in their arms and demobilize, as negotiations with the M-19 were to show later. As such, it was a major departure from the Betancur policy of in-place cease-fires. As the year ended, the results of this new dialogue were far from certain. However, the position of the Barco government was clear (although unlikely to be accepted by guerrilla leaders): "The Government understands that dialogue is a useful means to achieve national reconciliation, when and only when its reason is solely that of establishing the steps that lead to definitive demobilization."[19]

Meanwhile, army and police troops were dying in conflicts with the guerrillas. The nature of this conflict and the dilemmas of a democratic government fighting leftist guerrillas were well described by Colonel Amadeo González after four of his men were killed in a July 1989 ambush. He indicated his frustration over having to fight groups that did not fight face to face and that, in a "traitorous and cowardly fashion," caused the most damage possible and then immediately changed into humble peasants: "We are impotent facing subversion. . . . We have all the weight of justice on us, we are in danger of committing what in our law is arbitrary arrest, the abuse of authority, and we cannot really justify, prove, or demonstrate because we do not have the time to prove that an individual had, knew, participated."[20] The colonel meant that both Colombian and international law constrained the armed forces more than its guerrilla opposition.

By late 1988 various Colombian leaders denied that the Barco initiative was working. Toward the end of November, Fabio Echeverri Correa, president of ANDI, criticized the passive attitude of the government toward recommendations made by various groups to save the country from the grave situation caused by "a crazy, indiscriminate, and sickly violence." He said that the country was on the road to destruction. At the same time, ex-president Carlos Lleras Restrepo wrote, "The country today is under the empire of crime." He continued by saying that this was different from the situation that he and other presidents had confronted during the partisan *La Violencia:* "In conclusion, it is not a matter of the confrontation of two opposing forces as was that which characterized the 'first violence,' but rather a state of general decomposition. . . . The country is sick; but even more it is . . . under the empire of crime. . . . [O]ne arrives at the conclusion that a strengthening of the state and vigorous actions to restore juridical order, now absent, are necessary and urgent."[21]

Guerrilla Policy during Barco's Last Two Years

The context for negotiations between the government and certain of the guerrilla groups changed during the last two Barco years (1988–1990). On the government's side, the increase of paramilitary activities gave negotiation with the guerrillas a higher priority. The year 1987 soon became known as the "year of the massacres,"[22] and it was the paramilitary groups that carried out most of them. Something had to be done.

The guerrilla groups—especially the M-19—were also experiencing changes. Colombian sociologist Ana María Bejarano identified various reasons for the M-19 to take a different approach to negotiation with the Barco government. The M-19 was militarily weak, and the palace incident had led to their having less legitimacy in Colombian society. The movement had never had a coherent revolutionary ideology, and now there had been rapid leadership turnover, with three different maximum leaders in three consecutive years. Finally, the growth of paramilitary groups and their connections with drug monies had changed the whole structure of violence in Colombia.[23]

In mid-March 1989, the government and the M-19 signed a Declaration of Cauca, with the intent of beginning the process of the reintegration of the guerrilla group. Under the declaration the M-19 would occupy an area in the mountains of Cauca (five hundred soon arrived) where they would be protected from attack by the Colombian military. "Working tables" would be set up immediately so that the government and the group could arrive at "concrete political agreements" to bring the latter back into the political process before the beginning of the regular sessions of Congress in July. Although the Barco initiative had always called for the surrender of arms, when asked about this, M-19 commander Carlos Pizarro Leongómez said, "We are going to demobilize but we will keep our arms."[24]

On July 17, 1989, the government and the M-19 signed a pact that would lead to demobilization and disarming of the guerrillas over the next six months. The working tables would continue work on their conclusions.[25] Meanwhile, the National Congress balked at passing the Barco constitutional reform (see chapter 9). The lack of this reform and the canceling of the January 21 referendum on constitutional changes left the agreement between the government and the M-19 uncertain. In January 1990 a joint declaration of the government and the guerrilla group stated that "although suspended, the political pact remains in force and its content continues being valid." They indicated that the disarmament and pardon would not be on the date agreed to previously but that they would look for ways to make this peace formula viable.[26] In the end those ways were found, and, after seventeen years of combat, the M-19 entered into truce in March 1990. They laid down their weapons and offered candidates in the 1990 elections.

Conclusion

The Barco government increased the apparent power of the state by negotiating the M-19 demobilization. It successfully resolved the conflict with the M-19 because it was never as ideological in its Marxism as the other guerrilla groups were. Also, actions of various Colombian governments and their own foolhardiness (as in the case of the Palacio de Justicia) decimated the M-19, especially in the leadership cadre. The newsmagazine *Semana* stated: "Where the government of Virgilio Barco had greatest success was in the peace process. When the M-19 put out its hand after the liberation of Alvaro Gómez, the government of Virgilio Barco articulated a peace policy, maintaining its positions, with prerequisites, positions, objectives, and dates."[27]

Without detracting from this accomplishment, it should be pointed out that the state was not strengthened as much as it might have been because the two largest guerrilla groups—the FARC and the ELN—were still in combat with the government. It should be remembered that the cease-fires negotiated by the Betancur government with the FARC and the EPL failed during the Barco government. Therefore, it must be concluded that the Barco administration did not increase the ability of the Colombian government to implement its decisions; guerrilla groups prevented it in most of the country as much, if not more, than they did at the beginning of the government.

At the conclusion of the Barco administration the EPL was negotiating an agreement, similar to that with the M-19, that was to be signed in the beginning months of the Gaviria government. The general theme—success with small guerrilla groups but failure with the large ones—was to be continued in the Gaviria years.

4

Barco's Drug Policy

The government of Virgilio Barco pursued two different drug policies between 1986 and 1990. One was military in nature and included the seizure of drug properties, the attempt to capture drug dealers, and in many cases the extradition of the drug dealers to the United States. This military policy became paramount each time there was an assassination of a notable person that was allegedly carried out by drug dealers. The other policy was to try to find a negotiated settlement to the conflict. Semantics became important in this case. True negotiation was not possible, nor were direct conversations between the government and the drug leaders. However, intermediaries talked to both sets of actors.

Military Actions

Until November 1986, the Barco drug policy seemed to be little different in method or intensity from that of the last year of the Betancur government. The government continued cooperating with the U.S. Drug Enforcement Administration, destroying crops and factories, capturing some *narcotraficantes* (although not the "big fish"), and extraditing a few to the United States. Then a series of "total wars" between the government and the narcos began, all immediately following the assassinations of notable governmental officials.

There was, however, an important change of focus in the way government leaders thought about the drug war. Whereas previous administrations had considered the drug trade a particularly violent form of common crime, the Barco government considered it, above all, a problem of national security. That meant that the role of the armed forces in the fight against narcotraffic would be greater. For that reason, as President Barco stated to the National Congress, "The campaign against the drug trade should be understood not only as one of the law against organized crime. It is much more than that. It's a matter of the survival of democratic institutions and public liberty."[1]

Drug policy, then, became oriented to producing necessary changes to reduce tolerance of the drug trade and to strengthen the power of the government to confront it. Specific steps included (1) issuing Decree 180 of 1988, which increased the sentences for crimes against public safety and tranquility and redefined terrorism; (2) ending the prosecution of and the granting of judicial pardon for those who gave information that led to the arrest of criminals; and (3) offering rewards for information.[2]

The First War: The Cano Assassination

The Barco war policy gained momentum after assassinations. The first change came after the December 17, 1986, killing of Guillermo Cano Isaza, editor of the Liberal Bogotá daily *El Espectador* since 1952 and long a leading critic of the drug trade who constantly editorialized about its negative effects on the country.

On December 19, the Barco government issued a series of decrees in what the president called "an offensive without precedent" against the drug trade. New policies included the paying of rewards for information leading to arrests of drug leaders. Also included were the establishment of new identities, even outside the country, for individuals furnishing information to the government; the prohibition of the sale of motorcycles with motors larger than 125 cubic centimeters; and the conduct of military trials for drug-related crimes. When the Supreme Court later found such courts-martial unconstitutional, the Barco government replied with a decree establishing thirty-nine special courts for narcotics-related trials and ending the right to bail for suspects.

During the first month of this intensified drug crackdown, police officials carried out 1,666 searches, arrested 4,802 people (only 324 of whom were not released for lack of evidence), destroyed some 80,800 coca plants, seized 71 tons of marijuana and 322 kilograms of cocaine, burned 723 hectares of drug cultivation, dismantled 10 modern drug laboratories, and confiscated 43 radios, 4 helicopters, 22 airplanes, 40 automobiles, 698 weapons, and 47,774 rounds of ammunition. However, except for Evaristo Porras Ardila, none of the big fish of the drug trade were arrested; those arrested were released for lack of evidence.[3]

The biggest catch came on February 4, 1987, when Carlos Lehder Rivas was captured, secretly sent to Bogotá, and then extradited to Jacksonville, Florida, for trial. Although this case was surely important, as Lehder was one of the top Medellín Mafia leaders, it was not followed by the arrests of other leaders.

The *narcotraficantes* responded with violence to the Barco "offensive without precedent." Throughout the following year, they demonstrated their stranglehold over the country through the use of assassinations, or the threat thereof, and of bribes. By this time fifty-seven judges had been assassinated, as well as twenty-four journalists. On January 13, 1987, an assassination attempt was made against the former justice minister Enrique Parejo Gonzalez, then ambassador to Hungary, in the streets of Budapest. No one seemed safe. The country cocaine billionaires were trying to hold the country hostage.[4]

The Second War: The Hoyos Assassination

Colombia's attorney general, Carlos Mauro Hoyos, was killed near Medellín on January 25, 1988. Hoyos, who had been a known enemy of the narcos and supporter of their extradition to the United States, was kidnapped and killed the day after the drug traffickers had declared total war on anyone who favored extraditing Colombians to face drug charges in the United States. In a call to a radio network, an unidentified member of "The Extraditable Ones" *("Los Extraditables")* stated that Hoyos had been "betraying the country" and that "the war continues."[5] President Barco replied to this with new executive orders that became the Statute for the Defense of Democracy. Specific measures included increased military patrols, stiffer penalties for offenders, more judges, encouragement of plea bargaining by lighter sentences, and more protection for witnesses. Plea bargaining was practically unknown before this in Colombia.

How the narcos used violence and threats thereof, with the goal of paralyzing the justice system, was clearly seen in a letter sent to the Bogotá judge who was investigating the death of *El Espectador* editor Guillermo Cano. In it they stated that they knew "perfectly well" that there was no evidence against Escobar. Further, they warned the judge that she would not be safe if offered a foreign diplomatic post after the trial, saying, "You know perfectly well that we are capable of executing you at any place on this planet." They also promised that they would first kill all of her family, so that she would see all of her forebears and descendants die.[6]

Power also came from the narcos' wealth. The most notable use of bribery came in the case of narco leader Jorge Luis Ochoa Vásquez, who was arrested on November 21, 1987, when a routine speed check led to the Porsche in which he was riding being pulled over. Ochoa had left the Modelo prison in Bogotá on December 30, 1987, on a writ of habeas corpus after a judge ruled that he had been illegally detained because there was no warrant for his arrest. This happened despite the fact that it was known that the U.S. government wanted his extradition for trial and despite the Colombian government's having moved him to a Bogotá penitentiary to prevent his release due to bribery.[7] The Virgilio Barco government later saw to it that the judge was prosecuted.

The Third War: The Galan Assassination

The position of Luis Carlos Galán, leader of the New Liberalism movement, in opposing the drug trade had gone back as far as 1981 when the people of Antioquia elected Pablo Escobar as an alternate member of the National Congress for the Liberal Party in Antioquia. At that time Galán started his campaign of trying to get the narcos out of Liberal politics. In 1984 his friend and colleague in New Liberalism, Minister of Justice Lara, was assassinated by the narcos, logically increasing Galán's opposition. Lara's death proved to be the beginning of the total war; afterward, narcos found that no matter how much money they might make, their children would not be accepted in the best schools. They no longer could enter political campaigns as Pablo Escobar had done, and they had to live outside the major cities, hiding in the country.

Although none of the kingpins of the drug mafias were captured during the drug offensive of President Belisario Betancur, and although Barco was widely criticized for not doing enough, in 1988 and 1989 the government campaign had picked up. Cocaine was being confiscated, plants were being closed down, and seventeen hundred military and police officers who were on narco payrolls were fired.[8] As of August 14, the government had seized more cocaine in 1989 than in all of 1988. Seizure of precursor chemicals such as acetone and ammonia had also increased by 300 and 800 percent, respectively. Pablo Escobar lost US$75 million in a single operation.[9]

During 1989, drug-related violence increased, especially in the Medellín area. On July 5 a car bomb killed Antonio Roldán Betancur, governor of Antioquia. Narco death threats on Galán began on July 23, the day after the Liberal convention had approved the popular consultation—a kind of open primary (that he would win)—in which anyone voting in the congressional election could also make a presidential preference known. The threats were made by telephone and in writing. Then a friend of Galán's oldest son was kidnapped as he left school. When released half an hour later, the message conveyed was that this could be done to Juan Manuel Galán also.

The first attempt on Luis Carlos Galán's life came in Medellín on August 4, when he apparently was saved because a luncheon meeting went on longer than planned. In addition an anonymous call tipped off the police about three assassins waiting in a car. Two weeks later on the day he died, Galán told a journalist that he was nervous because "[i]t doesn't seem to matter to anyone that they were going to kill me in Medellín."[10]

Mid-August was bloody. On August 14 the judge in charge of the investigation of the assassination of Guillermo Cano resigned because of threats to his daughter. On August 16 another judge investigating drug dealers was killed in Bogotá. On the morning of Friday, August 18, the commander of the Medellín police was assassinated. In the afternoon of the day he would die, Galán stated during a visit to the newspaper *El Espectador:* "I know that they have me sentenced and I am taking precautions. For that reason, following the recommendations of security forces, I've asked my friends not to announce my public appearances ahead of time. But it is impossible to anticipate every possible attempt. I realize that."[11]

Although Galán made last-minute changes to many plans for the weekend rallies, at 8:45 P.M. in a rally with some seventeen hundred people in attendance, two assailants shot him down at close range immediately after he rose to the speaking platform. Galán suffered three wounds to the abdomen, even though he wore a bullet-proof vest. One of the bullets passed through the aorta, and although he was taken immediately to a hospital, he bled to death.[12] Later investigations were to suggest that the perpetrators were members of hit squads, trained by foreign mercenaries to assist the drug mafias in their fight with each other.[13]

President Barco went on television immediately and announced decrees that would fight the drug dealers. Most important were (1) the suspension of an article of the penal code that required a treaty for extradition, making it possible to use administrative methods—bypassing the courts—to extradite narcos; (2) the seizure of goods and real estate from suspected drug traffickers, giving individuals five days to prove that the property had been purchased with legally earned money; (3) the punishment of those who acted as proxies for the drug dealers in their purchases; and (4) in the case of drug trade and terrorism, an increase in the length of time suspects could be held without charges from one to seven days.[14]

The Barco government at once started carrying out its new policies—seizing real estate, airplanes, and other belongings of the narcos and arresting three *Extraditables* in the first week—although none of the twelve major leaders wanted in the United States, such as Pablo Escobar or Rodríguez Gacha, were included. The highest-level one was Eduardo Rodríguez Romero, who was under indictment in Atlanta for laundering US$1.2 billion of cocaine money. In sum, in the first four days, Colombian police made 800 raids, netting 678 firearms, 3,303 rounds of ammunition, 1,161 cars and trucks, 4 tons of coca paste, 62 airplanes, 18 helicopters, 141 homes, offices, and ranches, 30 yachts, 13 motorcycles, 42 two-way radios, and 5,222 farm animals and pets.[15] Although eleven thousand people were arrested, all but three thousand were released by the end of the month for lack of evidence.[16] Also, for the first time in almost thirty years, the Colombian government offered a reward for a criminal—COL$100,000,000 each for Pablo Escobar and Rodríguez Gacha.

Barco issued a second group of decrees on August 24, including four that had to do with the destination of seized and occupied goods, the end of the illicit enrichment by proxies (that is, having property put in the hands of third persons), and the control of air strips. The third and last issuance of decrees on August 31 consisted of a decree calling for the establishment of a Special Fund for the Reestablishment of Public Order and a decree about the rules for processing crimes related to public order.[17]

The narcos replied to these governmental initiatives, adding in the month after the death of Galán a new kind of violence to all the previous kinds that Colombia had suffered: a bombing campaign that combined psychological terrorism with material terrorism, applied in an indiscriminate way against all sectors of the society. This new violence began on August 24 when the drug dealers began bombings that continued until August 1990. A communiqué from the *Extraditables* stated: "We declare total and absolute war on the government, on the industrial and political oligarchy, on the journalists who have attacked and ravaged us, on the judges who have sold out to the government . . . on the presidents of unions and all those who persecuted and attacked us. . . . We will not respect the families of those who have not respected our families."[18]

This war was a logical consequence of the conflict that had begun many years before and had been escalating since. The narcos assassinated Galán not only so that he would not be president "but also as a message of terror to Colombian society to pressure for dialogue."[19] The series of bombings in October and November of 1989, according to the governmental authorities, was probably also the reply of the narcos to the extradition of three mid-range leaders. The narcos saw terrorism as a strategy employed so that Colombians, increasingly affected indiscriminately, would weaken and push for a negotiated settlement.[20] In the end, as was seen during the Gaviria government, that is exactly what happened.

There was no apparent settlement in sight during the last months of 1989. On November 27 an Avianca flight from Bogotá to Cali was bombed by the *Extraditables,* causing more than one hundred deaths. Then on December 6 the headquarters of the security police (DAS) was bombed; 63 died and 600 were wounded. President Barco, who was in Tokyo at the time, replied, "They will not defeat us. We are in the fight and will continue in it. . . . We are not going to allow ourselves to fall under the bloody tyranny of the narcoterrorists."[21]

The government won one of the most notable victories in this latest drug war when, on December 14, 1989, the elite corps of the national police killed Medellín Mafia leader José Gonzalo Rodríguez Gacha near Cartagena. Rodríguez Gacha was considered to be the individual in charge of the violent activities of the Medellín drug dealers. His death was interpreted as a turning point after the worst two-week period of the Barco presidency: when the plane and the DAS building were bombed and the constitutional reform was defeated (see chapter 9). The death of Rodríguez Gacha changed everything,[22] at least symbolically. As time would tell, very little of substance changed during the Barco years.

Indirect Negotiation

At the same time the drug wars were going on, representatives of the Colombian government were meeting with people who were meeting with delegates of Pablo Escobar. These conversations were always secret, with the government occasionally denying that they were even taking place. At times the government suspended the talks.

The First Talks: May–October 1988

Some time before 1988, Pablo Escobar had arrived at the conclusion that the way out of the war was to negotiate, as the government had negotiated with the guerrillas. In May of 1988, a Medellín lawyer named Guido Parra arranged a meeting between Escobar and Joaquín Vallejo. Vallejo then contacted the general secretary of the presidency and right hand of Virgilio Barco, Germán Montoya, who was his friend as well as a fellow Antioquenan. After a meeting with Montoya, Vallejo thought he had a green light. On his own he prepared a document of "preagreement" that was published in the newspaper *La Prensa* as the basis for the negotiation between the two parties. This manuscript never was sent to Montoya but was presented at a second meeting that Vallejo had with the Medellín leader. Escobar, informed that the government had not closed the door to dialogue, maintained that although he spoke in the name of the cartels of Medellín, Bogotá, and the coast, it would be better if all the leadership heard the proposal.[23]

Vallejo then organized a meeting in the mountains of Antioquia where he and Guido Parra met with Escobar, Rodríguez Gacha, and the Ochoa Vásquez brothers. The Medellín Mafia people said that, although they had a lot of money, they had no life. They said that their concern was for Colombia and for their families and that, with the goal of recovering tranquility, they were ready to retire from the business. In exchange for the end of extradition and a pardon, they were ready to turn over in their entirety their labs, cultivations, clandestine airports, and arms. In addition they would repatriate their capital. In general terms they tried to repeat the offer made in Panamá in May of 1984.

This was how things remained until September of 1988 when President Barco gave a speech on television in which he announced a peace proposal as a reply to the M-19's kidnapping of Conservative leader Alvaro Gómez. He said of the proposal, "We could say in simple terms that there is a violence related to the groups in arms and another that has nothing to do with subversion. This initiative is directed to those two great manifestations of disturbance."[24]

Guido Parra contacted Vallejo, who contacted Montoya, asking if this meant negotiation with the cartel. Montoya replied that the scope of the words was exactly what they said: the initiative was directed to all forms of violence. Those sentences of the speech had been drafted by the advisers from the presidential peace counsellors, who were thinking of the hired hit men and paramilitary groups when they wrote, not the narcos. Nevertheless the response of Montoya, transmitted by Vallejo to Parra and by the latter to the Mafia, was interpreted by Pablo Escobar and his people as a wink. Enthused, they drafted the document of September 15 that would become the peace proposal of the *Extraditables*.[25]

With this document in his hand, Vallejo returned to Bogotá and gave it to Montoya. The latter's position was that no negotiation would be possible unless it included also the government of the United States, which was, after all, the main consuming country asking for extradition. Although the negotiation process stagnated at this point, the actions of the government against the narcos became more intense and effective. Pablo Escobar, disgusted by what he considered an ambivalent governmental position, decided to send a message to the president: if the government wanted to give a sign of good will, it could change the commander of the Fourth Brigade in Medellín. Vallejo replied that he was not willing to pass that message on.

The Second Talks: 1989

During the first half of 1989, Vallejo and Montoya had various meetings and discussed numerous possibilities. For the Medellín Mafia the process had gone on for a year without accomplishing anything. While Montoya continued receiving Vallejo with courtesy, the military actions against the Mafia intensified. At the time of the assassination of Governor Roldán of Antioquia, the cartel decided to make the contacts between Vallejo and Montoya public. All the documents were obtained from Parra and left in the mailbox of a senator.[26]

On the day of the funeral for Luis Carlos Galán, Montoya and Vallejo met. The latter, in light of the violence, considered dialogue more important than ever. Montoya, who had always been skeptical, was even more so. On August 23 Montoya communicated to Vallejo that the doors to any type of dialogue were completely closed. Vallejo had met with Montoya ten times but never had any contact with the president. All the messages were communicated to Guido Parra, who in turn gave them to Pablo Escobar. Montoya emphasized that he did all this "personally and by my own decision"; Vallejo's impression was that the president was informed of everything.[27]

In addition to the bombings, the drug dealers responded with a proposed deal. On August 29, 1989, drug patriarch Fabio Ochoa Restrepo (not under indictment in either the United States or Colombia) wrote President Barco stating, "No more drug trafficking, no more war, no more assassinations, no more bombs, no more arson. Let's sit down and talk . . . Doctor Barco, let there be dialogue, let there be peace, let there be amnesty."[28]

The Third Talks: 1990

In January and February of 1990, there was a lull in attacks on the drug properties, and no one was extradited. Government critics charged that the government had negotiated a secret, nonaggression pact with the drug leaders, which was denied by both the government and the United States Embassy in Bogotá. At the same time the narcos proposed a "surrender," behind which there was a double motivation. The first was of humanitarian character, trying to secure the release of twenty individuals kidnapped by the narcos. The second, of political character, consisted of trying to accomplish through peace the same things that had been sought through the war, without any concessions or giving in on any principle. Escobar apparently thought that through surrender, he would be able to obtain the goal of no extradition. He was told that this was not possible but that if he surrendered and turned in his business, justice might be less rigid with him.

Pablo Escobar had entered the world of kidnapping after the death of Rodríguez Gacha. He used kidnapping as a life insurance policy, as a way to resolve problems of liquidity, and as a way to put the government up against the wall any time he wanted to. He used the families of the kidnapped to make demands of the government. These demands included the freeing of three men who were allegedly in the hands of the government; a limit of seven days was set for their release. If they were not released in that time, the narcos would kill Alvaro Diego Montoya, the son of the president's secretary, Germán Montoya.[29]

The Montoya family contacted two Antioquia industrialists, J. Mario Aristazábal and Santiago Londoño White, to handle the negotiations for the release of their son. They met with Guido Parra.[30] It was disclosed that President Barco and several cabinet officials met at least twice in January with the two Medellín businessmen who were also meeting with Pablo Escobar. One of the businessmen, Londoño White, and government officials verified that these meetings were only to obtain the release of Alvaro Montoya. But the traffickers asserted in a later communiqué that they had believed they were talking with government emissaries.[31]

The representatives of the families suggested that Escobar use the opportunity to work for the peace that he had always claimed he wanted, especially because now it was clear that he could not win the war. Escobar replied that during five years he had been trying to get the government to have a dialogue but that no one paid attention to him. He said that if the government wanted peace it would at the least have to listen to peace proposals and respect the lives of the wives and children of the narcos.[32]

Escobar, in a telephone conversation, expounded his points of view and made his demands. Among his demands were that the procurator keep a close watch on an investigation concerning a kidnapping in El Poblado and that guarantees be made for his family. It was then that the idea was proposed for Escobar's "surrender," which would be a concrete demonstration that peace was his major concern. Pablo Escobar said to the two intermediaries that his offensive capacity had not diminished and that twenty-five times a week he could explode bombs the size of the one at DAS. He also said that the government's military operations had done him no harm, that the money seized from him was insignificant in relation to what he had, and that all was the result of a disinformation campaign conducted by General Maza. Nevertheless, he made a counterproposal.[33]

The conversations led to two conclusions: (1) that any kind of dialogue was impossible if preconditions were demanded (as that was the reason earlier efforts had failed) but (2) that the petition that the lives of family members be respected could be allowed because it was a right guaranteed by law. It had been put to Escobar directly that the only possibility that anyone would listen to his peace proposals was if he were to give up. He presented his counterproposal: total and immediate surrender, including turning in the business and the arms, in exchange for being judged by the Colombian justice system. This proposal was given to former president Alfonso López, with the request that he pass it on to the government and to public opinion. He refused to do so, arguing that it meant no extradition and as such was not a surrender but a negotiation.[34]

Escobar's representatives insisted that he was willing to do anything except surrender to the authorities, who would put him on an airplane to the United States for trial. They added that ending the war and, more specifically, the narcoterrorism was more important than extraditing Escobar. For this reason, they argued that a counterproposal must be made.[35]

It seemed that the process had ended unsuccessfully until a new formula was suggested: to use the same mechanism as in the informal dialogues between the *Coordinadora Guerrillera* and the *Comisión de Notables*, with the same spirit, in order to create some conditions in which the government could expound its reactions to Pablo Escobar's proposed surrender. A commission was set up that included Mario Revollo Bravo (primate archbishop of Colombia), Alfonso López, former president Julio César Turbay, and Diego Montaña Cuellar (president of the *Unión Patriótica*). López wrote the draft of the government's response, including general principles but nothing specific.[36]

The problem that remained was that nothing was agreed to beyond the general language of the two communiqués, making it possible for each side to make its own interpretation. The government wanted a complete surrender, leaving the concessions that it might give until that was a reality. The *Extraditables*, although they said they would submit to Colombian justice, really wanted the status of political delinquents so they could obtain amnesty, something Colombians considered absolutely impossible.[37]

The *Extraditables'* communiqué included the following points:

We accept the triumph of the state, of the institutions, and of the legitimately established government. . . .

. . . We resolve to free immediately Patricia Echavarría and her daughter and the others retained. . . .

. . . We have decided to suspend the delivery of drugs and will turn in arms, explosives, laboratories, hostages, clandestine landing strips and the other elements of our activities, in the moment in which we are given constitutional and legal guarantees.

. . . There will be no attacks with explosives in any part of the national territory and we have ordered the suspension of all kinds of executions of political leaders, governmental and labor functionaries, journalists, police, and members of the military.[38]

In February 1990, the *Extraditables* "kidnapped" twenty-four journalists who were to be witnesses to the turning in of a laboratory complex for cocaine processing. The narcos also released a school bus with one thousand kilos of dynamite, as well as a helicopter. People were impressed. This was part of the unilateral surrender by the *Extraditables* in response to the call of the *Notables*. They also liberated the Montoya son, without the government giving anything, after Escobar made some unacceptable demands. The cross of communiqués between the *Notables* and the *Extraditables* made all of this possible.

The problem was that the two sides had different interpretations of what had happened and the implications of it. The position of the government was that it was accepting an unconditional surrender, with no agreements of any kind, and that it was up to the narcos to demonstrate their good faith by turning in their arms and dismantling their businesses. Only then could the government be generous, within the parameters of the law. For the narcos what was underlying all of this was the elimination of extradition. Although nothing was agreed to, it was understood that if they carried out these conditions, extradition would be eliminated—or things would move in that direction.

By early 1990, the problem for Pablo Escobar had become one of life or death, not of more money. From the perspective of the *Extraditables,* trial by Colombian law could lead to a pardon, if one were lucky, and if things went badly one might have to spend two or three years in prison. There had been few prison terms of more than eight years. Assassins usually served less time than that. In these cases few people thought that Colombian justice operated efficiently. *"Plata o plomo"* ("money or bullets") had worked very well for the narcos before. The truth was that Pablo Escobar hoped to get through *"rendición"* (surrender) all that he could not get through *"diálogo"* (dialogue), that is, to get the government to listen.[39]

In early March of 1990, President Barco said the narcos should stop making threats and surrender. Later in the month the drug chiefs threatened to start the war again after the two-month pause, with a communiqué from the *Extraditables* stating, "We will not remain indifferent in the face of betrayal, torture, and assassinations of our companions."[40] In effect the war was reinitiated and included many indiscriminate bombings by the narcos, including two in upper-middle-income sectors of Bogotá on the Saturday in May before Mother's Day. Fourteen Colombians died in those bombings, including four children shopping for gifts for their mothers.[41]

The government was divided, and there was not much clarity over what to do. For this reason the declarations of Virgilio Barco were contradictory; they oscillated between morning headlines like "The Narcos Must Be Listened To" and afternoon affirmations such as "There Never Has Been Or Will Be Negotiation."[42] The armed forces did not believe the narcos because Escobar's life history did not inspire respect for them. However, some civilians within the government had a different idea. They thought that if there were some way to obtain through peace the same things that might have been gained through war, then this alternative should not be discarded.[43] And some members of the Barco government had such close connections to the drug groups that war against the Mafia was war against them also.[44] On the side of the *"pulso firme"* ("strong pulse" or the hard line) were Generals Maza and Gómez Padilla, as well as Minister Lemos. The *"mano tendida"* ("outstretched hand" or the soft line) side included the president, who had said that "if the narcotraficantes give up and turn themselves in, an agreement could be considered."

But the situation exploded when it was least expected. The uncontrolled declarations of the minister of government to the effect that the *Unión Patriótica* was connected to the guerrilla activities of the FARC, and the disagreeable coincidence that a few hours later on March 22,

Bernardo Jaramillo, presidential candidate of the UP, was assassinated, opened a Pandora's box.[45] The cause here was the government's statement that the *Extraditables* had been the "intellectual authors" of the Jaramillo assassination.

Conclusion

As described in this chapter, the government of Virgilio Barco vacillated between a military policy and a policy of talks with representatives of the drug dealers. The final result was failure, as Pablo Escobar and other Medellín drug leaders were still at liberty, and violence continued at a level that was very high, even by Colombian standards.

One might ask, especially given the number of deaths that resulted from the military policy, why the government of Virgilio Barco did not make more attempts at conflict resolution through bargaining. One reason was that there was much opposition, both in the government and in educated Colombian society, for this kind of treatment for the narcos. The journal *Semana* captured the basis of the antagonism to bargaining with the narcos when it pointed out the difference between them and the guerrillas in juridical, ethical, and political dimensions:

> To begin with, the amnesty decreed in 1982 for guerrilla groups covered political crimes, but did not include aggravated homicide, terrorism, and murder outside of combat, which are precisely the crimes for which the Medellín cartel is wanted. On the other hand, the guerrillas are recognized as having a political status since, independent of their methods of struggle, the reasons that lead them to take arms are ideological. Those who have studied the question affirmed that the motivation of the narcos was the desire to make money and that any possible political motivation they might have came from the defense of that interest. However, this interpretation might be arbitrary if one keeps in mind that today there are many guerrillas dedicated more to making money than to political ideals. . . . But, in addition to this, perhaps the principal reason that the state does not consider any negotiation with the narcos possible is out of respect for the martyrs who have fallen in this struggle.[46]

The last reason—respect for the martyrs—should be emphasized, as guerrilla violence almost always was in the countryside, with the deaths and injuries being to the peasants and the soldiers. When others were affected by guerrilla violence, as will be seen in chapter 6, the whole nature of negotiations changed. The narcos not only placed their bombs in the major cities, hence killing people of various social

backgrounds, but they also assassinated "good people" such as journalists, judges, cabinet officials, and presidential candidates.

As a result of this kind of argument, all the efforts of the state during the Barco years were directed to capturing or killing Escobar and
Rodríguez Gacha, who, according to the government, were the two
people responsible for the narcoterrorism in the country. Within the
government there was consensus that if Escobar and Rodríguez Gacha
were captured or killed, narcoterrorism would end.[47] Although it
might have been certain that those two individuals were responsible
for the terrorism to that point, it seems disingenuous to think that
their removal would end it.

As in the case of the guerrilla groups, divisions within the government, both in Bogotá among policymakers and in the field, also had
their effects on narco policy. For example, during the first week of July
1990, when more than three thousand men of the *Cuerpo Especial* (Special Corps) of the national police, of the army, and of DAS searched
for Pablo Escobar in Magdalena Medio, the jealousies of the different
establishments were seen. As a result of inefficient coordination, even
though twenty-five people were arrested and 1,800 kilos of dynamite
were seized, as well as firearms and COL$25 million, Pablo Escobar
was not caught.[48] Nevertheless, the director general of the police, General Miguel Antonio Gómez Padilla, said that this "Operation Apocalypse II" marked "the beginning of the end of the empire of Pablo
Escobar," whose organization has been 80 percent dismantled.[49]

In an evaluation of the Barco narco policy, the Bogotá weekly,
Semana, concluded: "Perhaps one of the greatest gaffes of communication that Virgilio Barco committed was having said in his speech at
the opening of the congressional session on last July 20, that the war
against narcoterrorism had been won. That same day, the number of
police assassinated in Medellín in recent months passed 200 and an
operation had just failed, one in which for the umpteenth time, it had
been announced that Pablo Escobar would be captured. Although all
presidents use hyperbole in their farewell addresses, that time there
was an overdose."[50]

On a more positive note, *Semana* continued that, in spite of the government's not having captured Pablo Escobar, the Barco policy was a
success. The drug trade, as organized crime, had been badly damaged.
"At the beginning of the government, the drug trade was an independent power, practically parallel to the State. Now it is a power against
the State and it is retreating." Eradicating the drug trade would have
been impossible while the demand continued to exist. "But the orga-

nized drug network that existed in Colombia has had its back broken."[51]

But Colombians, the Bogotá weekly continued, were not as concerned with the trade as they were with the terrorism. Its infrastructure had been weakened, and, although it would always be possible to put a bomb in a supermarket, the terrorists, as was true everywhere in the world when they were losing wars, were getting weaker. Not all agreed with *Semana*'s analysis on this point, and, as was seen during the Gaviria government, the Pablo Escobar group still had significant power.

The Barco government also failed in its extradition policy and in addition had failed in the so-called narcodialogue. About the latter, *Semana* said, "In the drug war there was nothing more ambiguous, nothing more confused, and nothing more serious. Serious because many persons died, including presidential candidates, as vengeance for what the drugtraffickers considered foul play on part of the government."[52]

The government position was that it was one thing to listen to a proposal and another to accept it and change policy. The misunderstanding that was generated around these two interpretations was the most costly of all the problems of semantics that this government had, because the assassination of Luis Carlos Galán coincided chronologically with the breakdown of the first round of bargaining and that of Jaramillo and Pizarro with the breakdown of the second. *Semana* concluded that the bad handling of this situation was perhaps the most serious shortcoming of the government of Virgilio Barco.

The major conclusion of this chapter is in keeping with that of *Semana*. The drug dealers were more of a problem for the Colombian government after Virgilio Barco's administration than they were before. After all, the narcos controlled more of the national territory than ever before; had more wealth that no doubt entered Colombian democratic politics in increasing, albeit unknown, ways; and eliminated at a minimum the major candidate for president. If anything, Barco's government was even less successful in increasing the power of the state through weakening the narcos than it was in amplifying the state through diminishing the power of the guerrillas.

However, some argued that, even though the Barco government had failed to capture Pablo Escobar, it had won the war against narcoterrorism. Some government sources went so far as to say that the power of the Medellín drug group had been effectively dismantled.[53]

A statement by the patriarch of the Medellín Mafia, Fabio Ochoa, also made it seem as though the Gaviria government would be bargaining from a position of strength. Ochoa gave the impression that the drug dealers were weak when he stated: "This war was lost, and the important thing is that victory not bring revenge. . . . Well, ok, let's accept that the fight for negotiation failed and nothing is left that can be done except surrendering to the justice system. This could be done, but only if the people are put in jail in Colombia."[54]

Colombian political scientists Luis Javier Orjuela and Cristina Barrera P., however, conclude: "We could say that five years after the vehement declaration of war on the drug trade by President Betancur and despite the severe setbacks administered by the government of President Barco, things seemed to be much like they were at the beginning. Not only had the battle not been won, but the power of the drug trade was growing and violence in the country continued increasing."[55]

The information presented in this chapter and later ones suggests that this is the correct conclusion. Despite all of its initiatives, the Barco government had failed to end the drug terrorism—perhaps because too many of its high-level members were on the payroll of the drug groups.

5

Self-Defense, Private Justice, and Paramilitary Groups

The Final Piece of the Jigsaw Puzzle

In this chapter I describe how the Virgilio Barco government went from ignoring the vigilante groups to developing a mild policy to address them, while rejecting the idea that the groups were somehow tied to the government. In addition I demonstrate that the dynamics of Colombian society led to vigilante groups being a greater problem in 1990 than they had been in 1986; I show a continued weakness of the Colombian state to control law enforcement within the boundaries of the country.

Vigilante Groups in 1986

In the month of Virgilio Barco's election, National Procurator Carlos Jiménez Gómez started a controversy when he cited the names of military officials he believed were involved in the death squads operating in the country. Stating that he would not be following his constitutional mandate if he did not denounce what was taking place in the "Argentinization" of the country, which might be the precursor of its "Central Americanization," he concluded that "the National Congress should name a special commission as a citizen-complaint mechanism, not with investigative ends but as a forum for charges and of evaluation, in order for, with the help of the Office of the Procurator, the political class to become connected with the defense of the citizenry in general and of the democratic order in particular."[1] In the previous five months, the procurator reported, 350 unidentified persons had been killed in Cali alone.

Minister of Defense General Miguel Vega Uribe first admitted the possibility of excesses on the part of junior officers and promised that the military justice system would investigate and punish accordingly, but he later categorically denied the procurator's accusations. General (retired) Alvaro Valencia Tovar also disagreed with Jiménez, criticizing him for making accusations before normal criminal procedures had been followed, for naming individuals, and for suggesting that subordinates not follow orders. The Colombian Association of Retired Military Officers argued that the procurator, in addition to making unjust accusations, was placing the lives of military personnel in danger. This led Enrique Santos Calderón to write in *El Tiempo*: "It's possible that a good part of the Colombian public might not know—or might not want to know—that for a number of years a 'dirty war' has been carried out in Colombia, in which there is no human right with any value that is not lambasted by that sordid and underground side of the chronic political and social violence that we suffer."[2]

The controversy continued in the months that followed. The military procurator "found" 99 of the 313 people who were on the official list of "disappeared" since 1977. He contended that the "dirty war" was of the guerrillas against the military and that criticisms such as that of Jiménez psychologically benefitted the former. Amnesty International announced that there were six hundred deaths from the dirty war in the first half of 1986; the military procurator replied that many of the "disappeared" on that organization's list were common criminals.

Procurator Jiménez feared the country was nearing a military dictatorship not only because of the actions of the military but because civilians were becoming afraid to state their views or enter debates. Elected *Unión Patriótica* officials, including senators and representatives, were assassinated. In response to the assassination of one senator, Minister of Government Fernando Cepeda stated, "The Government is convinced that the military forces and the police are committed to the business of reconciliation" and not involved in the deaths.[3] The UP left the Congress for a time because of the violent deaths of its members. A member of the UP leadership, Alberto Rojas Puyo, asserted: "The crisis comes from the events created by the militaristic mentalities and behavior of the extreme right as well as the revolutionary groups. The activities of terroristic paramilitaries against popular leaders and amnestied guerrillas serve as sustenance for the guerrilla tendencies of the left."[4]

It is not surprising that, given these circumstances, increasing numbers of Colombians tried to protect themselves. In August 1987, a conflict erupted within the government when the minister of defense, General Rafael Samudio Molina, and the minister of justice, José Manual Arias Carrizosa, both came out in favor of "self-defense groups" such as were being formed by *campesinos* and landowners in the *departamento* of Huila. National Procurator Carlos Mauro Hoyos incorrectly replied, "Groups of self-defense, brought together and organized by their own members, are not authorized by the Constitution or the laws," and President Barco added, "In no way have the formation of self-defense groups been aided by the government, and I am sure that, when it is analyzed, it will be seen there is neither confusion nor differences of opinions."[5] Investigations in the years that followed, including ones by the government itself, were to show that military officers in many cases did play roles in the founding, financing, training, and arming of self-defense groups. As pointed out in chapter 2, the government had indeed authorized them.

The procurator began an investigation amid criticism of the Barco government from all sides. Rich people already protected themselves with bodyguards from private companies; self-defense groups for *campesinos* would serve the same purpose for them.

Thousands of incidents occurred in the dirty war during the first year of the Barco government. In many cases, neither the perpetrators nor the reasons could be documented. Frequently, the Colombian press described the deaths of dozens of citizens, concluding that the guilty parties were unknown. Two cases, one each from the following two years, serve as examples of the divergent activities of the paramilitary groups. The first was an individual assassination; the second was a massacre.

The first case was the October 12, 1987, assassination of the president of the UP, Jaime Pardo Leal, presidential candidate of the FARC-instigated party in the 1986 presidential elections. UP leaders, including Pardo, had long contended that its party leaders and candidates were being killed by right-wing death squads, perhaps with the tacit approval of military officials. The party claimed that some five hundred of its leaders had been assassinated since the establishment of the party under the Betancur "democratic opening." Pardo's assassination led to demonstrations, violence, looting, and deaths throughout the country, especially in Bogotá, Barranquilla, Bucaramanga, and Barrancabermeja.

As is often the case in such assassinations, there was considerable delay in establishing either who performed the act or who were the "intellectual authors" of it. In the Pardo case it was not until mid-

November that the minister of justice suggested that investigations, to that point, indicated that the assassination was instigated by the narcos as retribution over the inequitable division of drug profits between them and the FARC guerrillas who assisted them through armed protection of the drug-manufacturing process. However, he also suggested that self-defense groups and other paramilitary groups might also have been a part of this "involved scheme." Although the actual perpetrators had been captured, those guilty of planning and organizing it were "still in the shadows."[6]

Several weeks before Pardo's death, Minister of Government César Gaviria (who would be president from 1990 to 1994) revealed that there were 128 known death squads in Colombia. Some of these could not be considered right wing; indeed, some had been established by the narcos, including the widely known MAS, whose goals had more to do with protecting its members than with ideology.

The second case was in Segovia, Antioquia. On November 11, 1988, forty-three people were massacred. Although there were numerous incidents of death squad activity during the year, perhaps the most dramatic was this one in the turbulent Magdalena Medio area. Armed individuals took over Segovia and fired indiscriminately for several hours, wounding at least thirty in addition to the killings. The governor of Antioquia, Antonio Roldán Betancur, called it "the most shameless manifestation of violence" in the *departamento* in recent decades.[7]

Several days later, the Death to Revolutionaries of the Antioquian Northeast movement (MRN, *Movimiento Muerte a Revolucionarios del Nordeste Antioqueño*) sent a message denying that they had carried out the Segovia massacre and blaming the ELN and FARC. The statement continued: "Before the people of the Antioquian Northeast, the MRN promises to confront and annihilate militarily the barbarous material authors of the genocide and to turn the intellectual authors over to the authorities with the goal that the barbarous act be recognized and that there remain no doubt about who are the promoters of massacres and dirty war in the region and in the country."[8] This, in effect, was a promise to massacre the massacrers.

Despite this denial many thought that the MRN was to blame. People also wondered why the government troops stationed in Segovia did not leave their barracks during the attack. Military procurator Manuel Betancur observed, "Instead of coming to defend the people, the police entrenched themselves, even though the criminals had to come very close to the police headquarters to commit their transgressions." Meanwhile in Segovia new signs were seen on the walls that read, "Segovia, we will pacify you"; they were signed by the MRN.[9]

Even two weeks after the massacre there was a feeling of distrust. It was not easy to convince people who had never seen justice work that this time it would be different. The minister of defense, General Manuel Jaime Guerrero Paz, used a communiqué to differentiate "paramilitary groups" from "guerrilla groups" and in an occurrence without precedence in the history of statements by high-level officials said, "We had to make it known to the middle-level commanders throughout the national territory that both have to be combatted with equal strength."[10]

The Segovia case showed that by 1988 the paramilitary groups had become tired of just killing leftist leaders; rather, they decided to do away with the population in which they thought there might be a guerrilla presence. The year was later called the Year of the Massacres. In the majority of the cases the lives of the innocents—children, women, old people—were not respected. In other cases, such as one in Urabá, the massacre was done with a list in hand to specify the victims. Paramilitary groups of the extreme right, allied with drug traffickers who sometimes counted on the complicity of some military officers (according to the DAS and the procurator), formed a veritable picture of impunity, with the blessing of more than a few sectors of society.

In addition to the narco money increasingly getting involved with paramilitary groups, either through founding them or taking over groups set up by legitimate landowners, paramilitary groups grew in numbers and in numbers of activities during 1988. In addition to the MRN, others included *Muerte a Secuestadores* (which was set up by the narcos, as described earlier), *Ejército Rojo Facista* (Red Fascist Army, Granada), *Movimiento Obrero Estudiantil Nacional Socialista* (MOENS, National Socialist Student Worker Movement, Medellín), *Muerte a Revolucionarios del Nordeste* (Death to Revolutionaries of the Northeast, Medio Magdalena), *La Sociedad de Amigos de Ocaña* (Society of Friends of Ocaña) *Juventud Anticomunista Colombiana* (Colombian Anticommunist Youth), and *Movimiento Muerte a Revolucionarios del Oriente* (MMRO, Death to Revolutionaries of the East Movement, Meta). The investigation of one of the 1988 massacres demonstrated that deserters from FARC and ELN were received in a friendly fashion by death squads.[11]

Little hope for real change came in 1989, as the year began with a paramilitary group in Santander killing fifteen members of a governmental investigating committee. The war no longer was only between the right and the left but now also extended to those who investigated it. Confusion began within the very government. Although the director of criminal direction, Carlos Eduardo Lozano, did not hesitate to place blame on the paramilitary groups, General Farouk Yanine Díaz, commander of the Second Division of the army with headquarters in Bucaramanga, accused the Twenty-third Front of the FARC.

National Procurator Horacio Serpa said that the paramilitary groups were "causing more damage to the state than they are causing to their open, clear and certain enemies." Going back several years, Colombians had become aware that the paramilitary boom had begun to resemble the asphyxiating practices of extortion and kidnapping carried out by guerrilla groups in vast regions of the nation. For live-stock raisers in many places, the moment arrived when it was more practical to change from the "guerrilla vaccination" to the death squad "security tax."[12]

With the massacre of the governmental commission in mid-January of 1989, the paramilitary people sent the message that they did not want the noses of the investigative groups of the government poked into their affairs. This meant, according to Procurator Serpa, that there had been a qualitative change in the armed Right. No longer was it a matter of irregular counterguerrilla groups operating in some areas of the country but of a powerful organization of the extreme Right, just as subversive as the guerrillas that they claimed to be fighting. In Serpa's interpretation, "It is the matter of a force that is an enemy of the state and the society that it pretends to defend."[13]

In February 1989, the *Federación Colombiana de Educadores* (FECODE, Colombian Federation of Teachers) made known that a thousand teachers were threatened by death squads in 1988 and that eighty-eight were killed. Many more left their teaching positions—in isolated areas of Meta, for example. At the same time ten judges in Bogotá proclaimed, "The despicable acts that a paramilitary group took against honest employees of the judicial system are a peremptory declaration to the Colombian government that within the country there are small independent states that defy the law."[14]

On March 3, 1989, a death squad assassinated *Unión Patriótica* leader José Antequera in the Bogotá International Airport, at the same time seriously wounding Liberal senator Ernesto Samper, one of the precandidates for president at the time and later to be elected president in 1994. Antequera had given his analysis of the paramilitary groups in an interview with *Semana* early on the day of his assassination:

I believe that there is not the slightest doubt that it's the matter of a national paramilitary organization, very well coordinated. . . .

Those [drug dealers] are financing this crime wave. But they could not be carrying this out without a high level of complicity from entire structures of the armed forces. . . . In the regions there are structures of various officials and subofficials that are accomplices of the dirty war.

Let's look at the case of Córdoba, where Fidel Castaño walks "like Pedro in his house" around his three farms. Everyone, beginning with the Brigade, knows where he is but no one seizes him. There is complicity, of this there is not the slightest doubt.

We have a discussion with President Barco about this matter. He says that military justice should take charge of it. We believe that will not work. We have suggested to him the creation of a high-level court, an entity above all suspicion, to investigate the dirty war and purify the Armed Forces.[15]

The morning he left the position of general procurator, Horacio Serpa Uribe criticized both the guerrilla and the paramilitary groups. In an interview with *Semana*, he stated: "Actions to reduce and counteract the paramilitary phenomenon are absolutely necessary—judicial actions and actions of the public forces, as well as a pedagogic and therapeutic action with those sectors that have been stimulating or financing the paramilitary activity, so that they might understand that is the worst path to confront guerrilla violence."[16]

The Dynamics of Region and of Other Groups

The foregoing gives highlights of the development of paramilitary groups during the Virgilio Barco government. The deterioration of the Colombian state in the Barco years can be better seen by first studying regional variations and, second, by showing how both the armed forces and the drug dealers became involved with the paramilitary groups during the Barco years. The logical conclusion is that if both were working with the paramilitaries, ironically, the Colombian military and the Medellín cartel were working together.

Regional Dynamics: Magdalena Medio, Urabá, and Córdoba

Although paramilitary groups affected almost all parts of Colombia, no doubt the three areas most affected were Magdalena Medio, Urabá, and Córdoba. The ways they were affected varied to an extent, as the discussion to follow will show.

Magdalena Medio

Gonzalo de Jesús Pérez arrived in the Magdalena Medio in 1951 as a member of the ELN and as a nurse for the FARC. At the beginning of the 1970s he organized the peasant self-defense groups to fight his own former guerrilla chiefs. In mid-1987 he gave the command of those groups to his son, Henry de Jesús Pérez. Although Gonzalo wanted to fight as long as there was a communist in Colombia, Henry and the younger leaders thought that war only brought death, and they wanted to consider dialogue. In July 1991, Gonzalo was killed in Puerto Boyacá.[17]

In the Magdalena Medio, the paramilitary groups were originally supported by the Association of Ranchers and Peasants of the Magdalena Medio (ACDEGAM, *Asociación Campesina de Agricultores y Ganaderos del Magdalena Medio*), whose leaders were quite enthused with the idea. In 1983 bodies began to appear, sometimes mutilated or tortured, of those who were accused of having some connection with the guerrilla groups. By the end of 1983 the "Health Brigades" began appearing, preceding the "cleaning operations."

As the organization grew, new demands emerged for communications, armament, or equipment in general. The patrol members asked for better salaries, and, according to one of the testimonies collected by the authorities, money began to be scarce. It was not easy to ask the ranchers to increase their donations because there was a chance of danger that the self-defense contributions were going to be more onerous than the guerrilla protection money.[18]

Urabá

In Urabá as elsewhere, it was not clear who began the dirty war. But by the beginning of the Barco administration citizens lived in the "dictatorship of the proletariat," and a counterrevolution had begun. The general sentiment was, "Enough is enough." One banana farmer said, "It is a conflict between democracy and communism."[19] The conviction of many was that Urabá needed an anticommunist crusade in which the spilling of blood was inevitable. As the government was in no condition to assume that responsibility, they thought it depended on the "good people" of the region.[20]

The lack of means of communication, the terribly unsanitary conditions, and the lack of an educational policy were some of the constants during the first two decades of the settlement of Urabá. The EPL arrived in 1964, led by Francisco Caraballo, among others, at the time the banana industry was beginning. They dedicated themselves to organizing the banana workers, to teaching them self-defense techniques, and, along the way, to developing one of the strongest and most profitable kidnapping and extortion rings that had been seen in the country.[21]

The Fifth Front of the FARC arrived later. As a consequence in Urabá, a situation without precedent in the history of Colombia existed: the political and armed conflict of two guerrilla organizations, with a high penetration in the labor sectors. During the Betancur years, with a new guerrilla legitimacy, the labor unions achieved an unusual power; the rapid growth of unions was seen, as in the case of the agrarian labor union that went from 147 members before the treaty to 4,500 in 1985. If what had existed there had been a "savage capitalism," no less savage was the labor leadership and the working class and guerrillas that supported it.[22]

This reality led the medium and large property holders of Urabá to the conclusion that the eradication of the violence was their job. The by-product of this feeling was the formation and financing of paramilitary groups and the solidarity—even the complicity in some cases—of elements of the armed forces in this crusade.[23]

Córdoba

In January 1989, a group of ranchers in Córdoba sent a letter to President Virgilio Barco that read as follows: "We are ready, Mr. President, even to renounce that collective defense used so effectively in other regions." This was a tacit recognition of the supposed legitimacy of paramilitary groups and private justice. The president of the National Federation of Ranchers stated, "When the Army knows that there is a focus of violence, in trying to get to it, it takes the wrong road almost on purpose."[24]

The truth of the Córdoba drama was that the guerrilla groups had imposed their own law. The regional ranchers had a choice between the threats of the guerrillas if they did not pay the "vaccination" and the threats of the paramilitary groups if they did pay it. Paramilitary groups had not proliferated there as they had in other areas. Although it was evident that they did exist and were as bloody as those of Magdalena Medio, those groups were more the result of the appearance on the plains of Córdoba of the nouveaux riches of agriculture—the narcos—than of the traditional ranchers united in a common front.

Of the latter, the majority, although they had begun to calculate how much a private defense group would cost, had not dared to make the jump to paramilitarism.

What was certain was that if Magdalena Medio had been converted into the focus of the paramilitary groups and the Eastern Plains had become the principal nest of the narcos, the department of Córdoba was about to become both things. To this was added the army's difficulty in controlling the region, not so much because they did not want to as because they did not have the wherewithal. Tactical problems and the lack of equipment kept the army from responding immediately to guerrilla actions.[25]

The Military and the Drug Dealers in the Paramilitary Groups

The complicated picture became more so because of the involvement of the Colombian armed forces and the Medellín drug gang in the paramilitary groups. In the end, there were all kinds of combinations of people with the same enemy—leftist guerrillas, radical parties, and labor leaders.

The Armed Forces

In October 1988, Carlos Vicente Meléndez, a member of the municipal council in the Magdalena Medio, was assassinated. According to a 1983 report of National Procurator Carlos Jiménez Gómez, Meléndez (a major in the army) and Pablo Guarín were the founders of the paramilitary group MAS. More than once they were also accused by the leader of the *Unión Patriótica*, Jaime Pardo Leal, of being the organizers of paramilitary groups in Magdalena Medio. Meléndez had stated in a television interview: "The UP and the Communist party make those frightening accusations against me because when I was commander of the Army in Arauca I was hard on the guerrillas and later when I arrived at Yocopí and there was a hegemonic power of the Communist party there, because there was a lot of guerrilla pressure. But once the guerrillas left the area the domination that the communists had was ended."[26]

Over the previous few months, Meléndez had been in favor of dialogue between the government and the guerrilla groups if the dialogue included the paramilitary groups. For him dialogue alone with the guerrillas was not feasible if they left out "those who organized themselves against the extortion and fraud and who call themselves self-defense groups."[27]

Mid-level regional commanders of the military and the police were also directly or indirectly involved. More than two years of investigations about the paramilitary phenomenon allowed the authorities to draw the organizational chart of these groups. In the chart, drug dealers, ranchers, mid-level military commanders, and paid assassins were combined. The axis of their operations was between Puerto Boyacá and Puerto Berrío in Magdalena Medio. The narcos were added when they bought the best lands in the area.[28] The information about the connections among the paramilitary organization and the armed forces and the police was most jealously guarded by the authorities. Data showed how easily Henry Pérez could get safe-conduct passes and buy arms from the Bárbula Brigade.[29]

In May 1989, Colonel Luis Bohórquez, commander of the army in Puerto Boyacá, was transferred. In his tearful farewell message he said, "I thank deputy Leonardo Guarín [founder of self-defense group] for the money generously donated to help us maintain public order." This confirmed what had only been rumored before: the coexistence of armed forces and paramilitary groups. Bohórquez had been the subject of an investigation for his possible connections to the training of paramilitary groups, the granting of permits for arms used by them, and logistical support for the schools they ran in Magdalena Medio.[30]

The investigative organizations affirmed that the arms used by the paramilitary were bought from the military industry, through the Bárbula Battalion, and that the leaders had blank safe-conduct passes signed by the colonel. Also in the Magdalena Medio the military looked favorably on the "clean-up campaign" against communists, helpers of the guerrillas, teachers, labor leaders, and in general "anyone who might smell like a subversive." The authorities, particularly in some sectors of the army, participated in the campaign.

For many commanders of battalion and brigade, helping groups of peasants to arm themselves against the guerrilla groups was not a transgression of the law; rather, it was a defense of democracy and the constitution. The cliché "The enemy of my enemy is my friend" was shown to be especially apt when the internal rules of the army provided support for these groups. "To organize, instruct, and help the self-defense groups should be a permanent objective of the Military Forces where the population is loyal and aggressive actions against the enemy are manifest."[31]

In addition to doing their duty by helping the self-defense groups, the military also thought that, in agreement with the rest of the Colombians, the justice system did not work in the country. The belief was, "If one captures a delinquent, the judge either for money or out of fear will end up freeing him, that is, if they don't put a bomb in the jail to break him out. And if by a miracle he is sentenced, a Belisario arrives, frees him, and gives him a taxi."[32] The last reference was to the Betancur peace plans, which included funds for either education or businesses for demobilized guerrilla fighters.

The Medellín Drug Dealers

In the late 1970s a new aspect of "self-defense" was the formation of armed groups by the narcotraffickers; the groups were made up primarily of adolescent delinquents. The first of these groups had their origin in Medellín and were recruited in the northeast slums. Among them the group that stood out was the self-denominated Little Cheeses, whose members were connected to the assassination of Lara Bonilla. The assassination of Guillermo Cano was attributed to another called the Priscos.[33]

In the case of massacres of peasants in Urabá and Córdoba, the DAS confirmed that two narcotraffickers—Fidel Castaño and César Cure, who were owners of large farms in the south of Córdoba—paid a group of hired assassins to commit the crimes. The material authors of the crime had been set up as a self-defense group by Fidel Castaño, a kind of "Rambo" who dedicated himself to paramilitary activities after his father had been kidnapped by the FARC and then died at their hands.[34]

The participation and help of drug traffickers in this sinister mode of justice had a clear explanation. The narcos invested profits from their business in vast extensions of land and livestock. They did this principally in those regions where the traditional ranchers, because of the presence of the guerrillas and the absence of the government, began to sell their lands. The narcos' condition as new landowners, their custom of deciding their own affairs, and their status as nouveaux riches were the perfect mixture for a political-military project of the extreme Right. Struck by the apparent efficacy of this private justice modality and without hope, because of its inefficiency, that the state apparatus would protect their lives and property, many non-drug-traffic ranchers got on the paramilitary bandwagon, not thinking much about the consequences of the monster they were creating.[35]

There were also chance meetings of the paramilitary and drug gangs. At the beginning of 1985, for example, the paramilitary group in Magdalena Medio captured a cocaine shipment. The narco owners contacted the paramilitary chiefs in Puerto Boyacá, and negotiations led to an agreement that the guerrilla groups and the communists were common enemies of the two. This was the beginning of a romance that ended in marriage, with narcotraffickers and paramilitary members easily agreeing on their goals. With the passage of time, the chiefs of the organization in Puerto Boyacá got on a first-name basis with leaders of the Medellín drug gang. New capital followed. With more money it was easy to form new schools for paramilitary members, who then began to combine with the hired assassins.

It was also simple to extend the paramilitary organization to new areas and to move the groups from their original self-defense posture to one of attack. The Urabá–Córdoba–Bajo Cauca–Magdalena Medio axis soon was covered by the "tentacles of the paramilitary octopus," which had principal goals of (1) protecting the region from the extortion, kidnapping, and other practices of the guerrillas, (2) preparing and training escorts for the cartel and paramilitary leaders, and (3) resisting militants and leaders of the *Unión Patriótica* and other political and labor organizations, as well as representatives of the government, political parties, or other organizations of society, that might oppose narcotrafficking. To meet these objectives, the primitive self-defense training schools were replaced with two new ones—the Galaxias school in Pacho, Cundinamarca, directed by one Marcelino Panesso and financed by Rodríguez Gacha, and Cero-81, which was near Puerto Boyacá and was supervised by Henry Pérez.[36]

By 1987 the paramilitary organizations had attained a level that their financiers considered optimal. Their direction was definitely in the hands of the cartel of Medellín. General Maza Márquez explained: "The paramilitary groups, as we know them today in Colombia, are the particular interpretation that the narcotraffickers have made of the self-defense groups." In early 1989 some Israelis arrived to assist in the training. Fifty students were recruited. Henry de Jesús Pérez chose twenty from Magdalena Medio; Rodríguez Gacha chose twenty from Pacho; Víctor Carranza chose five from the Llanos; and Pablo Escobar and Jorge Ochoa chose five from Medellín.[37]

There was no doubt that Puerto Boyacá, cradle of these groups and what one functionary called "a kind of paramilitary independent republic," continued to be the epicenter from which the principal bases and schools were controlled and from which policies and objectives were designed. In that municipality, the paramilitary organization had a clinic, a printer, a drug store, an armory, a computer and (a datum that most concerned the governmental officials) a center of communication that worked in coordination with the state-run telecommunications office. A second satellite center was located in Pacho, Cundinamarca.[38] Rodríguez Gacha also had a farm in that small town.

The organization had thirty pilots and a flotilla of airplanes and helicopters. It had 120 vehicles, principally jeeps, but also bulldozers and levelers, without counting the boats. It collected a monthly fee from ranchers. The one paid by narcotraffickers was much higher, and, according to some sources, the paramilitary organizations were financed almost completely by them. One high functionary said, "In addition one can think that those men [narcotrafficking leaders] have stopped being mere common delinquents, as they were when they dedicated their activities to narcotrafficking only, and have begun to get a certain political status since they have changed themselves to the sponsors of the subversion of the right."[39]

As can be seen, it was possible that the narcotraffickers were trying to place themselves in positions in the country that might in the future allow them to become valid questioners of the government. Nevertheless, there was reason to ask whether the government was having a dialogue with guerrilla groups that were known to be heavily involved in narcotrafficking. Would the government, in certain circumstances, begin conversations with those other groups? In other words what some asked was, If there is dialogue with narco-guerrillas, why not with narco-paramilitaries?[40]

The Narco-Para-Militaries

Of special importance during 1989 was the substantiation of an alliance that had long been suspected—the "narco-para-militaries"—a coalition of money without limits (the narcos), violence without scruples (the death squads), and inside information and protection (the military). In late May 1989 there was no longer reason to doubt that such an alliance did exist when there was an assassination attempt against the head of DAS, Miguel Maza Márquez. For this purpose a large amount of money (COL$150 million or about US$400,000) was paid to professional assassins who had inside information from military intelligence about the route that Maza would take. Documents captured at the time indicated that criminals from the Magdalena Medio area had had access to minutes of the National Council on Drugs and to files of the judicial police of the procurator. The ring also had classified documents of the ministries of justice, government, and foreign relations about the narcotraffic and about negotiations concerning extradition.[41]

The Barco government tried to deny that this triple alliance existed, but the office of the procurator started an investigation.

The Barco Policy in Relation to the Paramilitary Groups

At its beginning, the Virgilio Barco government, with the possible exception of Minister of Government Fernando Cepeda, did not know about the vigilante situation, and the government developed no policies for the worse cases such as Urabá and Magdalena Medio. From that moment the wave of violence took off uncontrollably.

By the end of 1988, Amnesty International had called attention to the problem. In response Alvaro Tirado Mejía, Presidential Counsellor for the Defense, Protection, and Promotion of Human Rights, stated:

> The terrorism of the extreme right, in its most recent expression, aims at setting the Nation against the democratic policies of reconciliation, the negotiated solution of the guerrilla problem, the effectuation of a needed Land Reform, the creation of ample opportunities for citizen participation and the recognition of the rights and guarantees of trade unions. . . .
>
> In short, amidst enormous difficulties and unprecedented obstacles, this Government and the Nation will not cease in the struggle against violence and impunity, pledged as they are to attain the fundamental object of every democracy, which is the rigorous establishment of human rights in the fullest sense.[42]

The situation was such that the minister of government, César Gaviria, in an attack of sincerity, stated in May 1989: "Right now the government is incapable of eradicating the violence in recently colonized areas such as Urabá, Magdalena Medio, Arauca and Caquetá."[43] The paramilitary groups had become as important as the guerrillas with regard to their effect on Colombian society. The implications of this to the government were very serious. To begin with, the peace initiative presented by Virgilio Barco on September 1, 1988, was undoubtedly incomplete in the face of the dimensions of the new force the government had to face. When he launched the peace initiative, the government's own figures indicated that more Colombians had been killed in the previous year by paramilitary groups than by guerrillas.[44]

Nevertheless, the government seemed determined to defend its theory of cause and effect, according to which the paramilitary groups were a result of the guerrilla groups and that therefore focusing the peace initiative on the latter could in the long run take care of the problem. But by this time the government needed to realize that the paramilitary sickness needed its own therapy. Further, until the government demonstrated concrete results with the paramilitary groups, there was no real possibility of a guerrilla demobilization.

There were some signs of change. The military command finally agreed that the officials in charge of the military and police in Segovia would testify before a civilian judge. Something had changed since the time when the minister of defense, Fernando Landazábal, advocated collecting a day's salary from officers to pay the legal defense of military men charged with collaborating with paramilitary groups. The government, to face this threat, had to resolve its own divisions. One of the most serious was that between the judicial power and the armed forces.[45]

Investigations of the paramilitary groups did show results. The names of some of the most important leaders became known, as did their modus operandi and, in some cases, their location. But until April 1989, guilty verdicts and sentences were scarce, with a few exceptions like that of Los Nachos, sentenced to a combined 203 years of prison. The diagnosis was clear. The war was no longer against two enemies but against three: guerrilla groups, drug traffickers, and paramilitary groups.[46]

On April 4, 1989, two military operations against paramilitary groups—one in Bogotá and another in Magdalena Medio—led to ten deaths and thirteen arrests. The one in the south of Bogotá was against Los Justicieros (The Avengers), who, according to Maza Márquez, worked on orders from Rodríguez Gacha. The group in Magdalena Medio cared for the property of Pablo Escobar.

During the preceding months the intelligence organizations, the military authorities, and functionaries of the presidency had been compiling and analyzing the available information so that they could plan, with complete information, the solution to the jigsaw puzzle of paramilitarism. According to one source the information that the government had was ample and detailed; the origin, development, and current structure of the paramilitary groups was known. It was known how groups were financed, how they operated, how they communicated, and how they trained their men. The nexus between those groups and narcotraffic had been established. In addition there was exact intelligence information about who their top leaders were.[47]

In mid-April 1989, President Barco announced a crime plan, symbolically unveiling it in Medellín. Its major point was the creation of a special force of one thousand to combat the death squads, the narcos, the so-called self-defense groups, and the mercenary groups of hired assassins. The function of the force was "to combat the death squads, bands of psychopaths, and groups of self defense or of private justice, mistakenly called paramilitary groups, and to realize the other necessary actions to eradicate and impede their activities."[48]

In addition, at the end of April the government took two other steps against paramilitary groups. First, it ended the basis for their legality. Second, it set up a coordinating committee to direct and oversee government policy on the paramilitary groups, made up of the ministers of government, justice, and defense. The president also announced that he was preparing other measures to investigate the origin of illegally acquired wealth and to expropriate goods held by the drug lords directly or through proxies. There was support for the president in general, even from the Conservative leaders who had generally criticized the Barco peace efforts.[49]

Also in 1989, the next step toward a "Central Americanization" of the Colombian dirty war seemed to be about to take place when the Association of Ranchers and Peasants of the Magdalena Medio—the paramilitary group centered in Puerto Boyacá—founded a political movement called MORENA (*Movimiento de Restauración National*, Movement of National Restoration).[50] MORENA would be for the paramilitary groups what the UP was for the FARC or what ARENA (*Alianza Republicana Nacional*, Nationalist Republican Alliance) was for the death squads in El Salvador.

One case in which the authorities saw the shadow of ACDEGAM was in the assassination of the father of Martha Lucía González, judge of public order, who had indicted the leaders of ACDEGAM—Pablo Escobar, Gonzalo Rodríguez Gacha, and various officials of military intelligence—for massacres in Urabá. Hence, the problem lay in the connections, not with the paramilitary groups but with the narcotrafficking ones. Although the directors of MORENA denied it emphatically, they were certainly under suspicion.[51]

Because the Magdalena Medio region appeared to be more like El Salvador than like Bogotá (leading to comparisons between MORENA and ARENA), it seemed likely that the winning of numerous mayoralties would be neutral or even healthy for democracy if it were not accompanied by a very particular phenomenon in this case: the possibility that the violence, which in 1989 was lived in face of the impotency of the authorities, might be exercised after the 1990 mayoral elections by orders given from the office of the mayor. That is to say, the private violence might become state violence.[52]

In reaction to the appearance of MORENA, the Barco government issued a decree, partially changing the law of political parties. According to the decree, in order to get legal recognition a prospective political party would have to include in its bylaws an express statement that it would be governed by the Colombian constitution and laws. To this typical act of formalism from Bogotá (which assumed that national problems could be handled through formal governmental statements), MORENA leaders replied that if it were not approved as a political party, it would be a clandestine group.[53]

Conclusion

During the 1980s the self-defense groups that originally were informal and voluntary became institutionalized as small armies of men on salary. And when a man was paid for doing nothing more than going around with a machine gun and his efficacy could only be measured by the number of deaths, the dynamics of the situation could only lead to a bloodbath. The point was reached that the ranchers—the original supporters of the paramilitary groups—considered themselves the victims of their own invention. And by the end of the Barco government, it was difficult for anyone to establish with certainty exactly when the paramilitary groups were defending their rights and when they were violating the law.

Semana, written for the educated, urban Colombians editorialized:

> For a *bogotano* [citizen of Bogotá] in El Chicó [an upper-income section in the north of Bogotá] the paramilitary actions may be violations of human rights, but for a soldier in the Magdalena Medio, Urabá or the Eastern Plains, the death of each guerrilla fighter is equivalent to ridding the place of an armed enemy that might in the end kill him. For this reason, although the top leaders of the Armed Forces never have been pro-paramilitary groups and there are no indications that they have ever participated in any of the activities of those groups, neither can it be affirmed that they have fought them. Now every one recognizes that the country is headed towards a bloody orgy.[54]

Another aspect of the dirty war was that crimes were either not reported or were not solved, and there was a general breakdown of law and order. According to the Colombian government itself, at least 80 percent of the crimes were not reported. Of the 241,644 cases begun in 1989, 209,000 were dismissed. Nevertheless, Virgilio Barco said in his farewell address to the National Congress, "The struggle of Luis Carlos Galán and of millions of Colombians has not been in vain."[55]

Other details fly equally in the face of the Barco statement. In November 1989, Amnesty International reported that 2,500 Colombians had been executed "extra-juridically" in the previous eighteen months by the armed forces. This was denied by both the armed forces and the Barco government. In January 1990, the government stated that 380 Colombians had been held by kidnappers, including narcos, guerrillas, and common criminals. The average number of kidnappings per month climbed from forty-four in 1988, to fifty-six in 1989, and to eighty-six in the first eight months of 1990. Not only was the growth serious, but also serious was the fact that in recent years there had been no successful investigation leading to a guilty verdict. Although government statistics gave the proportion of kidnappings as between 17 and 22 percent by the guerrillas in those three years, all the rest were lumped together as "common crime." Evidence suggested that guerrillas, *narcotraficantes*, paramilitary groups, and common crime had a system of "lent services" through which assistance was shared according to circumstances.[56]

Further, the government was not capable of prosecuting the perpetrators of even the most important crime of recent years—the assassination of Luis Carlos Galán. By December 1989 it had been established that the Galán assassination had been ordered by Pablo Escobar and assigned to Rodríguez Gacha, who had contracted some twenty individuals to carry it out. However, one of the perpetrators, José Orlando Chávez, who had simply held a campaign poster an assassin could hide behind, was murdered on August 5, 1990. After he had turned state's evidence on Jaime Rueda Rocha, who had fired a submachine gun from behind the poster, Chávez was released on his own recognizance. His homicide was planned by Rueda, using his cellular telephone from his prison cell to plan the murder.[57]

Nowhere was this dirty war worse than in the second-largest city, Medellín. There, in the first six months of 1990, 3,160 people died violently, not counting the police who were assassinated.[58]

In the last days of the Virgilio Barco government, spokesmen of the paramilitary groups sought dialogue with the government. In a message on a radio network, Fidel Castaño promised to break up his organization if the EPL were sincere in their promises of peace. "The only reason for which we saw ourselves obligated to form a self-defense group in the Department of Córdoba was because of the continued attacks, kidnappings, blackmailings, and so on of the guerrilla groups that have strongholds in this region of the country."[59]

Also, for some weeks the minister of government had been meeting and exchanging messages with spokespeople of the self-defense groups of Magdalena Medio. On August 2 Horacio Serpa sent a six-page memorandum to Henry Pérez and Ariel Otero in which he replied to a letter sent by them and in which he made some statements about the possibility of dialogue. In the first place, he said that no kind of negotiation would be possible with groups of hired assassins or paramilitaries. Instead, he only mentioned that it might be possible "to take the necessary steps to obtain the method of finding the exoneration of criminal responsibility for those who might have committed punishable offenses for the illegal possession of arms and membership in an armed group, illegal acts that it is supposed are carried out by those facing certain circumstances and who assume a defensive attitude."[60]

Yet it seems reasonable to conclude that the Barco government largely ignored the problems that had caused the growth of paramilitary groups. At times the government seemed to overlook that the groups even existed and, at best, made weak efforts to combat vigilante groups toward the end of its mandate. In part this can be explained by the scarcity of resources; drug- and guerrilla-related violence was considered to be of greater importance.

Another part was that many top-level people in Colombia (both in the government and in the private sectors) thought that the Betancur peace process had been a mistake. Three questions were predominant in Colombian political debate. The first was whether there had been an agreement to hold a constitutional convention, which was denied by the Betancur government. The second had to do with the fact that the guerrilla groups accepting the truce did not have to turn in their arms. Some critics suggested that the subversive forces were really using this as a respite to regroup and rearm. The third issue had to do with the cost of the promise to rebuild the guerrilla-occupied zones.[61]

Because the vigilante groups had their origins in landowners fighting guerrilla groups, they were not only considered justified but were part of the Colombian tradition of privatizing functions of the state. Of course this matter became more complicated when drug monies became important in paramilitary groups, which might well explain why the Barco government had a policy to deal with them *at the end* of its tenure but not *at the beginning*, when drug funds were less influential in private justice.

In 1989 the U.S.-based Human Rights Watch wrote:

> Although we could not prove that Colombia's military high command directly ordered paramilitaries to commit atrocities, it should be obvious that their response to these atrocities "to close ranks and frequently to obstruct any serious investigation" compromised their obligation to uphold the rule of law. We concluded that the failure to investigate and prosecute military officers who have joined with paramilitaries to commit murders and mass murder indicated, at the very least, that their superiors had chosen to tolerate these crimes.[62]

I would add the following: either the Colombian civilian leadership did not know what its military was doing or, knowing it, either decided not to put a complete end to it or was not able to do so.

In conclusion, this chapter shows (for the third time) that the Colombian state was weaker after the Barco administration than before because it was even less able to implement its policies and because the human rights of more Colombians were being violated.

The César Gaviria Government, 1990–1994

That César Gaviria Trujillo was a different kind of president was apparent when he was inaugurated on August 7, 1990, as president of Colombia. For security reasons, the ceremonies were held in a plaza of the Congress before its members and invited guests rather than in a packed Plaza Bolívar, as is the custom. After all, three presidential candidates had been assassinated, including Luis Carlos Galán, for whom Gaviria had been campaign manager. So there was little wonder when the new president began his inaugural speech emotionally: "I welcome you and invite you to evoke with us, the Colombians, Luis Carlos Galán: the friend, the man of rectitude, the critical spirit who returned to politics both majesty and the capacity to transform reality. In homage to that leader, surprised by death when, smiling, he greeted his people who full of illusions acclaimed him, I wish to repeat his words when invoking the people of the Comunera Revolution: 'Colombians: Not a step backwards! Always forward!' "[1] Gaviria stated that his government would have the responsibility for strengthening the economy, pacifying the country, and transforming governmental institutions. Clearly, the latter two duties would be duties connected with state building.

The president said that he would lead the process of changing the political institutions through formation of a constituent assembly. The executive branch would gradually take over the task of investigating crimes. A permanent jurisdiction would be established that would deal with such matters as plea bargaining, collective judgments, protection of the identity of judges and witnesses, payment of rewards, and an increase in the sentences for crimes. The new president concluded:

> At the beginning of this new decade, where all over the world walls are being torn down and the glories of democracy and liberty are being opened, we are obligated to pacify and transform Colombia.
>
> This is the size of our challenge.
>
> If we assume it with valor, optimism, and decision, posterity will not say tomorrow that we were inferior to the responsibilities that our times imposed on us. It will say, to the contrary, that the 7th of August of 1990 we began a long journey of creation, of renovation, and of work. It will say that that day we began to make real the peaceful revolution that Colombians want and need.
>
> It is my hope, my promise, that on a day like today in 1994, when I turn over to the person that democracy designates the responsibilities that I have just taken over, I can do it with the affection and respect of you Colombians, because I deserved to exercise the power that you gave to me.
>
> Compatriots: Welcome to the future.[2]

The peace process proclaimed by César Gaviria in his inauguration speech targeted four sources of violence: guerrillas, narcoterrorists, self-defense groups, and paramilitary groups (which he seemed to be defining as the vigilante groups allied with the narcos). He was clear what he would do with each one. There would be dialogue for the guerrilla groups, ordinary justice for the self-defense groups, and total war with narcoterrorists and paramilitary groups.[3] It should be remembered that Gaviria, as minister of government, was the first to denounce the existence of paramilitary groups that, with financing by the narcotraffic, had become powerful criminal organizations.

6

Negotiations between the Government and the Guerrilla Groups

In this chapter I analyze the efforts of the César Gaviria government to negotiate a cease-fire with the *Coordinadora Guerrillera Simón Bolívar* in 1991 and 1992 and with parts of the CGSB after 1992. As I have shown previously, the Gaviria government negotiated in light of two different precedents: (1) for cease-fires, without concessions on either side, under the Belisario Betancur government and (2) for demobilization and surrender of arms in return for political rights and economic assistance under Virgilio Barco.

Prelude to Negotiation with the Guerrilla Groups

Referring to the guerrilla groups in his inaugural speech, President Gaviria stated that the transformations in the Eastern Bloc and the Colombian desire for peace had taken "all viability from guerrilla conflict" and converted many of the insurgents to common criminals.[1] In addition, because the process for establishing the constituent assembly was already under way, the government had something that the guerrilla groups apparently wanted: the right to participate in the writing of a more democratic constitution, the lack of which had been a justification for guerrilla conflict through the years.

Further, the early days of the Gaviria government included a number of positive events for the government in relation to the guerrilla groups. On August 10, 1990, FARC leader Jacobo Arenas died of a heart attack. Arenas had been the sectarian defender of "the combination of all forms of struggle," and for that reason many believed that while he lived, it would be difficult to arrive at a peace agreement with the guerrilla group. His probable successor, Alfonso Cano, said a few days after Arenas's death that the search should begin for a way that would not be a dead-end street allowing FARC participation in the constituent assembly. Following that statement, adjustments were made in the political agreement about the assembly, leaving open the possibility of a gradual participation of the guerrilla groups in the assembly if the peace process advanced; this was a way to arrive at an intermediate formula suggested by the guerrillas.[2]

Yet problems soon arose over the possibility of guerrilla participation in the constituent assembly. On December 9, 1990, the same day as the election for the membership of the constituent assembly, the Colombian military attacked Casa Verde, the headquarters of the FARC in the *departamento* of Meta. In the following months the guerrilla groups replied with a series of terrorist assaults, especially powerful on February 7, 1991—the day the constituent assembly began its sessions. Nevertheless, both sides continued their interest in having peace talks, at least on the side of the CGSB, in order to obtain seats in the constituent assembly, as did the M-19 and the EPL. At the same time, the Gaviria government decided to change the policy of preparing to fight an external war and instead to concentrate its efforts on the strengthening of the internal security of Colombians. As a way of elaborating its "strategic plan," which sought to improve the efficiency of the military budget over the following years, it gave the civilian Council of Economic and Social Policy the right to pass on military expenses. A high-ranking official of the government said, "The slight offensive capability that the armed forces has shown recently is because of the low budget allocation for internal security. The difference between an offensive plan and a defensive one is a matter of money. For that reason the decision of the government is to correct the orientation of the spending."[3]

It was this criterion that inspired Decree 416 of February 11, 1991, which created a "war tax." With this measure, which was taken under state-of-siege powers, the government made two things very clear: (1) the collections from the tax would be used to satisfy additional and extraordinary military needs to counter violence; and (2) the tax receipts could only be used for expenses related to fortifying internal security. Those expenses were to include additional funds for the intelligence services of the armed forces, the creation of two new "mobile brigades" of fifteen hundred soldiers, as well as patrol companies to protect pipelines, oil fields, and mines.[4]

Finally, Gaviria wanted to close the gap between the military and civilian government by, among other things, appointing Rafael Pardo as national security counsellor. Although a civilian in this position had been envisioned since it was created in 1965, it had always been occupied by a military officer. As one high official said, "Here there has been a collective irresponsible act that led to, since the National Front, a process of isolation which led to the Armed forces becoming a kind of 'golden cage,' totally distant from the civilian population." And a retired general added, "The ruling class doesn't even know we exist when there is peace in the country, but if the situation becomes very serious they immediately look to us and even coups d'état have been suggested."[5]

The Proposals Made in the Negotiations

In the context of that Gaviria policy, a series of negotiations between the government and the guerrilla groups took place in Cravo Norte, Colombia, then in Caracas, Venezuela, and finally in Tlaxcala, Mexico. This section presents the proposals of both sides.

The first negotiations, lasting two days, began on May 15, 1991, in Cravo Norte, capital of the *comisaría* (province) of Arauca. The principal representatives of the government were the vice minister of government, Andrés González, and a presidential peace adviser, Carlos Eduardo Jaramillo. The three representatives of the guerrilla groups had to travel from Caracas, Venezuela. A delegation from the constituent assembly, as well as one from the Colombian Bishops' Conference and the media, witnessed the meeting.[6]

At the beginning of these conversations, the Gaviria government summarized its bargaining position along the same basic lines as that of the Barco government: the acceptance of international supervision over any agreement that might be signed; the inclusion of nongovernmental participants in the conversations; the compliance with certain international protocols, according to the behavior of the guerrilla groups; and the willingness to begin peace talks immediately, without a previous cease-fire.[7] The agreement at Cravo Norte was simple: the two sides agreed to continue conversations the following month in Caracas, Venezuela.

Caracas, 1991

During the remainder of 1991, there were various meetings of the two sides in the Venezuelan capital. Bellicose actions by both sides within Colombia aggravated the difficulties caused by very different proposals from each.

The first round: June 1991

When in June of 1991, the Colombian government and the *Coordinadora Guerrillera Simón Bolívar* began negotiations in Caracas, both sides presented proposals on the first day in which there was agreement on some procedural matters (for example, the international supervision of agreements). But there were also fundamental differences. The government wanted a unilateral cease-fire of the guerrillas, who, after all, were the lawbreakers. The *Coordinadora* logically wanted a simultaneous end of hostilities on the part of the army. The government also wanted demobilization and surrender of arms, whereas the guerrilla organizations wanted more basic things such as a study of the disappearances of large numbers of people during the dirty war. As far as the constituent assembly was concerned, the government seemed willing to give some status to the guerrillas, but the guerrillas wanted a specific number of representatives: eight delegates, or a representation that would be over 10 percent of the total assembly.[8]

The most important change during the first day of conversations was that the government was willing to study new mechanisms for demobilization, including the establishment of "peace zones." After forty-six hours of conversations, the government and the *Coordinadora* agreed on a "preliminary agenda." Each side made its own proposal; there was no single plan. The guerrilla agenda was much more general, bringing up very broad matters such as "the demilitarization of national life," as well as "democratization," human rights, conflict in civil society, and economic policy. The government's position was that these were matters of substance rather than procedure and that they were being legitimately taken care of through the national government and the constituent assembly.[9]

After a beginning that the government considered promising, it announced that it would be decided during the next weekend whether the commander of the FARC, Manuel Marulanda Véliz (a.k.a. "Tiro Fijo" or "Sure Shot"), could speak to the constituent assembly. In other words, the executive branch would decide whether enough progress had been made in Caracas for Tiro Fijo to travel to Bogotá and speak before the assembly.

The problem soon arose that the talks were going on while there was no cease-fire. Jesús Antonio Bejarano, chief of the government's delegation, stated, "Obviously we are not in agreement with having the talks in Caracas with an atmosphere of pipeline bombings and terrorist acts. It is natural that a cease-fire would include a suspension of all those acts." Francisco Galán, commander of the ELN who was a member of the *Coordinadora*'s team, replied that the negotiation was taking place without a cease-fire on either side and that the Colombian army maintained a "general offensive," in the face of which, he said, "the guerrilla groups defend themselves. We have come here without previous agreements. The conflict continues."[10] This was the first indication of a phenomenon that was to be very common in the peace talks: while negotiating teams talked, in Caracas or Tlaxcala, belligerent activities by both sides continued. This might have been to increase the power at the bargaining table of one or more of the two sides. Alternatively, it might have been because some elements, on one side or the other, never believed in the peace process and were not effectively controlled by its leadership. Many times it was not clear which was the case.

Nevertheless, the government and the *Coordinadora* did agree to the following: to study a formula that would permit a cease-fire and the end of hostilities; to have the participation of the *Coordinadora* in the deliberations of, or at the least a presentation before, the constituent assembly; and to take actions against paramilitary groups and vigilante justice.[11] It is worthy of note that there was no agreement other than that these were things to be talked about.

As a result the two sides returned the next week with new proposals (see table 6.1). This time it was the government that had an extensive proposal, albeit dealing entirely with procedural matters. The guerrillas were unable to accept the government's first and second points, with a *Coordinadora* negotiator, Andrés París, explaining, "Accepting the proposal of the government would be the equivalent of our cornering ourselves. 'Demobilization zones' contradict the concept of guerrilla conflict that we are developing."[12] Hence the two sides had already reached the point that was to be the Gordian knot of the negotiations: In how many zones would the guerrillas demobilize? Both sides agreed that a *zone* meant *where the subversives "habitually" were*, but that lacked specificity. Thus the guerrillas' promise to enter a "bilateral cease-fire" on July 1 in "those areas where the distinct guerrilla fronts have a presence"[13] was of no value unless those areas could be previously delimited.

Thus as the first round ended, although the negotiation had not led to any agreement, there was some reason to think that the differences between the two sides were narrowing. Yet this did not prevent Jesús

Table 6-1. Proposals, Caracas, June 1991

Government	Guerrillas
1. All of the armed fronts of the guerrillas to be in specified areas where they usually had been located.	1. Mutual cease-fire, beginning on July 1.
2. A date and hour for the end of offensive actions in the specified areas. At the same time the guerrillas will stop all acts of war.	2. Cease-fire to apply in those areas "habitually with presence of the guerrillas, jointly and previously agreed to."
3. Three days before the cease-fire, armed forces will stop actions in zones neighboring the specified areas.	
4. Dates and hours to be agreed upon for the liberation of all civilians and military personnel kidnapped by the guerrillas.	
5. Nongovernmental agents to supervise the cease-fire in the specified areas.	
6. To develop the policy of human rights, specific procedures to be developed in coordination with the National Procurator.	
7. Procedures to be established, in coordination with the National Procurator, to study the guerrilla accusations of the effect of military actions on civilian populations.	

Source: La Prensa, June 12, 1991.

Antonio Bejarano from complaining that the guerrillas wanted a third of the country, while the CGSB replied that they would not be "corralled" as the government proposed.[14] Pablo Catatumbo, FARC member on the negotiating team, opined that the government wanted to confine the guerrilla to four or five municipalities of the country, while the *Coordinadora* thought they should stay where they were, without having to move to other areas. The government, meanwhile, said that the CGSB proposal would not permit verification and therefore could not be taken seriously.

Jesús Antonio Bejarano said that such difficulties were to be expected: "It is not strange for a cease-fire to cause so many difficulties. We will take the necessary time to reflect. This process might be long and very slow. It is necessary to begin constructing the will for peace, and that cannot be hurried. For that reason, it cannot be said that three weeks is a long time."[15]

The second round: June 1991

When negotiations began again the following week, the government conditioned a cease-fire to the guerrillas' staying in ten areas of "distension." The CGSB rejected that proposal and stated that it was ready to agree to a bilateral cease-fire beginning on July 1, with its 8,500 troops remaining in their one hundred fronts.[16]

By this time it seemed unlikely that the guerrilla groups would par-ticipate in the constituent assembly, although the guerrillas proposed a truce of two weeks so that their commanders could travel to Bogotá for the assembly. Bejarano replied that such a proposal was "an insanity," as they had met in Caracas to find a coherent plan for a cease-fire and not a short, fragile agreement.[17]

By the end of June, at the close of this second of the five proposed stages of negotiation, the government and the *Coordinadora* agreed on various oversight commissions: an international one that would supervise the negotiations in general and various regional ones to verify the eventual cease-fire. Nevertheless, the agreed-upon commissions still had nothing to supervise because the two sides had still not been able to define the cease-fire formula. This was the most important matter considered—and also the most difficult.

The two sides agreed to meet again on July 15, this time with an international witness (still undefined) in order to delimit the "demobilization zones" and to set dates for the cease-fire. But the government insisted that the international witness begin when there was an agreed-upon accord; the guerrilla groups asked that the accord start immediately. Meanwhile, to verify the eventual cease-fire, four kinds of commissions were agreed upon: regional ones for each demobilization zone; a national one of *"notables"* (group of notable people); and two other national ones, one from the government and another from the guerrillas. The regional commissions would be nongovernmental, with membership not greater than seven coming from the church, the interest groups, social organizations, and "local personalities." The national oversight would come from a Committee of Evaluation and Vigilance. The *Coordinadora* would nominate various ex-presidents for its membership.

About the contradiction of defining the verifiers without having agreed on a cease-fire, Counsellor Bejarano explained that, having been unable to arrive at an agreement about the "demobilization zones," it was decided to have conversations about "collateral aspects" so that a level of confidence could be reached that would permit a discussion of the priority topic in the next round. For Bejarano, all aspects of the cease-fire, with the exception of the demobilization zones, were already agreed upon.[18]

A governmental commission began writing a report on the negotiation, the principal point of which would be the criteria for the definition of "demobilization zones." The commission, headed by Bejarano, would also work during the three-week recess on a "general perspective of the process," which it would read to the *Coordinadora* delegates on July 15.[19]

The government saw positive aspects of the bargaining so far on three points: having agreed on an agenda, having begun discussion of the cease-fire zones, and having agreed on regional commissions for the verification of the cease-fires.[20] Bejarano said, "The balance is adequately positive. For the first time in a negotiation with the FARC and the ELN, we have an agenda and a verification mechanism. What we have achieved up until now is an important advance."[21]

An escalation of terrorist attacks by the guerrillas in the following weeks resulted in the third round of conversations being postponed. Such attacks had been going on during the meetings in Caracas; however, in the first week of July they picked up greatly. The terrorist attack of the *Coordinadora* on the first day of the month caused energy rationing in the Atlantic Coast region, left Bucaramanga without natural gas, and destroyed two police stations in the *departamento* of Norte de Santander. ECOPETROL (*Empresa Colombiana de Petróleos*, Colombian Petroleum Enterprise) suffered ten terrorist attacks in four days, with damages of over COL$10,000,000.[22] Then, electricity towers were bombed on July 3 (the day before the promulgation of the new constitution), and the seven *departamentos* of the coast were having blackouts, especially during peak-demand hours. As a result the inhabitants of the coast began protest days against the *Coordinadora*. On their part, the spokespersons of the guerrillas announced from Caracas that the actions would continue, as no agreement on the cease-fire had been reached.[23]

On July 6, minutes after the broadcast exhortation of President César Gaviria to the *Coordinadora* that they abandon their military actions, the latter replied with a series of dynamite attacks in various parts of the country. The most serious was directed to the antenna of the radar that controlled the air traffic of the entire Caribbean region of the country, seriously affecting air transport in the region.[24]

Then, after lifting the state of siege following the proclamation of the new constitution, the government declared the guerrilla activities completely illegitimate. In response the guerrillas increased their violence, attacking other radar stations, pipelines, and electrical towers.[25] They continued doing the same in the following days, despite a call from M-19 leader Antonio Navarro for them to stop the terrorist activities and accept the new constitution.[26]

On July 10 President Gaviria confirmed the obvious when he said, "The possibilities of dialogue with the Coordinadora Guerrillera Simón Bolívar have deteriorated. . . . We believe, like the great majority of the Colombian people, that the climate of peace and reconciliation is severely affected and the peace process will lose credibility greatly if those terrorist acts are continued."[27] The *Coordinadora* replied on July 11 with a blast that destroyed a runway at the Aeropuerto Internacional Rafael Núñez of Cartagena and on July 12 with an attack only 13 kilometers from Bogotá.[28]

Counsellor Bejarano, in his reaction to this military policy of the *Coordinadora,* made the following argument to the effect that the terrorist activities of the guerrillas were decreasing their bargaining power rather than increasing it:

> Certainly we are in a critical phase, and I believe that it is important to improve this mood because if it gets much worse, we are surely going to arrive at a point at which the dialogue will become a useless gesture of the government. . . . It is evident that the credibility of the guerrilla groups is getting worse in the country. . . . It is indubitable that if we had achieved the building of confidence, now it has been erased by a calculation—which appears to me mistaken—of thinking that the criteria of the government are going to be changed by a terrorist escalation. . . . Terrorism must be distinguished from armed confrontation. In fact there is no evidence that the guerrilla groups are stronger in military terms. . . . The fact that they use terrorism, with all its political costs, is because evidently they do not have the capability of facing armed conflict in any other way.[29]

Gaviria's first year as president ended before the talks resumed. In that year, it became obvious that progress was not being made with the guerrilla groups, even though the new constitution was written and plea bargaining was advancing with the Medellín drug gang. The violence of the guerrillas had increased at an unprecedented pace, and the government did not seem to have sufficient capacity to handle it. And the subversive groups of the *Coordinadora* had not been able to help write the more democratic constitution, which had long been one of their demands.

In the guerrilla negotiations, the Gaviria record had not been good. If there was one big error during his first year, it was the December 9 attack on Casa Verde. Not only was this an inopportune day for the attack (it was the day of elections for the constituent assembly), but militarily it was a disaster. All indications are that the error of the government was not only in overestimating its offensive abilities but in underestimating the capacity of the enemy to respond. In January, while the guerrilla groups were blowing up the infrastructure of the country, the minister of government stated on television: "We will talk with the guerrilla groups when we want to, how we want to, in any way and in any moment that it might want." From that moment on, the traditional demand of a cease-fire as a prerequisite for conversations with the government was abandoned. Some analysts saw a parallel with the narcos, who got the greatest concessions because of the number of deaths they were causing.[30]

The third round: September 1991

In September the government changed its strategy by having its delegates "talk more strongly" at the negotiating table. By presidential directive, the negotiators took a new position: the conversations could not be continued while public order degenerated because of subversive acts. For this reason the government delegates asked the *Coordinadora* for a demonstration of their interest in peace as a condition of continuing the conversations. In making these points, Jesús Antonio Bejarano pointed out that the government had accepted international oversight of the process and the ratification of the Geneva protocols at the bargaining table, not to mention the new constitution adopted by the constituent assembly. Guerrilla groups had done nothing to indicate their interest in peace.

For the Caracas negotiations to have meaning, Bejarano continued, the guerrillas should liberate kidnapping victims and accept a specific methodology to discuss the agenda. He also suggested that the cease-fire be given priority on that agenda. The peace counsellor concluded: "The problem is that we make a demand, threatening them that if they do not comply the Government will leave the table. Very surely we will have to return to the country with no agreement and nobody wants

Table 6-2. Proposals, Caracas, September 1991

Government	Guerrillas
1. Two-stage process, with fewer areas in the second stage coming after six months.	1. Agreed to put its troops in determined areas.
2. Bilateral cease-fire, verified by regional committees in each area and with national and international verification at the same time.	2. Agreed to bilateral cease-fire.
	3. Called for a neutral zone around those areas.
	4. Cease-fire should end all effects, from both sides, on the civilian population.
3. Possibility that some guerrilla leaders would be able to travel for political activities.	5. Need still to clarify the space of the areas of the guerrillas.
	6. Government should dismantle the paramilitary groups.

Sources: El País, September 12, 1991; El Espectador, September 11, 1991.

that. Nevertheless the entire country will understand and will support the position of the Government."[31]

As a reply, Alfonso Cano said that the rebels were prepared to give on some points. "We came with the order to be flexible in our positions in order to advance with the agreements." Nevertheless, he said, the government had not come to the new round with innovative proposals.[32]

The minister of government, Humberto de la Calle Lombana, argued that the delegation did bring specific proposals for the delimiting of areas where the guerrillas would stay, under verification by independent commissions. As a reply, Cano attributed the violence in Colombia to "the fratricidal war that 42 years ago the Conservative and Liberal parties began." He insisted that the government revise its national security policy, proposed demilitarization of society, and rejected the bombings of civilian targets and extrajudicial executions. He said that the country was rich in natural resources that were being exploited without benefits for the people.[33]

A week later the two sides did present new proposals, as shown in table 6.2. Novel in the government's position was that the guerrillas would be placed in localities in two different phases. In the second phase, coming about six months into the process, the guerrillas would have to be in fewer zones. In the first phase each point would be a district (vereda or corregimiento) and would not cross municipal lines. Also new in the government's proposal was the idea that the demobilization zones would be determined by the administrative structure of the country. According to the government's information, the FARC had forty-seven fronts, although some were inactive and others had fewer than fifty members. The ELN, according to the government, had eighteen fronts.

Also for the first time the government accepted a bilateral cease-fire. In addition the government proposed that both the government and the guerrilla members be able to move freely in the areas formerly controlled by the guerrillas. The purpose of this concession was to allow the guerrillas to spread their political proposals as part of the new democracy of the constitution of 1991. Those with such mobility would be protected by government troops.[34]

After what seemed to be meaningful concessions by the government, the *Coordinadora* delegates said that they were prepared to put their members in determined zones, as proposed by the government; they stated once again that the cease-fire would have to be bilateral. But, after agreeing for the first time to put their troops in determined zones, they said, "There must be a neutral zone between the demobilization zone and its periphery." Alfonso Cano added, "We still have to clarify criteria. The government talks of points and zones to put the guerrillas troops in, but it does not clearly define the space. . . . A formula should be sought that guarantees the mobility of all the guerrilla members, and not just a few.[35]

Francisco Galán made clear that the principal worry of the *Coordinadora* negotiators was the paramilitary groups when he stated, "To agree with the government about some guarantees for our political action during the cease-fire, without defining first the problem of paramilitary groups, is a utopia. For that reason, this theme has become fundamental during the Caracas negotiations."[36]

One of the formulas that the *Coordinadora* would study was asking the government to "demobilize" such groups. For such a purpose, according to Galán, the guerrilla groups would send a complete list of such groups to the government, as well as of the individuals who made up their memberships and of members of the government, "principally members of the Army," and economic leaders who support and finance them. The government replied that they were prepared to agree on an army offensive against the paramilitary groups in each region where the guerrillas charged that the vigilante groups were active.[37]

As a result, the principal difference was once again the matter of where the guerrilla troops would be located. Bejarano admitted that the two groups were still very far from an agreement, while Cano agreed that much progress had been made. Antonio García, ELN member of the negotiating team, said that the demobilization regions could not be very small, whereas the government repeated that such zones could not be an entire municipality.[38]

At this juncture, the question became whether the cease-fire could be completed by October 27 so that the demobilized guerrillas could participate in the congressional election made necessary by the reform of the constituent assembly. Counsellor Bejarano thought that the formula for the cease-fire might be reached by that time but added that there would be a delay between the signing and the application of the cease-fire. Hence, it would be very difficult for all logistical and legal problems to be resolved by that date. Alfonso Cano did not disagree greatly, promising that the military officials held by the FARC would be released soon. He was slightly more optimistic than Bejarano, pointing out that there were differences of criteria but not of focus.[39]

The next week Francisco Galán again brought up the problem of the paramilitary groups. Stating that the government should admit that it financed and assisted those groups, he made it very clear that it would not be enough that the army announced that it would combat them. Rather, the responsible governmental officials would have to give explanations for their past behavior.[40]

By late September, then, all observers agreed that the dialogue was at a crucial stage. The two sides presented new proposals. Although more specificity was seen in the Gordian-knot problem of demobilization zones, Bejarano immediately rejected the guerrilla proposal, arguing that the ninety-six demobilization areas proposed by the guerrillas would mean that the regular armed forces would be excluded from at least two hundred of the one thousand municipalities of the country. "That is to say, a third of the national territory would be in the hands of the guerrillas." Besides being unacceptable, the counsellor added, it "lacked all sense of reality." Furthermore, he considered the new guerrilla proposal to be a step back from the proposal they had made earlier in the month and concluded that the subversives were attempting "to achieve at the bargaining table a territorial domination that they could not gain in the years of armed conflict."[41]

The guerrilla representatives replied that the government had forgotten that they were at a bargaining table. As Antonio García expressed it, "What is happening is that the Government wants to achieve a kind of cease-fire by decree and not by negotiation. We are not asking that they accept our proposal, but that they discuss it."

Alfonso Cano added that the guerrillas' asking for two hundred municipalities was a military concession, as the *Coordinadora* dominated more than six hundred towns.[42]

The second change in the late-September government proposition was the proposal that the national police remain in the demobilization areas to protect the guerrillas from the paramilitary groups.[43] Although, as was shown in chapter 5, the Colombian army had more to do with the support of the paramilitary groups than the national police did, this still had an aspect of "the fox guarding the chicken house" and as such surely could not be considered seriously by the *Coordinadora*.

The third theme of the late-September proposals, albeit not a new one, was the CGSB proposition that three meetings follow the cease-fire—meetings in which to discuss economic development, human rights, and natural resources.[44] This was a return to a peace proposal like that of June 1991 in which, in addition to procedural matters, policy matters were to be considered. There was a logic to this. The constituent assembly reform had made many procedural changes. It seemed that guerrilla groups could no longer base their appeals solely on making the country more democratic; that is what the assembly had done.

The CGSB proposal, however, also had two new procedural propositions. The first was that there be an immediate cease-fire before agreement on demobilization zones. This was a suggestion of a Betancur-like cease-fire (in-place cease-fire, leaving everything else for negotiation) rather than a Barco-like one (placing the guerrillas in set places, with demobilization and surrender of arms preceding governmental concessions). The second proposal was for a compromise between the two paradigms: a two-step process in which the Betancur-like truce would occur that week, coming from statements from the two sides, and the Barco-like cease-fire would come at some later time.[45]

The first week in October, for the first time (but not the last, as shown later) a guerrilla action disturbed the negotiating process—in this case by kidnapping the president of the lower house of Congress, Aurelio Iragorri Hormaza. The government immediately suspended the conversations. The CGSB called that decision hasty but at the same time condemned the kidnapping. Further, the subversives added, the authors of the kidnapping had not been established and neither had the motives. ELN leader Pablo Catatumbo called President Gaviria, attempting to get him to modify this decision.[46] Nevertheless, the government did not change its position. Minister of Government Humberto de la Calle Lombana said, "This is a matter of an action of such a magnitude that the Government has no doubt in attributing it to an important armed group. That is the reason for which we have proceeded in this way."[47] In an analysis of informal dynamics, one M-19 observer in Caracas said, "This was very important because of what the Bogotá press, especially *El Tiempo* editorialists were saying. The government had to reply. Bejarano especially reacted to the media, and when they criticized him he felt like he had to be even tougher in the negotiations."[48]

A few days later Alfonso Cano indicated that the *Coordinadora* was awaiting the response of the government to a new proposal, made after the suspension of the talks, of a cease-fire to begin on October 20.[49] In the context of the kidnapping, the government made no response. It is worthy of note that the massive bombings of the guerrillas affecting anonymous civilians were less important to the government than the kidnapping of a well-known person. Hence, it seems that the guerrillas were learning from the drug dealers' strategies.

The fourth round: October 1991

There was not much reason for optimism when the dialogue began again in late October in Caracas. A week before, the *Coordinadora* had sent an "extensive study" of the paramilitary groups to the government negotiators, thereby highlighting one of the two basic problems already discussed.[50] It had previously been agreed that this round would last only eleven days. To make the matter even worse, guerrilla activities increased a few days before the conversations began.[51] The official position was that the cease-fire, with demobilization areas and political guarantees, had to be considered first, bringing up the Gordian-knot problem as the first priority.[52]

Before beginning to discuss the cease-fire formula, the two sides did a complete reckoning of all that had been accomplished through the negotiations to that point—which demonstrated just how little had been achieved. Agreement had been reached on the definition of a *cease-fire* but not on one of *hostilities.* The problem of demobilization zones was shown, as was that of the paramilitary groups. Kidnapping was a crucial tactic to the government but apparently not to the guerrillas. The CGSB demanded that a report be made public on the actions taken by the state against the paramilitary groups—a report to include the result of the investigations of the multiple massacres and political assassinations that had taken place in the last six years. Also to be included was a pronouncement of the government that said, "It is not the state policy to promote activities of paramilitary groups" and the ratification of rescinding of military or administrative laws, decrees, and resolutions that "authorize, order, or favor the creation or constitution of paramilitary groups." In short, there was at least agreement on what the fundamental disagreements were.[53]

On November 10 the government delegates returned to Bogotá. It had been agreed that the dialogue would start again in the new calendar year. The government delegates agreed that there had been no progress in this latest round. Bejarano even stated that there had been retrogression, as the CGSB's new proposal of a two-step peace process was in conflict with its earlier agreement on locating in demobilization zones.[54] Hector Riveros, vice minister of government, added, "I am not satisfied with the result of this round, despite the fact that the exercise might prove useful and the two sides were able to exchange multiple opinions about many themes and even come closer on some." But he continued by saying that he would have preferred a formula for the cease-fire or even other, more specific advances.[55]

After five months of dialogue in Caracas, the government concluded that the greatest obstacle to achieving a cease-fire at the bargaining table was that the guerrillas continued vindicating armed struggle. For the authorities the guerrillas only had two things to give: cease-fire and demobilization. To that point no movement had been seen in either respect. Bejarano opined, "What they like is the process, not peace." And about the next round, the peace counsellor said, "We have the intention of developing new initiatives. But if the guerrilla groups are not interested in peace, it will be very difficult. And what is certain is that we will not accept a cease-fire without demobilization zones."[56]

Tlaxcala, 1992

By March 1992 the new, serious change was the guerrilla strategy to keep the country in an even bloodier war than in the past. The leadership made this decision at a meeting at the beginning of the year in the *departamento* of Norte de Santander, where representatives of all the guerrilla groups (with the exception of the EPL) agreed to step up the war and introduce new tactics, including attacks on major cities and on localities seen as the areas of socioeconomic conflict such as Barrancabermeja and the Magdalena Medio. A second change was in negotiating partners, with the goal of having simultaneous negotiations with the government, the Congress, the governors, the industrialists, the armed forces, and so on. A final goal was to unite with labor in their disputes.[57]

The cease-fire that until the end of 1991 was the immediate, putative objective had ceased to be so for the guerrillas. Now they considered it to be the final step in the process, with the intermediate steps of extracting concessions from the state in economic matters and concretely sabotaging the Gaviria economic opening policy, which the guerrillas considered calamitous for the country. In other words, the priority of the guerrilla groups was to derogate the central economic project of César Gaviria's government. Left behind were the times when the guerrilla groups said they only wanted a change of the rules of the game in political matters, understanding that under those new rules they would carry out their economic battles in a democratic framework. Now after the constituent assembly, economic concessions had become a precondition to the cease-fire. And it was a cease-fire that, for the first time in recent years, they did not offer in time for the next election.

The consequence of all this was that the peace process was going nowhere. Neither the government nor the *Coordinadora* believed that the reinitiation of the conversations would lead to anything. Both sides, for reasons of strategy, had an interest in maintaining the concept of dialogue, but neither had faith that it would lead to a cease-fire.[58]

At the beginning of the new year, Horacio Serpa, the new peace counsellor, said that the government did not feel pressured by the continued terrorist activities by the subversives and would seek an immediate cease-fire when the dialogue began again in Caracas on February 10. In his opinion, "The cease-fire is the indispensable point in order to continue with the negotiations because the people demand that peace. . . . We cannot carry out the negotiations if every day there are more attacks. It wouldn't be logical to talk in Caracas while we receive news of attacks and deaths."[59]

Other themes of the negotiation, according to Serpa, would be the restructuring of the armed forces, the social question, paramilitary groups, foreign commerce, and international relations.[60] This indicated that, for the first time, the government had decided to converse about substantive policies as well as procedural ones.

At the beginning of February the *Coordinadora* sent a message to the National Congress listing twelve themes that they wanted discussed in Caracas. As shown in table 6.3, the majority of those themes

Table 6-3. Proposals, Tlaxcala, March 1992

Government	Guerrillas
1. Kidnappings. 2. Cease-fire. 3. The other points of the third round agenda, as they were agreed to, parallel to the development of the other themes of the cease-fire. 4. Elements corresponding to the minimum agreements that guarantee the continuation of the conversations in the future.	1. The substitution of the economic opening with a policy that stimulates above all national industry and protection of agricultural production. 2. Colombian natural resources should be produced, administered, and marketed with a patriotic criterion, giving value to the country's ownership condition. 3. The social function of the state should be strengthened, guaranteeing its administrative efficiency, protecting it from politics, and developing its productive capability through high efficiency and productive enterprises. 4. Administrative corruption is one of the principal factors of violence in our country. Mechanisms of popular oversight must be fortified. 5. The Colombian state should change its military policy of total war and the internal enemy. 6. The paramilitary and self-defense groups should be dismantled, punishing their inspirers, instructors, financiers, and leaders, as also should be those held responsible for assassinations and massacres. 7. Human rights in Colombia should be reconstituted and made real. 8. Impunity should be attacked by revising the judicial branch of government and doing away with the military *fuero* (right to try its members accused of crimes). 9. Democracy without fraud, without antiterrorist statutes, and without militarization of electoral campaigns.

Table 6-3 (continued)

	10. Lands in areas of latifundia should be redistributed, with transportation, rural roads, and cheap credit for the peasants. 11. National unity should be fortified, without centralist arrogance and with the participation of minorities. 12. Those affected by violence on the part of private enterprise, the international community, and the state should be compensated.

Sources: El País, February 6, 1992; *El Espectador,* April 26, 1992.

concerned substantive policies, although some familiar procedural issues remained, including paramilitary groups (6) and democracy (9). Without doubt the most widesweeping was the demand that those affected by violence on the part of private enterprise, the international community, and the state should be compensated. This lacked specificity about how any government might carry it out.

In general, as the Colombian sociologist William Ramírez has commented, the CGSB document sent to the Congress had a tone of strategic reforms, without any methods suggested to carry them out. As such it contrasted with the conclusions of the Sixth Summit of rebel commanders, held in January 1992. In those conclusions, clear tracks of struggle and precise tactics to achieve political results were affirmed. Further, discussion of demobilization zones was discarded for the following conversations with the government, and in this way a cease-fire was postponed.[61]

A new attitude on the part of the guerrilla leaders was also seen in other actions. The ELN, in the first place, announced that it would not send its military commander to Caracas until the government sent its minister of government and President César Gaviria. Second, according to the *Coordinadora,* the central theme of the next round would be Gaviria's policy of "economic opening" and its effects on the people. The localization of the guerrilla fronts would not be discussed. Their strategy was to carry out meetings with the nation, struggle against the economic opening, break the negotiating strategy of the government, and "fight against the paramilitary groups and the dirty war."[62]

The negotiations were renewed at the end of February in Tlaxcala,

Mexico, instead of Caracas because of an attempted coup d'etat against Venezuelan president Carlos Andrés Pérez. As a beginning, Antonio García, member of the guerrilla negotiating team, berated the economic opening and said that the internationalization of the economy was "an accomplished fact that was imposed in spite of the laws and subjective appraisals." While insisting on a socialist model, he criticized the administration and said that "the State cannot avoid, through privatization, primary duties like the supply of public services, social security, health, education, and housing."[63] This last statement leads to the conclusion that the *guerrilleros* had not been following the constituent assembly or the new constitution, in which (as is pointed out in chapter 9) such policies were promised more than ever before.

Armando Montenegro, director of the National Planning Department, replied by explaining the government's social policy. The government was not going to negotiate its economic opening, social policy, or investment plans with the *Coordinadora*. Rather, "The Colombian government is attending the dialogue with the guerrilla groups to listen to their positions, and not to negotiate the economic policy of President César Gaviria." On his part, Horacio Serpa added, "It is important that the guerrillas give their points of view in all the other issues, so that the government can examine clearly the progress and possibilities of the process, and the Colombian people will have the opportunity to take a position on what the Coordinadora states."[64]

The conversations in Tlaxcala began with two fundamental disagreements. First, according to the guerrillas the cease-fire and demobilization zones would be discussed at the end of the process, in open contradiction to the position of the government. Second, regional dialogues (which had become a guerrilla procedural suggestion) would only be possible, according to the government's position, when a cease-fire was declared.

Meanwhile, back in Colombia, the thinking of some top-ranking officers of the armed forces was contained in a "confidential" document that was circulating in the highest levels of that institution and in the Bogotá press:

> There is no doubt that the subversive groups have come a long way. But not so much that territory should be ceded to them or doors of acquiescence opened for all that they demand. Until now, the power of the State has not been used in all its magnitude and there is still a great deal of dissuasive power to apply. The FARC and ELN have made a lot of noise about their great capacity to cause damage, but

not of their destabilizing power. To attack and attack without getting clear military or political victories, without advancing in territory, without winning over new members, and without receiving
popular support, is to be completely out of it. Until now, the Coordinadora wants peace—peace of the State with them, but not their peace
with the State. Any negotiator of the government should understand that he is going to discuss transcendental, national themes with
people soaked in rigid Marxist ideologies, whose philosophy teaches
its practitioners to be masters of deceit. With the Coordinadora negotiators, one cannot improvise nor take an action without knowledge
of cause, nor go armed with good will and patriotism.[65]

On March 10, in a document titled "Goals to put an end to the
armed conflict," the government presented thirteen points as "pillars"
of their conversations with the guerrillas. All had to do with conflict
resolution procedures, including guarantees of disarmed guerrillas,
verification of the cease-fire, regional forums after disarmament, and
international oversight.[66] In Tlaxcala the following day, the government was categorical: other themes could be discussed, but the first
priority had to be a cease-fire.

Not surprisingly, the *Coordinadora* representatives did not agree
with that position. They thought it brought the dialogues back to the
same themes as in Caracas the previous year (as indeed it did). Cano
energetically stated that the document was the same as presented by
Jesús Antonio Bejarano. "I see no progress."[67] Horacio Serpa pointed
out that the *Coordinadora* had ignored its written agreement of November 10 that there would be no attack on civilian populations. And
Vice Minister Riveros argued, "The Coordinadora does not know of
the political and democratic achievements that have happened in Colombia."[68]

The next day, ignoring those comments, Alfonso Cano returned to a
criticism of the Gaviria economic opening, charging it with the "physical annihilation of all opponents," as it was imposed by the International Monetary Fund. He continued, "This elitist design has as its
support the authoritarian concept that replies to all social protest with
militarization and force." He warned that patience was wearing out
in the delay for the promise of economic improvement and accused
Gaviria of "exposing Colombia to the bludgeoning of savage capitalism."[69] To that rhetoric, Vice Minister Riveros argued that the guerrillas were "falling in the vice of violence" while the government was
willing to negotiate without delay. He dared the guerrilla representatives "to have the courage to defend their ideas without arms" and

asked for the immediate release of all kidnapped individuals.[70] At this point the government proposed an agenda.

Suddenly, there seemed to be a way to begin the discussions. The agreement was that first the economic opening would be discussed, then the new constitution, followed by administrative corruption. Finally, the elements that would make up the formula for the cease-fire would be discussed, although that theme would "hover around" the table at all times. It was also agreed that experts on all these matters would come to Tlaxcala from the government.[71]

There was some optimism at this point because the *Coordinadora* representatives seemed prepared for more reflection and restraint than in Caracas the previous year. Nevertheless, just a few days later the mood changed when Alfonso Cano blamed the government for administrative corruption, for sponsoring the paramilitary groups, and for not correcting abuses of the armed forces. When Cano finished, Horacio Serpa brought up the conclusions of the Sixth Summit of Guerrilla Commanders and accused the *Coordinadora* of preparing for war in 1992.[72]

Conflict continued in the following sessions. After both sides presented their positions on the economic opening, the two sides searched for agreement, although the *Coordinadora* had called it "a factor that generates violence in Colombia" and the government defended it as "a generator of wealth and alternatives for the 400,000 unemployed of the country."[73]

Then, for a second time, an action of a guerrilla front damaged the dialogue. Similar to the first case, the problem came from the kidnapping of an important person. This time the EPL dissident group that formed part of the CGSB kidnapped political leader Argelino Durán Quintero. After the government called for the liberation of Durán, they decided not to meet with the guerrilla representatives the next day. Later that day the government's delegation returned to the room to announce that it would not negotiate again until Durán was liberated.

The EPL dissident group said that they would liberate Durán when regional dialogues began, but according to the government there could be no regional dialogues before a cease-fire.[74] When it became known that Durán had died in captivity, President Gaviria ordered the government negotiators to return to Bogotá and announced that the conversations were suspended indefinitely.[75] For the first time since the negotiations had begun, the guerrilla groups started attacking each other. Alfonso Cano said that the kidnapping was "an act of craziness. We always insisted on the liberation of Durán Quintero. It is, from beginning to end, a half-crazy episode and hopefully there will be an internal judgment of what has happened."[76]

After Tlaxcala: Unsuccessful Efforts
for Renewed Negotiations

There seemed to be a possibility of renewed dialogue after the death of Durán. However, Horacio Serpa, after a meeting with President Gaviria, said that without a cease-fire the dialogue was very fragile. "While that condition is not met, the negotiating table, if it functions again, will be fragile and will be conditioned by the things that can happen in such a cruel, senseless, and sterile war like that which we Colombians are suffering." In addition, Serpa underlined that there was no precise plan for new talks. As for the guerrilla leaders, "In Tlaxcala the delegates of the Coordinadora have to inform themselves about what is going on in Colombia; they need to know of the reaction of the citizens to the kidnapping and death of Argelino Durán and to the pugnacious and fragile circumstances of the war."[77]

On his part, Alfonso Cano warned that "there will be total war" if the government decided to end the dialogues. He reported that FARC leader Tiro Fijo and ELN chief Manual Pérez had ordered the delegates not to back down on the agenda.[78]

In early April Horacio Serpa and his advisers returned to Tlaxcala to notify personally the CGSB delegates of the ultimatum of the government not to continue the dialogues if they did not agree to an immediate cease-fire and release of kidnapped persons. President Gaviria, on March 26, had said that "the response of the government is to strengthen our security capabilities, our armed forces, to be sure that the outcome of the peace process that is being carried out in Mexico does not matter."[79] This was the first indication, to be repeated numerous times over the next year, that the Gaviria government had decided to "win" the war militarily rather than by negotiating.

In Tlaxcala, meanwhile, the discussion had no new elements. Serpa underlined the necessity of a cease-fire and the liberation of the kidnapped people. The guerrilla delegates insisted that the paramilitary groups would have to be disbanded before there could be a cease-fire.

The government then accepted mediation from the Roman Catholic Church. Twenty-four hours later the former president of the lower house of Congress, Norberto Morales Ballesteros, was released by the EPL.[80] Optimists thought that negotiation still had a chance. The mediation was headed by Father Nel Beltrán, who had been a member of the Peace Commission of President Belisario Betancur and of the Departmental Council of Rehabilitation in Barrancabermeja during the government of Virgilo Barco. The process began when Alfonso Cano called Beltrán's office, right after the government's withdrawal from Tlaxcala. Cano's call was a plea for help in saving the negotiations.[81]

On April 8 Beltrán traveled to Tlaxcala and, after a week and a half of conversations with the guerrilla representatives, returned to Colombia saying that they had a "spirit of peace." The government's commission returned to Mexico on April 22 but accomplished nothing. Beltrán felt betrayed because in his secret conversations with the guerrillas they had promised to change the agenda, but in the formal meetings they rejected such alterations.[82] Indeed, on April 26 the government proposed that the agenda be changed to have kidnapping and a cease-fire up for discussion; on April 29, the guerrilla representatives refused that change. On May 4 the *Coordinadora* asked for an indefinite recess "in face of the stubbornness of the National Government to change the agenda." At the same time, they asked that the paramilitary groups be demobilized, the dirty war ended, and the concept of the "internal enemy" terminated. They suggested the urgency of developing regional, local, municipal and departmental dialogues.[83] Clearly, there was nothing new on either side.

It took until May 5 to arrive at an agreement that would allow the guerrilla negotiators to return to Colombia. There was no doubt that Tlaxcala, and indeed negotiations in general, were over until the following October 31. As a high government official said confidentially to *El Espectador:* "We have no doubt that it is the end of the new round of conversations and that months of great guerrilla belligerency are in store. For those reasons we believe that the solution is to assure militarily that the guerrilla groups have increasingly less [bargaining] space, so that they have to return again to the political solution of the conflict, be it on October 31 or in three or four years."[84]

In the following months, the CGSB tried to change the actors in the negotiation when it called for the creation of a "Great National Roundtable" that could explore and define the mechanisms that could bring peace. Such a roundtable would include representatives of all three branches of government, political parties and movements, social forces and economic organizations, and spokespersons of the insurgents.[85]

At about the same time, the president of the Congress proposed a three-step process. In the "preparation phase" of two months, a commission would be set up from the three branches of government, the church, and the political parties. Its objectives would be to achieve initial agreements about human rights. The second phase, with a duration of six months, would be one of the founding of a Council of National Consultation, in accord with the formula agreed upon in the first step. It would deal with national matters and would be coordinated by the executive branch. Its task would be to examine and reach consensus on measures to bring peace.

The third phase, of ten months, would be one of demobilization and consultation under Article 104 of the new constitution. Its final result would be a calendar of demobilization and the transformation of guerrilla organizations into legal political parties.[86] Nothing came of this proposal.

Conclusion

In its last year, the Gaviria government had three notable successes in negotiating with small guerrilla groups—with the CRS, the militias in Medellín, and the Francisco Gárnica Front of the FARC. In all cases, government's sights were set at the subgroup level, not at that of the *Coordinadora*.

The number of CRS troops was uncertain, with one source putting it at three hundred, in addition to some one thousand militants operating clandestinely in the country.[87] Another said that their exact number varied from two hundred (government) to seven hundred (them). According to some, the ELN killed some of the CRS members after they began talking of negotiation with the government.[88] A sociologist who was interviewed reported yet a smaller, different, and fluctuating number: "The size of the CRS changed over time. Bejarano told me that they first said that they had ten men, later twelve. They had connections with some of the *militias populares* and some of their troops joined in the CRS negotiation. Also Bejarano told me that some of the people who got reinsertion with the CRS already had received the same kind of benefits with the M-19 demobilization."[89]

In the second most important success of Gaviria's final year, as a follow-up to the CRS demobilization in May of 1994, 630 members of three militia groups of Medellín—the *Del Pueblo para el Pueblo* (Of the People for the People), *Del Valle de Aburrá* (Of the Valley of Aburrá), and *Metropolitanas* (Metropolitans)—signed an agreement to disarm and demobilize. The 630 young people who demobilized represented some 85 percent of the organized armed groups of Medellín.[90]

The third most important success of Gaviria's final year was the de-mobilization of part of the FARC, the Francisco Gárnica Front. The 130 former guerrillas turned in seventy weapons on June 30, 1994, which were thrown into the ocean.[91] The terms of the agreement were similar to the CRS agreement.

Yet the Gaviria government failed with the CGSB and hence with the two largest guerrilla groups in Colombia. In many ways, the nego-tiating power of the government with the guerrilla groups was at a high point during 1991–1992 because of its success in writing a new constitution and in plea bargaining with the drug leaders. Between May 1992 and May 1993, however, it became even more difficult to think of a negotiated settlement of the Colombian civil war because of the weakening of the government's negotiating power, the terrorist es-calation on the part of the guerrillas, and the increased military action of the armed forces.

In the first place, the escape of Pablo Escobar from his "high-secu-rity" prison on July 22, 1992 (see chapter 7) caused the government to negotiate from a weaker position. If the government had not been able to negotiate successfully with one "enemy" (the guerrillas) when an-other (Pablo Escobar) had surrendered, how could they when that sec-ond "enemy" was again on the loose?

Second, the terrorist escalation of the guerrilla war led to a civil war at a new intensity: terrorists placed bombs in the principal cities for the first time. Third, new weapon systems, additional troops with greater mobility, and more money (from new taxes) gave the "hawks" of the government fresh hopes of winning the war in spite of terrorist escalation. The presidential speeches after Tlaxcala exhibited a rheto-ric in which the harsh adjectives used for the guerrillas seemed to have the purpose of putting them into the general delinquency category and hence taking away from them any status as rebels against the state. Thus can be understood the declaration of the commander of the army in June 1992 when, in his optimistic evaluation of the military actions of the first half of that year, he said, "With what has happened this year the axiom that the army cannot win the war is being proved wrong. The army will win the war because it already has political and economic support, it is training, and it feels completely backed by the President."[92]

The general could have been right. However, twenty-eight years ear-lier President Guillermo León Valencia had daily predicted (and it was reported in the national press) that the next day they would capture

Tiro Fijo in Marquetalia. The government never did capture that guerrilla fighter, and in 1993 he was still the maximum leader of the *Fuerzas Armadas de la Revolución Colombiana.*

César Gaviria was successful, later in his presidency, in negotiating an agreement with the *Corriente de Renovación Socialista,* the Medellín militias, and the Francisco Gárnica Front. Yet, no conclusion in this study seems clearer than that the Gaviria government failed, despite favorable circumstances, in its negotiations with the FARC and the ELN. In spite of the two proposals mentioned earlier, there were no additional meetings between the government and the CGSB either before or after October 31, 1992.

When one concludes that the peace conversations between the government of César Gaviria and the *Coordinadora Guerrillera Simón Bolívar* ultimately failed, especially intriguing is the idea of a Colombian historian who when interviewed said that the government lost a good chance in this case when, in 1990, FARC tried to bargain for seats in the constituent assembly. Beginning in a typical bargaining position of asking for twenty seats—many more than they really wanted—Alfonso Cano told the historian that they might have accepted fewer. But, the government, knowing that the public opinion polls suggested that the demobilized M-19 was going to win many seats, feared a constituent assembly dominated by guerrillas. Hence it never replied with a number and thereby lost an excellent opportunity to have a cease-fire with the largest guerrilla group.[93]

But at a more basic level, the failure of the Gaviria government to arrive at an agreement with the CGSB can be explained in five (not mutually exclusive) ways: (1) different ways of looking at the problem; (2) the belief on the part of some of the leaders of both sides that they could still win the war; (3) the economic strength of the guerrilla organizations; (4) the lack of viable proposals from both sides; and (5) the lack of unity on both sides.

Different Views of the Problem

Perhaps the most basic problem was that the two sides conceptualized peace differently. For the government, peace meant a cease-fire and demobilization, with the two actors being the guerrilla groups and the armed forces. For the guerrilla groups, there could be no peace while the paramilitary groups still existed; and for the guerrilla groups, peace had to do with many other things, including agrarian reform and economic policy. To borrow a phrase from liberation theology, the *institutional violence of capitalism* would have to end. Although seen most clearly in Tlaxcala, the different conceptions were fundamental in all the negotiations.

Different Ideas about Winning the War

Second, there were individuals, both in the government and in the guerrilla groups, who believed—even after more than twenty years of civil war—that their side did not have to negotiate because they still could win the armed conflict. This was seen in the government's strategy to increase its military power. And, although it might seem impossible, there were also guerrilla leaders with the same kind of thinking. As a sociologist who is expert in this matter says, "There are some guerrilla leaders who still think, despite what is going on in the world, that communism is not dead and can win in Colombia. They think that the economic opening is going to create so much unemployment, so much misery that they can win. I believe that they are crazy, that they don't understand what's going on in the world, but they do believe that communism can win in Colombia."[94]

This belief on the part of the guerrillas was clearly seen in their public statements. In May of 1992, Tiro Fijo sent a recording to *La Prensa* in which he expressed his belief that they could still win; he stated that he hoped that the guerrillas would not have to go to the extremes of the narcotraffickers. "But in the case that the dialogue is ended, our only new reply will be urban terrorism. . . . We have all the national territory to move around in . . . and the help to come out in any part of it."[95]

This opinion was shared by the leadership of the *Coordinadora.* According to May 1992 communications between the heads of the FARC and the ELN that were intercepted by intelligence organizations, their strategy during the next six months would be to increase their fronts to more than one hundred, while increasing their strength through the following three tactics:

1. Internationalization of the Colombian guerrilla movement toward Central American countries and Spain, where it might be possible to obtain some type of political recognition and economic assistance, although the latter was not really needed
2. Intensification of urban terrorism, along the Medellín drug group style, especially against financial institutions, multinational corporations, banks' automatic tellers, and public buildings, in the be-

lief that this kind of attack would be more effective with fewer cau-
salities than direct combat with the police and army
3. Imposition of the thesis of regional dialogues, whose principal ob-
    jective would be to sabotage the military operations in places
    where it is known that there are guerrilla camps[96]

The government, meantime, thought they could defeat the guerrillas. This option of a military response was considered even before the
failure in Tlaxcala, as when President Gaviria in a speech of March 26,
1992, stated, "Colombian society has to respond, as a punishment to a
group of political delinquents that every day are becoming more like
common criminals, like real bandits that are hurting Colombian life
and who deserve a strong response, a response of solidarity of all the
Colombians, because I also want to invite all Colombians to support
our armed forces."[97]

After the failures in Caracas and Tlaxcala, with few hopes of a
peaceful solution to the conflict, the government decided to take the
military option. Horacio Serpa seemed to be the only one to point out
the human costs of renewed violence.

The Gaviria government realized that the watchword of preceding
governments had been "hitting the guerrilla sufficiently hard that it
would sit down to negotiate its demobilization." The rationale for the
attack on *Casa Verde* was similar. Nevertheless, the questionable results
of the military operations had not met the expectations of the Colombians; the guerrilla groups, instead of losing ground, were gaining it.
During 1991 there were 22,468 murders in Colombia, including 2,058
peasants, 741 soldiers, and 495 police personnel. The statistics indicated that the ELN had attacked eight military bases, the EPL one, and
the FARC fifteen. The guerrilla groups realized 67 ambushes against
the armed forces and the police, to which were added 210 urban attacks against the police forces, primarily of the narcoterrorist type.
And there were 1,990 kidnappings.

One serious matter shown in the analysis of these statistics was that
even though the budget assigned to the military had increased, that
had not led to increased efficacy in the field of battle. In 1990 the military budget was COL$93 billion, three times greater than that for edu-
cation and twice as much as for health. As a proportion of the gross
domestic product, the military budget increased continuously after
1975, going from 0.8 percent in that year to 1.3 per cent in 1990. Especially large increases came after 1987.[98]

Although Colombia was far from being first among the Latin American countries in military expenditures, people asked why the military had not had more success, given the budget increases. There were two reasons. First, in Colombia there was very little or no military presence in most rural areas. And second, the armed forces had given priority to different investments, emphasizing those oriented to fortifying the defense of the country in face of potential foreign powers; this created a distortion in the matters of strategy, tactics, and military equipment. Most investments had come from foreign credits. Of the US$800 million spent between 1986 and 1990, 43 percent was assigned to the air force, 30 percent to the navy, and only 26 percent to the army and the police.[99]

So the Gaviria government thought that a change was needed. The first step was to fortify the operational capability of the armed forces, based on the war tax previously decreed. This included the creation of more mobile units, as well as antiextortion and antikidnapping groups. Investments were also made in the intelligence services through an improvement of the professionalism of the troops and their aerial transport. More than COL$20 billion was invested in *Agrupaciones Aéreas de Apoyo Táctico* (Aerial Units of Tactical Assistance). In less than six months the number of air force planes and helicopters was increased so that the government could fight continually.[100]

The strategy had three parts: (1) the most specialized units (about twelve thousand men in the elite units) were to fight the guerrillas; (2) new aircraft were added, including A-37 and *El Fantasma* (Phantom) combat planes, fifteen additional Black Hawk helicopters for transport of up to fourteen men, and armed helicopters; and (3) new weapons were added, including lasers, night vision lenses, and M-60 machine guns.[101] All of this was the Gaviria strategy based on the assumption that the government could still win the war.

In an interview with Silvia Galvis of *El Espectador*, Minister of Defense Rafael Pardo made it clear that more money would be going to the military. Increasing military budgets had been the policy before Gaviria became president. It would continue because, as Pardo stated:

> If the policy is to increase the presence of the public forces in the national territory, then money is needed to increase the number of police personnel. That is foreseen in the plans of the government. It is not an immediate increase from one year to the next, but a program for the coming three years. In terms of determined kinds of specialized units to fight given kinds of crimes, this objective is also expressed in financial resources, for example to create new counterinsurgency

Table 6-4. Income of Colombian Guerrilla Groups, 1991 (in millions of Colombian pesos)

Activity	FARC	ELN
Kidnappings	$14,800	$14,400
Gold	6,000	11,000
Protection, livestock owners	6,000	
Coca	50,000	
Amapola (poppies)	17,000	
Extortion	5,000	8,600
Appropriation of government funds		6,500
Coal		8,000
Transportation enterprises		4,000
Total	$98,800	$52,500

Source: Semana (Bogotá), July 7, 1992, pp. 28–29.

units and of anti-kidnapping units. Those are considered with the budget of this year.[102]

Economic Prosperity of Insurgent Groups

Another cause of the failure of the conversations had to do with the economic prosperity of the guerrillas, especially in comparison with the opportunities available in demobilized life. In July 1992 the magazine *Semana* estimated the annual income of the FARC and ELN, shown in table 6.4. A member of the executive branch of government added: "There is no doubt that *Semana* is right that the subversives are making a lot of money, although their figures might be either slightly low or slightly high. We have to change our cost-benefit equations knowing of their wealth. We have to make sure that their costs go up, if they continue as guerrillas, so that they will be prepared to negotiate."[103]

Further, the experiences from the reincorporation of other guerrilla groups did not give many reasons for optimism. The money promised for education or to start businesses had been lacking for smaller guerrilla groups such as the M-19 and the EPL. In addition, in many cases the amnesty granted by the government did not receive recognition from private groups and individuals, who for reasons of vengeance killed demobilized guerrillas. So, *guerrilleros* might ask, "Why leave guerrilla life, with substantial wealth, in order to enter civilian life, with the probability of less wealth and a possibility of being killed that was at least equal to that of guerrilla life, if not greater?"

Lack of Viable Proposals by Either Side

Under these circumstances, what could the government offer to the demobilized guerrillas? And there was no explicit proposal by the *Coordinadora*. Even in Tlaxcala, when the guerrillas tried to talk about substantive issues, they had no more than slogans coming from their ideology, and few well-developed programs.[104]

The best conclusion is that it was never clear what either of the two sides wanted, other than *peace*—a term that had different meanings, as discussed earlier. Perhaps that was because neither side was near enough defeat to have to think of proposals to end the war. And neither side had suffered as much as their counterparts in El Salvador, for example, had suffered.

Lack of Unity on Both Sides

Finally, there was a lack of unity within the two sides—the government and the guerrilla groups. Nothing could be farther from the truth than that there were two unified sides bargaining.

Possibly the lack of unity was more obvious in the case of the CGSB. In the first place, it was assumed that the CGSB coordinated three different guerrilla groups. But in addition, the FARC and the ELN had internal divisions. In the case of the FARC, although there had been attempts to create a hierarchical organization, including a purge in 1990 that led to the murder of front leaders who had not followed the orders of the central command,[105] there were still divisions of different parts of the country and of time in the guerrilla conflict, among others. A sociologist who has written a great deal about the FARC said:

> The most important difference within the FARC is between the fronts in colonization areas and those in areas which were previously populated. The two parts of the FARC are very different. The colonization areas have more of a political character. In the other areas, like the coffee zone, there is little difference between the guerrillas and mere bandits. In the colonization areas they direct a de facto government. . . . Another difference has to do with the fronts commanded by individuals who were in Marquetalia [an "independent republic" of FARC, attacked by the government in 1964]. They are the old ones, with a lot of experience and mystique. The others are the newcomers and in many cases they are of different social strata than the *Marquetalianos*.[106]

There were three principal groups in the ELN: (1) a radical group that believed they could still win the war; (2) the *Corriente de Reno-*

vación Socialista; and (3) the group directed by "Father" Pérez, a Spanish ex-priest.[107] In 1992 the ELN had just reelected Pérez as its leader (the ELN was more democratic than the FARC) for its internal organization. Before its representatives went to meetings of the CGSB, the fronts had meetings and arrived at agreements about their positions, which were the only ones they could propose in the negotiations.[108]

Finally, there were social differences within the guerrilla groups. Although there were some exceptions, as in the case of the leader Alfonso Cano, the majority of FARC members were agrarian workers. Many of the members of the ELN had university education.[109]

There were also differences in government; an obvious one was between the civilian and military leadership groups. There was always the possibility that the army would not follow the orders of the president and his minister of defense. For example, one source insisted that President Gaviria did not know ahead of time of the army's December 1990 attack on *Casa Verde,* command center of the FARC. He also reported: "If one talks with Serpa and with Pardo [the civilian minister of defense named in 1991] one has the impression of two different worlds. Serpa is the optimist, thinking that something can come from negotiations. Pardo, on the other hand, is the 'hawk.' It's necessary to use more force. The question is, which does President Gaviria listen to?"[110]

Finally, one has to consider the organizations that perhaps are not directly part of the civil war but that do play a role from time to time. There are various "self-defense" or "paramilitary" groups. Some have the help of guerrilla groups (including the "Bolivarian Militias" of the FARC); others of the army, with or without the knowledge of the president; others of landowners; and others of the drug groups. These, which are discussed further in chapter 8, play a role in any negotiation between the government and the guerrillas.

The final result is a set of players that will not fit into the models of game theory in which it is assumed that there are two participants. As shown throughout this book, Colombian reality is of a multiplicity of players—some cooperating sometimes, independent at other times, and fighting at still others.

Irony of Gaviria's Failure with Guerrilla Groups

Regardless of which of the preceding explanations are correct (and again, they are certainly not mutually exclusive), there is a great deal of irony in the failure to reach an agreement. First, it is ironic because the constituent assembly (see chapter 9) had brought to Colombia much of the democracy and many of the human rights (at least on paper) that the guerrilla groups had been claiming to be fighting for during so many years. If they had accepted the explicit invitation of Antonio Navarro, who himself had spent time in guerrilla activities, they could have claimed the constitution of 1991 as their victory. That assertion could have been justified, as they were a major contributor to the violence that led to the calls for a new governance structure.

The second bit of irony comes from the internal organization of the guerrilla groups, especially the ELN. They made decisions internally in a democratic fashion, so why could they not accept the same kind of structure for the entire country?

The conclusion, however, is that whatever the basic reasons for the failure, no matter who was responsible and how ironic it was, the two major guerrilla groups in Colombia—the FARC and the ELN—were still functioning at the end of the Gaviria government. This must be considered his major failure in trying to democratize Colombia.

7

Gaviria's Drug Policy

In this chapter I analyze the César Gaviria drug policy from its early days, to the elaboration of a decree to which many narcotraffickers would surrender, to the saga of the Pablo Escobar bargaining-surrender-flight-bargaining-death. I demonstrate how César Gaviria abandoned the policy of Virgilo Barco (either total war or conversations with intermediaries) and substituted a consistent policy of plea bargaining.

The Initiation of a Policy Shift

At his August 7, 1990, inauguration, César Gaviria made it very clear that he considered the drug-dealer problem the most important in the country:

> Narcoterrorism today is the principal threat to our democracy. We will confront it without concessions. There is no other way to rid the country of regicide, of hundreds of deaths from car bombs, of children fallen on Mothers' Day, of soldiers and humble people who are victims of all kinds of attacks, of the agents assassinated in the destroyed floors of the DAS building, of the police shot in the streets of Medellín.
>
> Since the leadership of this struggle cannot be delegated, the President will lead the actions of the Armed Forces, the National Police, the DAS, to turn back the terrorists and to put an end to the barbarous acts.[1]

More specifically, Gaviria stated that Colombia needed international help with the drug problem and that help was justified. "Never in the history of humankind has a nation paid as high a price as Colombia has in confronting a crime of international character, by confronting the most powerful criminal organizations that can be remembered."[2]

Modern mechanisms would be used to confront the narcos: a national organization would be formed to deal specifically with organized crime; a change would be made in the burden of proof in the matter of economic wealth; and more protection would be provided for judges—special places for them to live were a possibility. Also, more would be expected of the consuming countries. They would be expected to campaign against consumption, the laundering of money, the arms traffic, the distribution networks, the sale of precursor chemicals, and the growth of coca leaves.

During his campaign Gaviria made the distinction between *drug terrorism* and *drug traffic*—the former being a Colombian phenomenon that would be confronted without concessions and the latter being an international phenomenon that called for collaborative action by the affected countries. In the first place a police and judicial settlement should be given to the drug-traffic problem, in contrast to the almost exclusively military solution the Barco administration favored. Gaviria also announced the establishment of a permanent jurisdiction that would contemplate novel and modern instruments to confront drug trade, and once more he referred to extradition as another tool, not the only and principal instrument of the struggle: "It is a matter of a tool of discretional use on the part of the Executive."[3] In effect he then said that if the bombs, the assassination of police officers, and terrorism in general ended, and if there was a legal apparatus that functioned, then extradition would be less necessary.

In the early days of the Gaviria administration, it was not clear which direction drug policy would take. Some thought that because Gaviria's mentor Luis Carlos Galán had been murdered by the narcos, he was sure to continue the Barco policy of total war and extradition. This seemed to be the case when, on August 11, Gustavo de Jesús Gaviria, first cousin of Pablo Escobar and second in command of the Medellín mafia, was killed by the *Cuerpo Elite* (Elite Corps) of the national police. Although this was a most severe blow to the group, instead of the customary retaliatory bomb following such a death, the *Extraditables* issued a conciliatory declaration in which they announced that they would continue their truce.[4]

The question of extradition was also put into doubt when, in late August, the verdicts in the drug trial of Mayor Marion S. Barry, Jr., of Washington, D.C., caused anger in Colombia. Barry had been arrested for crack cocaine violations, and the police had a videotape that showed the mayor engaging in that illegal activity. The light sentence given him appeared to threaten extradition—a keystone of U.S. policy.

The reactions in Colombia were to that effect: "It's going to be difficult to convince our people of the necessity to extradite our nationals given these kinds of verdicts," National Procurator Alfonso Gómez told foreign reporters. His response followed two weeks of angry reactions, which included editorials in Bogotá newspapers. "Surprising and scandalous" was the editorial reaction of *El Espectador*. Enrique Santos Calderón of *El Tiempo* said, "In this climate it is going to be difficult to renew extraditions." Francisco Santos wrote in *El Tiempo*, "It's worth asking whether the war on drug trafficking should be fought in this country." *Semana,* the weekly, editorialized, "In the war against drugs, the United States is ready to fight to the last Colombian." Minister of Justice Jaime Geraldo Angel stated, "If such an important public servant is not punished for a crime against which we are struggling so arduously, then we feel bad." DAS director General Miguel Masa Márquez said, "The impression for the world is that, for North American courts, a gram of cocaine produced deserves a life sentence, while a grain of cocaine consumed is worth a pardon." And the perception of a judicial double standard was echoed when Foreign Minister Luis Fernando Jaramillo Correra said, "The Colombian people feel deceived by the harshness with which the law is applied to our compatriots—in contrast to the laxity of the case with Mayor Barry, which produced only a light penalty." Although fourteen Colombians were in jail waiting extradition, there had been none since the inauguration of César Gaviria Trujillo.[5]

The Surrender Process: Decrees and Requests for Changes

After careful study the new government arrived at the conclusion that a new policy was possible. As in the case of the Barco government, the bargaining process that followed between the César Gaviria government and the leaders of the Medellín drug group was never one of the principals of the two sides sitting at a table. The transgressions of the narcos simply made that unacceptable. Rather, various intermediaries talked to those principals.

The First Step: Decree 2047

On September 5, 1990, César Gaviria issued Decree 2047, which represented a radical change of government policy regarding narcoterrorism. Basically, it said that those who surrendered to the authorities and confessed their crimes would not be extradited and would receive in return a lowering of their sentences and an even greater reduction if they gave evidence regarding their accomplices. Those benefits would cover crimes committed before September 5, 1990. The big problem for the *Extraditables* was that the government could still extradite a person for crimes not confessed.[6]

Paradoxically, Gaviria was applying the slogan of Barco of "the hand held out and the pulse strong," *("el mano extendido y el pulso firme")*, but he was doing it publicly and in a more pragmatic way. According to the first Gaviria decree, if one did not confess all the crimes committed, once arrested one might be connected to other crimes not confessed. The latter would not fall under the benefits of the decree. But if Pablo Escobar were to surrender and confess each one of the crimes of drug trafficking and terrorism that he had committed in his life, he would not spend more than eight years in prison.[7]

The initiative came from the government exclusively and was not the product of a dialogue or of exceptional circumstances like the kidnapping of the son of someone important, as in the Montoya case. Neither did it come from any kind of explicit or implicit bargaining between the government and the narcos. The narcos had tried to establish lines of communication with some representatives of the new government, but Gaviria had been categorical in prohibiting all contacts. Nevertheless, he gave them what they had asked for in the famous Panamá meeting of 1984 and what the narcos offered in the surrender as a reply to the communiqué from the *Notables* at the beginning of 1990.[8]

From the standpoint of the narcos, Decree 2047 had two problems. The first was the necessity of confessing all crimes, which in some cases would have meant literally thousands of cocaine shipments, not to mention acts of terrorism and other crimes. The second was establishment of the September date, as crimes had been continuing since that time. In short, there were two ways the government could extradite someone who surrendered: (1) if the person did not confess all crimes and another was proven or (2) if the person had done something since September 5.

The Second Step: Decree 2372

The first problem was taken care of on October 8 when the government issued Decree 2372, which said that it was not necessary to confess all crimes in order to avoid extradition. With the confession of just one violation the government promised not to extradite. Further, un-confessed crimes could not constitute the basis for extradition.[9]

Yet this was not enough for the *Extraditables*. Francisco Santos, scion of the family that ran *El Tiempo*, the Bogotá newspaper, was kid-napped. Two demands accompanied the first communication about him: rejection of the decree and the demand for political treatment for the *Extraditables* as the M-19 had been given. This made many think that Pablo Escobar was copying the Alvaro Gómez kidnapping.[10]

As a result, in October and November 1990 bargaining with inter-mediaries took place between the government and the Mafia. In the early days of October, Alfonso López, Misael Pastrana, Cardinal Mario Revollo, and Diego Montaña Cuéllar offered, as the *Notables*, to nego-tiate the release of seven journalists whom the narcos had kidnapped. On October 27, as a response, the Medellín lawyer Guido Parra sent a letter to the *Notables* in which he made a proposal about the treatment of the kidnapped people and the *Extraditables*. He proposed, in addi-tion, a meeting of the U.N. Council for Drug Matters and following the rules of international law.[11]

In reply the *Notables* recognized the use of international law as le-gitimate. Then in early November, the *Extraditables* sent a communiqué that justified the kidnapping. In reply to that communiqué, the mayor of Medellín sent a letter to the *Notables*, expressing his willingness to collaborate in the negotiations to free the kidnapped ones. President Gaviria agreed to call for a meeting of the U.N. Drug Council and stated that international treaties would be honored.[12]

On November 2 Guido Parra sent a letter to the *Notables* in which he proposed three topics for discussion: (1) the possibility of changing the decree that made extradition by administrative methods possible; (2) the suggestion that the methods used in 1957 (in which the guer-rillas of the two political parties were declared to be common delin-quents and later given pardons) be used in this situation; and (3) the possibility of a surrender, underlining the need to follow international law and guidelines on human rights to protect the victims of armed conflict.[13]

The document that the *Notables* took to the president in mid-November had five points that were the conditions of the *Extraditables*, which were that:

1. They not be required to admit guilt
2. They not be required to turn evidence on each other
3. They be guaranteed that they would not be extradited

4. All be confined to the same prison, under the protection and guard
   of the army, the navy, the police or some organization of international supervision
5. Any possibility of revenge be warded off[14]

The key thing now was the elimination of confession as a requisite.
To the *Extraditables'* desire for a government guarantee of no extradition to those who surrendered, although they confessed nothing, the
minister of justice replied, "I want to point out that the totality of the
crimes do not need to be confessed, but only some of them, since it
should be remembered that the government can make plans for justice
for those that have cases pending with it, and not for those who consider that they have not committed any punishable offense."[15]

The majority of the *Extraditables* (Pablo Escobar being one notable
exception) were charged with crimes in the United States but not in
Colombia. Therefore, the *Extraditables* also wanted the government to
have the burden of proof, even after they had surrendered. The goal of
the government, as was evident through its decrees, was completely
different. In the first place, individual—not collective—surrenders
were anticipated. The person who surrendered voluntarily had to recognize the commission of one or more crimes. To the extent that they
declared who their accomplices were, there would be a lessening of
sentences. If after the confession the judge received proof that the person had lied, the benefits of the decree—including no extradition—
would be lost.[16]

According to Guido Parra, if there were to be an agreement, no door
to extradition could be left open. As a result the possibility for peace
in Colombia depended on the removal of two articles of two decrees:
(1) Article 12 of Decree 2047 ("In these cases there would be no extradition, unless there is added to the case evidence that spoils [the con-
fession] or alters it substantially") and (2) Article 4 of Decree 2372, having to do with escape ("Those tried under the procedures set forth
in Decree 2047 of 1990 and of this decree will lose the right that they
could have obtained by confession if they flee [from jail] or if they intend to do so"). Guido Parra said that it should be understood that the
kidnapping victims would not be released if these articles were not
changed.[17]

So it appeared that much still remained to be negotiated before the
leading Medellín narcos would turn themselves in. The impasse came
because the government and the narcos both knew that the former was
unlikely to prove anything about the narcos without their confession.

At the end of November 1990, however, the *Extraditables* announced, "Because of the election for the National Constituent Assembly, we have decided to declare a truce, so that the people can vote in a free and sovereign manner."[18]

Then in December, Fabio Ochoa surrendered, surprising the Gaviria government, which had thought that their decrees would appeal primarily to second-level narcos. However, one of the members of the family revealed the conditions in which the Ochoa brothers had been living. They lived in huts, unable to see their children or their wives or to be with their parents in their "golden years." They lived with the fear of being assassinated. All of this was much worse than being in any Colombian prison. Fabio Ochoa had written to the minister of justice, stating his intention and asking for more detail on the decree. His principal concern was that he not be extradited to the United States. He was convinced that if the *Cuerpo Elite* found him, they would kill him.[19]

The Third Step: Decree 3030

On December 4, in reply to the concern of having to confess to at least one crime, President César Gaviria stated, "We are prepared to modify that decree, because we are interested in the pacification of the country." Nevertheless, on December 17 the government announced Decree 3030, considered by the cartel lawyers to be a "declaration of war." Instead of more concessions, it was more rigid than Decree 2047.[20] No reference was made to the five demands.

Decree 3030 stated a clear position on two juridical issues. The first was to reconfirm submission to justice and confession of at least one crime, as indispensable prerequisites to getting the benefits of both decrees. Although this was not what the *Extraditables* wanted, Minister of Justice Jaime Giraldo Angel insisted that the position of the government on this would not change, as he demonstrated when he said, "Perhaps some thought that the government would not extradite a person simply because he presented himself before a judge. Or that they were going to be given special treatment because it was a collective crime. That is not the essence of this system. The spinal column is the submission to justice and the base of that column is confession."[21]

Decree 3030 was substantially different from Decree 2047 in the juridical mechanisms that it used to guarantee the two basic benefits that the government was offering—concurrent sentences and no extradition. Decree 2047 only considered the concern for confessed crimes, with the sentences not added together for the crimes confessed but added for unconfessed ones. In the second place, sentences for crimes committed after confession could be accumulated; Decree 2047 only offered no extradition for confessed crimes. In the new decree there would be no extradition for any crime committed before September 5, 1990, if the person had confessed a crime that had sent him to prison.[22]

The combination of flexibility and inflexibility was due, according to one legal expert, to the government's attempt to maintain equilibrium between its dignity and the effectiveness of its policy. In a statement to ABC News, Gaviria said:

> This is not a peace plan. Neither are we doing any kind of political negotiation. What we are trying to do is to fortify our judicial system, because extradition is only the second best option. The best and most efficient way to confront the problems is for justice in Colombia to be strong enough for those people to give up and confess their crimes. . . .
>
> The cooperation of the North American authorities with this drug policy is absolutely indispensable, because they are the ones who have to supply the evidence of the crimes committed in that country by the Colombians that surrender to the justice system. If they only confess part of their crimes, not all, we hope that the US authorities will supply us with the evidence that they have and thus we will be able to judge them on the basis of all the crimes that they have committed.[23]

By January 1991 Pablo Escobar and his lawyers were working on three items. First, they were concerned with the date that the decree would lose force. They preferred that it be at the time of the surrender. Second, they would ask that the constituent assembly form a committee to consider the principle of no extradition of nationals as a constitutional one. Finally, they were studying the "strategy of confession." They were considering which crimes should be confessed (as they were likely to be proved anyway) and which ones should not be (as there was little probability that they would be proved independently).[24]

In practice all of the problems could be reduced to this: Escobar wanted a legal guarantee that he would not be extradited, and the word of the Colombian president was not enough. For Escobar the international pressures to have him extradited were so strong that he would only be content if that possibility were completely eliminated. It was likely that the new constitution would consecrate the principle of no extradition because the majority of the members of the constituent assembly campaigned with that platform. Therefore, it was correctly anticipated that Escobar would wait until that happened before surrendering.[25]

As 1990 ended with the surrender of Fabio Ochoa, 1991 began with bad news. A narco from Manizales, Gonzalo Mejía Sanín, who surrendered before Ochoa, was freed after spending only a few days in jail. In order to make sure that this did not happen again it was necessary to issue more decrees to cover the judicial loopholes.[26]

A new letter from Guido Parra after the government issued Decree 3030 made more demands: that the effective date be the date of surrender; that the new penal code, including the use of anonymous judges, not be applied; and that evidence on cohorts not be included. Two modifications of the decrees followed. First was a series of procedural norms so that those who surrendered could not be released immediately by judges. The second was the requested change of date. This was Decree 303.[27]

The Surrender of Pablo Escobar

To work out final details, an "interlocutor" was needed between Pablo Escobar and César Gaviria. This turned out to be Alberto Villamizar, a congressman whose wife and sister had both been kidnapped by the *Extraditables*. Jorge Luis Ochoa, from his cell in Itagüí, insisted to Escobar that Villamizar was the person he had been looking for. After Escobar waited, Ochoa sent him another message in which he said, "I have studied all the possibilities of Villamizar; he is the man that you need. Don't complicate the matter more."[28] Escobar finally agreed. When Villamizar was contacted and went to the Ochoa home, he received a message from Escobar saying that if Gaviria followed through on the public denouncements that he had made about the violation of human rights, it would be very easy to begin a dialogue with him and search for a solution to the problem. Villamizar reported to high-level officials in the government and to the procurate.[29]

The last missing piece was discovered on April 18 when the octogenarian Roman Catholic priest, García Herreros, had a prayer on his daily *"El Minuto de Dios"* national television program in which he called for Pablo Escobar to meet with him. Villamizar and a member of the Ochoa family were watching the program together and agreed that they had found the solution to the puzzle. García Herreros was contacted in Bogotá and traveled to the home of the Ochoas in Medellín the next day.[30] Days later the response of Pablo Escobar arrived, expressing his willingness to surrender if there were justice, by which he meant that the law would be applied to those who had harmed his people. Specifically, he identified seventeen individuals who had violated the human rights of the members of his organization and hence, according to Escobar, could not remain with impunity.[31]

When he met with the priest, Pablo Escobar said that the basic problem if he surrendered was his personal security. The dirty war between the security organizations and the narcos had been of such a magnitude that lives were in danger, not only the lives of those directly involved in the business but also their families' lives. The response to the massive assassinations of police in Medellín was often police action that went beyond what was legal, with summary executions.[32] He insisted that he would not go to the Prison of Itagüí, where the Ochoa brothers were, because it was not secure. He had many enemies who were capable of anything, including bombing the prison. The more urban a jail was, the more dangerous it would be. For that reason he preferred a prison in Envigado, near Medellín. He left the impression that if the political will existed to create the conditions to protect his life, the problem could be solved. Another requirement was that there could be no members of the military in the prison.[33]

In the case of the prison for Pablo Escobar, it was decided that the number of guards was to be forty, half chosen from the different prisons of the country and half by the municipality of Envigado. The control of the prison would be carried out by a committee made up of the mayor of Envigado, the regional procurator of Antioquia, and the director of the prison. Another point of contention was the presence of the army at the jail. In the contract signed by the minister of justice, it was established that they would not have access to the internal part of the prison, as they did in all the other jails in the country. The *Extraditables* demanded that they be at least three kilometers away from the jail, but the government did not accept, being of the opinion that they could be anywhere outside the fence.[34]

On May 27 the government let Escobar know that they recognized his worries about his enemies getting positions in the prison but that they could not allow him to choose prison personnel. Pablo Escobar objected to the person chosen to be director because he only trusted "people from his land." The government did not heed his objection. A committee made up of the mayor of Envigado, the regional procurator, and the director of the jail would choose the guards.[35]

On June 18, 1991, at 5:11 in the afternoon, Pablo Escobar surrendered. At 1:00 P.M. that afternoon, the constituent assembly had decided that the new constitution would prohibit extradition. Seven years before, Pablo Escobar had decided to carry out a war to the death until Colombia eliminated extradition. At the basic level, from the time of Gaviria's first decree until the surrender, the government made only one really controversial concession: to change the cut-off date from September 5, 1990, to the date of surrender.

On July 3 the *Extraditables* announced their plan to demobilize, stating in a communiqué that the decision was due to the constituent assembly vote to eliminate extradition. The *Extraditables* were accused of the assassination of a number of judges and of four hundred members of the Medellín police force, as well as for the series of bombings.[36] They had sent some fifty communiqués through the press expressing their demands and threats while denying culpability for kidnappings, attacks, and assassinations.

Hence apparently ended the organization of the *Extraditables,* first known through a communiqué on November 6, 1986. In that first message they had "demanded the end of extradition of Colombians in the name of the rights of families, of human rights, and of national sovereignty."[37] On June 18, 1991, the constituent assembly had met that demand.

Pablo Escobar's Thirteen Months in Prison

The judicial processes working against Pablo Escobar began within a week after his surrender. Investigations had resulted in about fourteen charges being brought against him, and the anonymous judges soon arrived at Envigado to take his confession.[38] By the end of June he had confessed to only one crime: sending one shipment of cocaine to France (where he had already been tried and convicted in absentia). He denied, however, sending cocaine to the United States, kidnapping the journalists, bombing the Avianca flight, and participating in various assassinations, including Guillermo Cano and Luis Carlos Galán.

Pablo Escobar's summary of his life of crime was seen in early July when, in addition to stating his hope that his trial would be public, he stated to the Medellín newspaper *El Colombiano:*

The Medellín cartel exists only for the communication media. I consider myself a friend of the Ochoas and I knew Rodríguez Gacha, but I was never his partner in his war with the guerrilla groups. I never signed a communique of the *Extraditables.* That was a clandestine group. I only respond for documents that have my signature and my thumb print.

When I met in Panamá with López and with the Procurator I was not extraditable, but I represented the *Extraditables* politically. I am for the *Extraditables* what Diego Montaña Cuéllar was for FARC. That is, I am the political part. . . .

I have committed no crimes in the United States. . . . I can not understand why they accuse me of crimes there. If I committed crimes it was here, and not in the United States.

The communication media are uninformed, talking about the cartel of Medellín and the citizens that make up that cartel are not from Medellín. There is great confusion: the communication media say that I have problems with people from Valle and that is not true, my wife is even from Valle. Another thing is that the Rodríguez Orejuela brothers placed the first large bomb that exploded in this country, at the building where my innocent family lived.

The Rodríguez Orejuela brothers are dedicated to denouncing me and they are associated with Gómez Padilla, Maza Márquez, and Colonel Pelaez Carmona in order to assassinate people in bars and on corners in lower income neighborhoods and in order to torture, execute, and make disappear my family and friends. . . .

Maza Márquez wants to be President. For that reason he asked for the right to vote for members of the military [in the constituent assembly]. The presidential candidates were assassinated with the collaboration of the DAS bodyguards.[39]

By the time Pablo Escobar had been in the prison in Envigado (nicknamed *La Catedral*—the Cathedral) for a year, the government had concluded that, aside from the modest confession, little or nothing could be proved against him and the three Ochoas that the world had signaled as the principal traffickers of cocaine from Colombia.[40] The government knew that to convict these individuals, the Colombian government had to change and strengthen the judicial system. But there was little that the system could do in the Escobar case because judicial authorities and security organisms had spent years acting in function of extradition, gathering elements of intelligence and not evidence. As a result, the Colombian government saw that evidence from the United States was going to be crucial in the conviction of Escobar. The minister of justice was sent to Washington to talk to officials of the U.S. government, while in Bogotá a team of that ministry, the direction of the criminal justice system, and the national procurate was set up to receive, evaluate, and process the information coming from foreign countries.[41] Thus it was clear a year after Pablo Escobar's surrender that more remained to be done than had been done. Public opinion, nevertheless, supported the process, and many believed that the policy had worked better than they had thought possible.

The case in Colombia against Pablo Escobar that was most developed was the Guillermo Cano assassination. In March 1992, an anonymous judge in Medellín indicted him for this crime, charging him with being its "intellectual author." The process by which evidence was collected and witnesses examined was practically finished, with a date already set for sentencing. The possibilities that Escobar would be found guilty were considered good.

Escobar had also been connected to the January 1988 kidnapping of Andrés Pastrana, the assassination of ex-procurator Carlos Mauro Hoyos, the attempted assassination of General Maza Márquez, the assassination of Luis Carlos Galán, and three bombings: the airplane, the DAS building, and the Las Villas building. In all he had been shown to be a party in more than twenty crimes, the majority of which were incidents of terrorism. In the United States there were eight indictments against him—three for money laundering and five for drug trafficking. In the end, as the sum could not be arithmetic, the integration of the sentences could not be more than thirty years. "Whatever the final verdict was, what appears to be clear was that he was going to be spending much more time in prison than he probably calculated."[42] Because an additional reduction of sentences could be achieved through either productive work or educational advancement, the Ochoa brothers set up a plastic plate factory; Pablo Escobar expected to study journalism. Their lawyers calculated that, after the reductions, none of the Medellín drug leaders would receive a sentence of more than eight years.[43]

The Escape of and Second Search for Pablo Escobar

Things did not go as the government had expected in *La Catedral*, however. First, there were scandals about the opulent goods (television sets, VCRs, and jacuzzis—to mention only a few) purchased and brought to the prison by Pablo Escobar and his cohorts. Then, there was another episode of Colombian politics that seemed to resemble the "magical realism" popular in Colombian literature: the man who had been the most sought-after in the world only thirteen months before would walk out of his "maximum security prison" to have that status once again.

Escobar Conducts Business As Usual

In June of 1992, in a "lightening operation" nearly all the leaders of the Medellín cartel who were not in jail were kidnapped.[44] Pablo Escobar considered that it was he who had begun the battle against extradition and that his victory permitted the others to continue with the drug trade. The cost of this was that Escobar was in prison, while the others were still free. And he wanted them not to forget who the chief was and to pay him a certain percentage of their profits.

It was later reported that the security organizations had begun investigating on June 25, 1992, intercepting radio telephone conversations that gave the first indication of the crimes being committed from *La Catedral*. From one of the conversations the detectives discovered that the "farm" to which the drug leaders had been taken was the very prison of *La Catedral*. Two of the potential victims escaped. Their testimony, together with that of eight others, led to the conclusion that the prison of Envigado was a business office and a recreational farm where the chief of the Medellín cartel met his friends without any authority preventing it.[45] This led Chief Prosecutor Gustavo de Greiff to ask for a meeting with President César Gaviria. He told the president that he had decided to move Pablo Escobar from Envigado to the headquarters of the Fourth Brigade of the army in Medellín and his lieutenants to the prison of Itagüí while a solution to the problem was found and the officials who were responsible were identified.[46] Documents obtained by *Semana* showed that since the previous January 27, some officials of the government had known what was going on in the prison of Envigado, although it is not clear that President Gaviria did. Later, by the end of July, the general prosecutor's office reached the conclusion that there had been numerous uncontrolled visits to *La Catedral*, with evidence of kidnappings, tortures, murders, and incineration of some people—crimes planned and ordered from the jail. Some of the people had even been brought before Escobar at *La Catedral*, where they were judged for being disloyal.

Even before those conclusions were reached, for the president and his advisers it was clear that they had to assume military control of the prison and cut off immediately a situation that could only mean that Pablo Escobar, the most dangerous drug trafficker in the world, was making fun of the government's policy of submission to justice. *La Catedral* had been converted into the general headquarters of Escobar's organization, under protection from the government, from which he could order not only drug trafficking but also narcoterrorism.[47] The capacity to kidnap many of the best-guarded drug dealers did not portray Escobar as an indefensible person who surrendered to justice and was behind bars but as a man who had all the infrastructure with which to do what he wanted. The concern of the authorities was fundamentally that if this were true, it was a new and impressive demonstration of Escobar's power.

The general prosecutor's office also believed that Escobar could be considering an escape. The government checked out the legalities; on July 21, the letters to be exchanged between the ministers of justice and defense were transcribed—letters to formalize the solicitude of justice to defense that the armed forces take charge of the internal vigilance and not just the external role until that time.[48] During the discussion it was suggested that this might not be sufficient, given the studies of the general prosecutor's office suggesting that an escape might be in the planning stage. Hence it was decided, especially because security construction was being done to the prison, that Escobar should be sent to another place. To give the proceedings a judicial appearance it was decided that Vice Minister of Justice Eduardo Mendoza and the director of prisons, Colonel Hernando Navas, should travel to Envigado.[49]

The Escobar Flight

A little after nine that night of July 21, 1992, a radio station transmitted a "flash" stating that Escobar was going to be moved. As a result the government released a communiqué, directed more to the prisoners than to the public, to inform them that the operation going on was an official one and that it was being done for reasons of security—including theirs—as jail improvements were going on and that caused risks. Later many considered this a half-truth.

When Colonel Navas entered the prison (the commander of the armed forces feared becoming a hostage), it was decided to send the special forces from Bogotá, who were especially trained in rescue operations. Vice Minister Mendoza then entered the prison and had a personal contact, for the first time, with Pablo Escobar. They talked for more than half an hour, during which time Mendoza tried to persuade Escobar that the move was necessary. The narco leader insisted that there was a misinformation campaign going on against him, accusing him of continuing to break the law from inside the prison. Then the vice minister decided to leave and was prevented from doing so. Mendoza and Navas were hostages.[50]

At seven the next morning when people in the office of the presidency thought that the operation was finally being carried out, there was a new call from Navas, who said that Escobar wanted to negotiate. Navas's call brought an even bigger surprise: since 3:00 P.M. on Tuesday afternoon the order to the Fourth Brigade to take the prison had gone various times through the chain of command from president to minister of defense to General Murillo to General Pardo—but Pardo had not carried out the order by the next morning.[51] The only military group that entered the prison was at 7:30 A.M. on Wednesday, when the special forces group rescued Mendoza and Navas and subdued the prisoners with them. The delay in the special forces' effort was also unclear. The order was given to them before 11:00 P.M. on Tuesday, but their trip to Medellín was only possible the next morning.[52]

The definitive statement that Pablo Escobar was free again was made only late on Wednesday, partly because of the able maneuver by Escobar's organization to inundate the media with the false information that the group was hidden in a basement, with sufficient food and ammunition for many days. Another reason was perhaps more emotional. Colombians, from President César Gaviria down, refused to believe that the nightmare had begun again.

The escape of Pablo Escobar clearly complicated the discussion of a second surrender. The decrees of submission to justice under which Escobar turned himself in the first time stipulated that the benefits of sentence reduction received would be lost if the person continued committing crimes while in prison or if he escaped.[53] Now Escobar had clearly done both. But on the other side, as his lawyers pointed out, when he surrendered, the government had promised in writing that he would not be moved and that army troops would not be stationed in the jail. Therefore, there was panic when those conditions were broken by the government. Pablo Escobar had escaped, they argued, because the government had broken its promises.

Escobar's lawyers soon began talking about a new surrender process. The major obstacle to that came from the government's side. The room for maneuvering for the government was practically nonexistent. In principle the president would accept only an unconditional surrender. External pressures were also felt. Soon after the escape, twenty-five helicopters from the United States, as well as slightly more than one hundred Drug Enforcement Agency operatives were working with the *Cuerpo Elite* of the police.[54]

In early October three close associates of Pablo Escobar—Roberto Escobar, José Jairo Velásquez, and Otoniel González—surrendered, making all think that the second surrender of the *patrón* was close. Those three men had been his "life insurance policy" since long before his first surrender in 1991.[55] That Pablo Escobar did not surrender then was probably because several hours after the surrender of the three, two bodies of other narcos were found. As Escobar's lawyers stated: "This assassination shows that there were dark forces that do not want peace in Colombia. Pablo Escobar was completely willing to surrender. We were not negotiating any conditions with the government. We only asked that the lives of family members and those not in jail be respected. These two assassinations were connected to the actions of the Medellín SIJIN [police intelligence]."[56]

Escobar's other concern was for the security mechanisms between the place where he would surrender and the prison. If he were to be taken to Itagüí, there was no way to do so by helicopter. Furthermore, Itagüí was a fortress of the Moncada and Galeano families, the heads of which were assassinated by Escobar and who were offering a reward of COL\$1.5 billion for Escobar, dead or alive.[57]

By mid-October seven of the nine men who escaped with Pablo Escobar had turned themselves in. It appeared that the men's task was to convert the prison in Itagüí into a center that would be safe for their boss.[58] When Minister of Justice Andrés González had visited it in October, Roberto Escobar told him that if he wanted Pablo Escobar to surrender, there was the condition that a fourteen-meter-high wall that would leave Escobar incommunicado from his lieutenants be razed. The people who had constructed the wall said that several workers could tear it down in a few hours. But they thought the real problem was the security system in Itagüí where each movement of the prisoners was watched through closed-circuit television. A source in the national prosecutor's office said, "If he surrendered, that was going to bother Escobar and his people a lot, since the liberty there was in *La Catedral* was not going to be repeated."[59]

The Resumption of War

By the end of 1992, when it was thought that the government operations would diminish with the imminent surrender of the head of the cartel, on the contrary, those actions intensified. Although a new negotiation seemed attractive, by the end of 1992 the government had decided to use force. The cartel then reactivated its terrorist apparatus. In that way—occupations and captures on one side and car bombs and assassinations of police on the other—positions hardened. A wave of violence against police in Medellín was unleashed, with forty-five agents killed. Because of the number of surrenders and deaths of Escobar's close associates, the authorities were convinced that he was alone and that they would soon capture him.[60]

To Escobar, the government's refusal to let his lawyers place conditions on his surrender was not the only reason that a point of no return had been reached. The men that Escobar had turned over in a continuous manner during the last half of the year—among other things, to see how it went for them—had to endure especially severe conditions (by Colombian standards) of incarceration. There were more limitations to conjugal visits and to whatever convenience public opinion could consider a luxury. The following of all the movements of the prisoners by closed-circuit television cameras and the transfers without prior notice from the old to the new prison of Itagüí worsened their spirits. It was possible that the authorities—because of the embarrassment of *La Catedral*—had gone too far. Further, by that time the chief of the Medellín cartel had accumulated a series of new charges, arrest warrants, and subpoenas for trials that had changed the possibility of receiving a light sentence should he surrender.

Because of the military actions against Pablo Escobar, some said that his days were running out. The only thing that was absolutely predictable, they said, was that the more time that passed, the more terrorism there would be and the bloodier would be the lashing out *(coletazo)* of the cartel.[61] This was surely the case when, in January 1993, after a two-year hiatus, the narcos exploded a car bomb in Bogotá. This was surprising because, since Escobar's flight from *La Catedral*, the bombings had been in Medellín. It was the "chronicle of an announced bomb," as Pablo Escobar had written on January 15 to Prosecutor de Greiff: "In light of all the circumstances, no alternative remains but to discard the juridical struggle and begin and assume an organized armed battle. . . . I wish to communicate to you in an official and public way that my determination is to found and lead an armed rebel group that will be called 'Rebel Antioquia.' " In an earlier letter to the prosecutor, he had written, "What will the government do if as a reply to the tortures and disappearances, a bomb of ten thousand kilograms were placed at the national prosecutor's office, at the Administration of National Taxes or at Inravisión or *El Tiempo?*"[62] The bombing signaled the move of the war to Bogotá and meant that the action front of his so-called *Antioquia Rebelde* was going to be national.

At the same time, two captured terrorists gave information revealing that the terrorist plan was going to be in three stages. The first, which had begun the previous Thursday night with the bombing, had as its general objective to generate panic among the citizens. The second was to explode twelve car bombs of one hundred kilos of dynamite, each in state entities and in communications networks. The third and last step would have the commercial centers of the capital as targets.[63]

In February 1993, twenty members of the Medellín cartel turned themselves in, confessed, and turned state's evidence on others. By that first week of February, the reward for Pablo Escobar was COL$5 billion (about US$6.35 million) offered by the Colombian government, as well as US$3.5 million from the Central Intelligence Agency, the Drug Enforcement Agency, and Interpol. A decree was announced that would give benefits, including impunity, to whoever "ratted" on the *patrón*. Another new benefit was that someone already in jail could get a conditional liberty, reduction of term, or end of sentence. To avoid a debate, all of this was at the discretion of the national prosecutor's office.[64]

Response to Renewed Terrorism

At the same time three groups were actively trying to rid Colombia of Pablo Escobar. In keeping with Colombian political patterns, they were a paramilitary group (calling themselves Those Persecuted by Pablo Escobar—*Los Perseguidos por Pablo Escobar, Los Pepes*), a legal interest group called Free Colombia (*Colombia Libre*), and the Colombian government.

The *Pepes* were a serious threat to Escobar because they knew better than anyone his world and his vulnerabilities. Their philosophy was that terrorism could only be confronted with a greater terrorism, and thus they burned his wife's ranch, his warehouse where he had antique cars worth more than US$5 million, and his sister-in-law's art gallery. Later two other properties of his were attacked. In addition, they killed forty people and gave evidence on a half-dozen cartel members, who ended up dead or in jail.[65] According to some, the *Pepes* came from the so-called group of Itagüí, led by the Moncada and Galeano families, the first affected by the "justice" meted out by Pablo Escobar in *La Catedral.*

Others thought the *Pepes* were former members of the Medellín cartel that received help from the Cali cartel. Still other information suggested that behind them was Fidel Castaño, the so-called Colombian Rambo. Castaño had, over the preceding two years, been distancing himself from his old friend Pablo Escobar for several reasons. First, he and his friends criticized Escobar's 1991 surrender. For Castaño, it ended the possibility of negotiation with the government. He thought that because he and other paramilitary chiefs had done their part in the peace process that demobilized several guerrilla groups, they had gained a political status that should be sufficient to obtain a negotiated settlement for the paramilitary groups and their allies in the drug traffic.

Another motive was the war started by Escobar against the paramilitary groups of Magdalena Medio, and especially against Henry de Jesús Pérez, a close friend of Castaño. The definitive cause was the influence of Fernando Galeano, who was one of Castaño's closest friends.[66] Many of the affiliates of the *Pepes*, beginning with Castaño himself, thought that their actions against Escobar would permit all of them to obtain legal benefits in the framework of the new legislation about giving evidence and collaborating with the justice system.

Then in mid-February, 1993, the enemies of Pablo Escobar formed an apparently new "interest group." Based in an office in a secret place in Medellín, it called itself Colombia Libre. In an interview with *Semana,* a leader of the organization said, "Our function is to carry out an intelligence job through the payment of rewards to informants who turn over information about the location of Escobar and his men. We will give that information to the authorities so that they can be the ones who act in the name of the law."[67] Later intelligence information revealed that Colombia Libre was something like the civilian arm of the *Pepes,* a front with the goal of obtaining support from business people and other sectors not connected with drugs, but equally interested in doing away with Escobar.[68]

The third group acting against Escobar was the Colombian government. Between Pablo Escobar's escape from *La Catedral* in July 1992 and March 1993, the *Bloque de Búsqueda* (Search Block) killed ten of his principal lieutenants and imprisoned twenty-five. Of all, the cruelest blow that the chief of the Medellín cartel received was the death of Mario Alberto Castaño, who had had the security of Escobar delegated to him. By March 1993 only Alfonso León Puerta Muñoz accompanied Escobar. In *La Catedral* Castaño had had the difficult task of trying all the food that his chief would eat. Now he was the only man who had been at the side of Escobar since his escape.[69]

The Final Nine Months of Pablo Escobar

The terrorism continued, with a bomb exploding on April 15, 1993, in the fashionable El Chicó neighborhood of north Bogotá. Ten were killed and more than one hundred wounded. After this the authorities thought there could be only one definitive solution. The government decreed an increase in the length of sentences for terrorism, now up to sixty years, and eliminated the lessening of sentences for confession or surrender for those connected to acts of terrorism; there would only be sentence reduction if the person collaborated with the justice system by turning evidence on the other authors of the crime. A "terrorist" would be considered to be not only the person who placed the bomb or ordered the placing of the bomb but also anyone who helped to transport the explosive or who robbed a car so that it could be filled with explosives.[70]

The Gaviria policy toward Pablo Escobar had clearly changed. In 1991 the terrorist acts had pushed the general public and the government to offer ample concessions to Escobar and his people. But in 1993 the opinion that was gaining ground among many Colombians was that, after all the opportunities the cartel members had had to surrender to justice with favorable conditions, the bombing on April 15 had been the "crossing of the Rubicon." Concessions that were tolerable in the past no longer were so.[71] But it was also possible that Escobar's desire to respond with the strongest of his forces to the daily, sustained persecution that he was suffering was hidden behind this bombing. To each terrorist action by the cartel there was a reply of the *Pepes*, who, a few hours after the bombing, burned some luxurious farms of Escobar lieutenants and killed the lawyer Guido Parra, his son, and a third person after a brief kidnapping.[72]

The security organizations had various hypotheses about Pablo Escobar's motivations in the Bogotá bombing. One had to do with retaliation for the death of two lawyers who worked for the lieutenants of Escobar who were in the Itagüí prison. Another had to do with the two most recent warrants from the national prosecutor's office against Pablo Escobar. Issued on April 13, they were for the kidnapping and death of Lisandro Ospina Baraya, after the new antikidnapping law (see chapter 9) and therefore carried the potential sentence of up to sixty years. The final one had to do with the transfer of some of the men closest to him from the maximum security prison of Itagüí to different prisons as a result of information from the prosecutor's office about alleged plans for criminal activities in the Itagüí prison.[73] As a high official of the *Bloque de Búsqueda* stated, "From Escobar, anything can be expected. When he finds himself more cornered and more isolated, he carries out the most demented acts, perhaps with the remote hope that some day the country will surrender to him."[74]

César Gaviria compared this situation with that in 1984 when the war was begun against Escobar after the assassination of Rodrigo Lara. The only thing they had then were allegations, without any proof that the cartel chief was behind the assassinations. The situation stayed basically that way until 1991, when the office of the national prosecutor was established. That permitted what until then had just been intelligence reports, without any weight of proof, to be "judicialized." Gaviria stated that the hundreds of members of the cartel in prison or killed were proof that the strategy was making possible important achievements that a few years ago few thought could be accomplished.[75]

The president's words proved to be true. On December 2, 1993, Pablo Escobar was killed during a shoot-out with the *Bloque de Búsqueda* in Medellín.

Conclusion

Once again, on the surface it would seem to many that the "bottom line" was that President Gaviria, like President Barco, had failed with his policies in controlling drug terrorism. Yet, there were thirteen months during which it appeared that the policy of César Gaviria was quite a success. And in the end drug terrorism was significantly reduced during the Gaviria years, albeit not because of his conflict resolution policies but because of the death of Pablo Escobar. That finality was more likely because of Escobar's alienation of former allies during his time in prison, and the alienation was largely based, either directly or indirectly, on Escobar's accepting the Gaviria plea bargain.

Several conclusions can been drawn about the attempts of the Gaviria government to find a peaceful solution to the conflict with Pablo Escobar, the *Extraditables,* and drug leaders in general.

First, Gaviria was not bargaining from a position of strength at the beginning of his government. It seems more reasonable to conclude that his strategy was based on his understanding that during the Barco years the Colombian government had been losing the war. Despite powerful setbacks to the narcos and the death of Rodríguez Gacha, the big fish of the Mafia were still free, directing their troops and threatening the institutional stability of the country. As *Semana* pointed out, "The new policy of Gaviria recognized implicitly that incapacity of the state to capture and put the leading narcos in safe keeping."[76] When one inspects the proposals over time, it seems logical to conclude that from Panamá in 1984 to Bogotá in 1990, the narcos were becoming stronger and hence were willing to give up less.

Second, the Gaviria government always had to deal with two camps: Colombians who wanted a softer line and others who wanted a harder one. What for the former was pragmatic policy, for the latter was a surrender of principles. After the first decree, the next three that were issued coincided with the kidnappings of journalists and the petitions from the *Extraditables,* through their lawyers, to modify the decrees. If

the multiple demands that the narcos made and the government rejected are enumerated, the conclusion is that the government did *not*
accept more than it did. César Gaviria was accused of having con-
ceded much; in reality, he gave little. But in such delicate matters, having given little *is* giving much.

Third, all of the bloodshed resulted when the government changed
the rules on Pablo Escobar. There was evidence that DAS knew that
Pablo Escobar and his cousin Gustavo Gaviria had begun a cocaine
business as early as 1976. In the early days the drug business was like
many others in Colombia—on the border between legal and illegal,
like contraband or the black market. If arrested, a person could spend
some months in jail and lose money "tidying up" officials. Now the
government had played dirty and changed the rules. The penalty
would be life behind bars in a foreign setting. This was something that
Escobar was not willing to accept, even if it meant losing his life.

Fourth, the Colombian government could not win militarily during
ten years. It tried but it could not win, and the public got tired. Faced
with the prospect of continuing the bloodshed that many considered
useless, Gaviria sought a decorous exit to an inconclusive military situation.

Fifth, there were two ways the policy of surrender to justice could
fail: (1) if serious verdicts and sentences were not handed down by the
anonymous judges and (2) if those verdicts and sentences were a
mockery of justice—if the conditions of incarceration of Escobar and
the Ochoa brothers did not guarantee their departure date to be what
the authorities said it would be.[77] The Pablo Escobar activities in *La
Catedral*, his escape, and the inability to capture or kill him for over a
year show that, however well intended, the Gaviria policy of plea bargaining was a failure with Pablo Escobar, just as the Barco policy had
been. The Colombian government—including its penal administration
and its military—was simply too weak to really punish someone as
wealthy and powerful as Pablo Escobar. The Gaviria policy was, however, more successful with others, most notably the Ochoa brothers.

Even before the illicit activities in *La Catedral* and the escape, two
sources of opposition arose to the plea bargaining that brought Pablo
Escobar and the Ochoa brothers to prison. The first was from families of people killed by the narcoterrorists. On July 11, 1991, they sent
a message to President Gaviria asking that the law be applied to
the authors of those crimes. Signed by about three hundred people,
the message stated their relief that the leaders of narcoterrorism were

behind bars. They did not want retaliation or vengeance, just full justice "and reparation for the damage caused to humanity, to Colombia, and to the victims of those horrendous crimes."[78]

President Gaviria's response a few days later was that the policy had an objective beyond putting an end to the violence: "To strengthen a branch of government that has traditionally remained inert in face of the criminal organizations and has been severely compromised by the challenges of recent years. . . . That was the reason that we developed mechanisms like lowering of sentences, an ideal mechanism for countries like Italy and the United States, that also have had to face this type of crime. This system, known internationally as 'plea bargaining' [in English] has shown its efficacy in those places, here it has allowed the dismantling of powerful organizations."[79]

The second opposition was from the former justice minister, Enrique Parejo González, who, while ambassador to Hungary, had been the victim of a narco assassination attempt in the streets of Budapest. Parejo, in a letter to *El Tiempo* journalist Enrique Santos Calderón, criticized the negotiations of the Gaviria government with Pablo Escobar for allowing Escobar to choose a prison where he had his troops and protection from civilians; for guarding him with the army and not the police; for acting under pressure from Escobar through the kidnappings and assassinations; and for the constituent assembly being pressured to do away with extradition.[80] In the months that followed, Parejo wrote editorials in *El Espectador* criticizing the concept of plea bargaining, arguing that rewards should not be paid to people who furnished information to the police as that was a civic duty, and enjoying many "I told you so's" after Escobar escaped.

In the end it might be concluded that the drug dealers using terrorism—Pablo Escobar and the Medellín group—were weaker by 1994 than they had been before 1986. Although they still perpetrated terrorist activities from time to time, the high point of August 1989–August 1990 was never reached again. Of course the drug trade still continued, but increasingly in the hands of the Cali group, of new groups, and of new individuals within the Medellín group.

8

The Gaviria Policy for Paramilitary Groups

One might argue that the greatest conflict-resolution accomplishment of the government of César Gaviria was that the paramilitary groups came to be less powerful than before. This surely did not mean, however, that all or even most were in truce. And for the ones that did finally surrender, the procedure was made more difficult by their prior alliance with the drug traffickers.

That complicated peace-making process is the subject of this chapter, which will also show that the relationships between the government and the paramilitary groups remained unclear. Several themes show this, the first being the government's consideration of the groups. To repeat a statement from a member of the office of the presidency that was quoted in chapter 2: For the Colombian military, a self-defense group was one they themselves had armed, whereas a paramilitary group was one armed by someone else.[1] Second, this chapter will show that even a paramilitary man who had been tried and convicted of a crime was freely circulating in Puerto Boyacá, at the least indicating that the government was not able to incarcerate a convicted criminal. Third, this chapter will show that even when paramilitary groups officially demobilized, not all members surrendered and not all weapons were turned in. Fourth, the chapter will show that the information that the office of the presidency had about paramilitary groups was very suspect. Finally, as was seen in chapter 7, the Gaviria government was willing to accept a tacit alliance with a known paramilitary leader in its attempts to capture Pablo Escobar. Hence the conclusion that this was a success for the Gaviria government must be tempered.[2]

The Truce Process with Paramilitary Groups

With the new policy for the drug dealers, the government of César Gaviria made it very clear that paramilitary groups and drug dealers would be grouped with common delinquents for judicial processing; they would not be given the political status that guerrilla groups had. The Gaviria policy change included the discretionary use of extradition (which had no relevance in the paramilitary case) and the reduction of sentences, which did affect the paramilitary groups if they surrendered and confessed to at least one crime.

Specifically, the Gaviria government used the same decrees that it had with the drug dealers to encourage the surrender of members of the paramilitaries.[3] An official in the presidency commented about the success of this Gaviria policy up until July 1992: "Yes, there is a policy, very similar to the one with the narcos: lower penalties for those who turn themselves in. And there were notable successes: Fidel Castaño in Córdoba, Ariel Otero en Puerto Boyacá negotiated with the government. The two combined turned in over 700 weapons. . . . All of these people are being investigated and will be tried. They are not in jail, but the judicial process is in the works."[4]

As a result of this new policy the self-defense groups tardily tried to clear up their image. They argued to the government that, having been the invention of military men, they were then abandoned to their own luck after having lent enormous counterinsurgency services to the army. In one memorandum they demanded to be treated like the guerrillas, who were allowed to turn in their arms, demobilize, and enter into national political life. They assured the government that they had nothing to do with the narcos and, on the contrary, said that they were threatened by an alliance between Pablo Escobar and the *Ejército de Liberación Nacional*. Yet, a little while before that, the commander of the ELN, Manuel Pérez, had said to a Spanish journalist, "Nothing with the narcotraffic. We have not had nor have anything to do with the narcotraffic."[5] Of course this was another case in Colombia of various conflicting statements being made, with no reliable way to reach a conclusion about their truthfulness.

Henry Pérez and Fidel Castaño were the two great leaders of the paramilitary groups in Colombia. The army of Castaño was operating in Córdoba; that of Pérez was in the Magdalena Medio.[6] In Magdalena Medio, perhaps the most successful of the groups surrendered and turned in weapons in May 1992. Ariel Otero, who had become the leader of the Magdalena Medio paramilitary group after the death of

Henry Pérez, made it clear that there had been no negotiation with the government. "There was a conversation about security to facilitate the moving of the people and the surrender of arms." As for a guarantee that the group turned in all of its arms, he replied, "We have a computerized list of every weapon, all ammunition that we bought. Likewise the resumé of each member who formed part of the movement."[7]

Further, Otero was optimistic that the paramilitary group's war was over. Even if the conversations with guerrillas failed, he said, "We definitely will not return to arms. That has no meaning. The only crazy people who remain in this country are those of the Coordinadora." They had demobilized because "by that time we understood that war was not the best route to solve the country's problems. We arrived at the conclusion that armed struggle was worthless and that continuing in it was an error that we could not commit. The solution was not in the guns but at the political level."[8] Commander Julio César agreed that self-defense groups were a thing of the past. Further, they would be marginal as long as the army and the police guaranteed that Puerto Boyacá remained free of guerrillas.[9] At that time it was the only territory in Colombia without guerrillas.

The Paramilitary Groups and the Drug Trade

One reason the Gaviria policy was successful was that in 1991, paramilitary groups went from working closely with drug traffickers to warring with them. In other words, if "the enemy of my enemy is my friend" was the constant theme of Colombian group relationships, then paramilitary groups that had worked with Pablo Escobar and were enemies (because they were friends of an enemy) became "friends" when they became enemies of an enemy.

One clear case of this was in the Magdalena Medio region. In an interview with *Semana*, Henry de Jesús Pérez explained the war against Pablo Escobar in the following way:

An evaluation of the situation of the country was done and of who was the enemy that was doing the most damage at this moment in the country, and we concluded that there was evidence of an alliance between narcoterrorism, terrorists, and guerrillas and that created a very special situation. A situation of alliances of every kind in which in the end they sought the same objectives in order to defeat the government and create a kind of narcoterrorist state of Colombia. . . . In the end this is what Escobar wants. To take the government. . . . Then he [Pablo Escobar] sent us a message that we would have to put our organization in his control because if we didn't he would make us nothing, he was going to eliminate us. . . . He began to kidnap our friends, ranchers of the area.[10]

In explaining the "worst error" that the Magdalena Medio paramilitary group had ever made—the war against Pablo Escobar—Julio César, another of the leaders of that group, said that it was promoted from Bogotá by General Miguel Maza Márquez, head of DAS. Maza put the paramilitary group between a rock and hard place when he said to them that if they did not attack Pablo Escobar, he would see that they were annihilated.[11]

Pérez argued that Escobar realized that the Magdalena Medio paramilitary group would fight him until death when he saw that the group was helping the government in Operation Apocalypse—Escobar's men were used as guides for the government troops. The paramilitary group of Magdalena Medio, Pérez said, had never been tempted by narcotraffic. They did not deny that "we received aid from a person who had connections with the narcotraffic: Gonzalo Rodríguez Gacha. . . . What there has been is a question of coexistence."[12]

For Pérez the reason for this alliance was the "enemy of an enemy" reason. "The only thing that we shared with that man [Rodríguez Gacha] was that he had a war against the guerrilla and we also had a war against the guerrilla. He used us and we used him."[13] Ariel Otero explained the narco connection in more personal terms. "The friendship of some people who belonged to the self-defense groups with some narcotraffickers in no moment compromised the organization. In this case the connection was made because of the friendship that existed between Henry Pérez and Rodríguez Gacha."[14]

Status of Paramilitary Groups after June 1991

One might have thought that the surrender of Pablo Escobar in June 1991 and the conversations between the government and the *Coordinadora Guerrillera Simón Bolívar* would have made the surrender of the paramilitary groups more likely. After all, both the original enemy (the guerrillas) were at least negotiating with the government, and the more recent enemy (the narcos) had apparently decided to stop their terrorist activities. However, such was not immediately the case, and the process took almost a year.

The Pérez assassinations in Magdalena Medio

First, the founder of the Magdalena Medio self-defense group, Gonzalo de Jesús Pérez, then his son, and then the subsequent leader,

Henry de Jesús Pérez, were assassinated in July 1991. The paramount question was the matter of responsibility for the murders of the paramilitary leaders. Although the second division of the army blamed it on the guerrillas,[15] Pérez's successor, Ariel Otero, blamed it on Pablo Escobar. He contended that the narco chief had offered a reward of COL$40 million for anyone who would kill Pérez.[16] Some saw this as a continuation of the war between the two groups that had preceded Escobar's surrender, but others suggested that this was a way in which the surrendered narcos were attempting to eliminate people who might testify against them.[17]

From *La Catedral* Pablo Escobar issued a communiqué in which he said that he had nothing to do with the death of Pérez and added, "The autodefense groups of Puerto Boyacá have internal problems since they are in an internal struggle for power. For this reason they informed public opinion that the death of Henry Pérez had been an accident, when really it was caused by people of that very organization."[18] Otero denied this and announced that his band would reply with a war against the Escobar association.

To complicate matters further, Minister of Justice Jaime Giraldo Angel believed that there was no logic in accusing Pablo Escobar of this crime. In perhaps the most unrealistic and naive statements made in Colombia recently, Giraldo continued: "I see no logic in the hypothesis that it might have been Pablo Escobar who ordered the death of Henry Pérez. It is ingenuous to think that a person who pretends to continue committing crimes puts himself in a prison. A person who is outside, free, who has been sought for ten years, whom the government has not been able to capture, and who is going to continue to commit crimes does not put himself in a prison in order to continue committing crimes or ordering them."[19] A communiqué of the paramilitary groups replied, "With horror and shock we have seen how a Colombian with the position of Minister of Justice has come out in open defense of a person who is in judicial difficulties."[20] And Ariel Otero, in a statement to be substantiated over time, added, "Now he [Pablo Escobar] can give his orders without risk, he has a telephone, he is with his bodyguards, but not with the troops of the Medellín Cartel, and in addition now it is the army that guarantees his safety in jail."[21]

The identities of the people behind the death of Henry Pérez remained unknown. The fingerprints of the two people arrested did not appear in national files.[22] This became yet another criminal case in Colombia in which impunity reigned.

Another question about the Henry Pérez assassination was, How could it be explained that Pérez, who had been convicted of a peasant massacre, was allowed to walk down the streets of Puerto Boyacá, unarmed, and was not arrested?

The army simply denied that it was their responsibility to arrest people in such cases. That was the job of the national police. The assistant director of the national police, General Muñoz Sanabria, explained, "In a given moment it is possible that the information about the order to arrest Henry Pérez had not arrived to the local authorities, and for that reason we have to establish where the mistake was."[23] A similar idea was suggested by a member of the executive branch—that the national police and the paramilitary group had, at least tacitly, agreed that the two armed groups would have authority in different parts of Puerto Boyacá—the police around the docks and other key transportation points, the paramilitary group in the rest of the city.[24]

For a Colombian sociologist who was interviewed, however, the explanation was much simpler: the paramilitary troops of Henry Pérez in Puerto Boyacá were much better armed than the national police. Any attempt to arrest the leader was likely to be resisted by a superior force; hence no attempt was made.[25]

The groups led by Carranza, Castaño, and Otero

Several key areas and paramilitary groups warrant more description as we consider the status of paramilitary groups at the end of the second year of the César Gaviria government (August 1992). They were Víctor Carranza in Boyacá and the Orinoco Plains, Fidel Castaño in Córdoba and Urabá, and the Magdalena Medio area.

Before the arrival of the drug cartels, the man with the most money in Colombia was Víctor Carranza, who was based in the emerald-producing area of Boyacá. Many accused him of having connections with narcotraffickers, but he denied it. By early 1992 Carranza considered that, after so much shooting and so much bloodshed, the moment had arrived to clean up his image and that of his business, once and for all. As he was not under indictment within the justice system, he was in a position to do so.[26] The Carranza group demobilized after negotiating a settlement with the local government and the bishop of Chiquinquirá.[27]

One sociologist told a story about the Carranza group and how well armed it was: "A student of mine, who was trading emeralds to finance his way through the Universidad Nacional, was held by them for several days. They were well dressed and fed. They drove Nissan jeeps, with machine guns mounted on the rear. They had semiautomatic rifles, of the latest available in the world market. I think it is naive to think that they will disappear simply because the guerrillas sign a peace treaty."[28]

Then there was Fidel Castaño in Córdoba. Before he emerged with the *Pepes* in the fight against Pablo Escobar (see chapter 7), Castaño continued living in hiding in Córdoba, while trying to improve his image as a benefactor of the community. To do so, with the assistance of the local bishop he distributed one thousand hectares of his land to poor peasants. Nevertheless, he continued being a bitter enemy of guerrilla groups.[29]

A Colombian political scientist described the conditions he and some colleagues found in the Castaño camp: "Three of us visited La Tanga, the base of Castaño in Córdoba. It was impressive. We were taken there by an army officer and someone from. . . . They were well armed. Around La Tanga there were farms controlled by Castaño, and on each of them there were twelve paramilitary troops. If he wanted to carry out an operation and needed forty-eight men, he would radio four of the farms. If he needed more, he would call more. They were better trained than the Colombian military and better armed."[30]

Even in the Magdalena Medio, despite the truce of May 1992 just referred to, things were not settled. As a member of the office of the presidency said, "In the case of Otero, only about 250 of his 750 men turned themselves in. The others split into three groups, one led by the person who killed Galán. He later was killed and his people dispersed."[31]

Overall Statistics on Paramilitary Groups

A general picture of the state of paramilitary groups in Colombia in 1992 can be deduced from a study by the *Departamento de Seguridad Administrativo* and from another by the Inter-American Commission on Human Rights. The first suggested only a moderate power of such extralegal groups. After the Bogotá journals reported an estimate of paramilitary groups with a membership equal to that of the guerrillas, an official in the Council for Peace of the presidency stated:

> I doubt seriously that there are 7,000 men and I don't know what is meant by 28 major groups. That would be a matter of definition. In Meta, for example, if there are *paramilitares* in many *municipios*, it is difficult to say whether they are separate groups or one large one. The best way to look at it, I think, is by considering the *municipios* in which they are active. I can show you that on maps, but I should warn you that this is very incomplete. For example, there should be some in the south of Antioquia and in the north of Valle, but none are reported.[32]

Table 8-1. Paramilitary Groups in Colombia, February 1992, According to the Departamento Administrativo de Seguridad

Department	Name	Number of Members[a]
Antioquia	Muerte a Revolucionarios del Nordeste	30–50
	Autodefensa de los Tangueros	300–350
Santander	Muerte a Secuestradores	—
	Autodefensa del Magdalena Medio	—
	Autodefensa Chucureña	80–100
Boyacá	Autodefensa del Magdalena Media	—
	Banda de Coseaez o los López	150–200
	Grupos Justiciero y Recuperar Minas y Esmeraldas de Boyacá	90–130
Cundinamarca	Autodefensa Campesina	120–200
	Autodefensa USME	20–25
	Autodefensa de los Chachacos	15–25
	Autodefensa a los Gaitanez	35
Córdoba	Autodefensa Tangueros	—
Choco	Autodefensa Tangueros	—
Magdalena	Autodefensa Chanizos	—
Cauca	Frente de Amistad Juvenil	280–350
Nariño	Frente de Amistad Juvenil	70–100
Putumayo	Autodefensas	30–40
Caqueta	Autodefensas	20–30
Meta	Frente Revolucionario Campesino	250–350
Casanare	Six municipios named with autodefensas, no names or numbers of troops	

Source: Departamento Administrativo de Seguridad, "Grupos de Autodefensa," February 7, 1992.
[a]No data available for some groups.

The interviewee was referring to the DAS report. However, it was suspect, at least as given to the peace council of the presidency, as was clear from the very first page. No definition of *self-defense* or *paramilitary groups* was employed. Rather, mayors of all of the municipalities of the country were asked if they had any *autodefensa* (self-defense) groups within their territories. The results were also presented in an inconsistent fashion, as is shown in table 8.1. An interesting question is whether DAS or military intelligence had a more rigorous and complete study that they failed to share with the presidency.

The second set of figures was contained in a report on human rights in Colombia by the Inter-American Commission. Using "some news

Table 8-2. Paramilitary Groups in Colombia in 1992, According to the Inter-American Commission on Human Rights

Department	Number of Groups
Nationwide	10
Antioquia	18
Atlántico	7
Bolívar	1
Boyacá	3
Caldas	2
Caquetá	2
Casanare	1
Cauca	14
Cesar	2
Chocó	1
Córdoba	5
Cundinamarca	12
Huila	4
La Guajira	1
Magdalena Medio	9
Meta	11
Norte de Santander	5
Quindío	3
Risaralda	4
Santander	18
Sierra Nevada	1
Tolima	1
Valle de Cauca	19
Miscellaneous	5

Source: Inter-American Commission on Human Rights, *Second Report on the Situation of Human Rights in Colombia* (Washington, D.C.: General Secretariat, Organization of American States, 1993), 37–42.

sources and nongovernmental human rights organizations," the commission reported that 147 paramilitary groups had operated in Colombia during the previous ten years.[33] Table 8.2 shows these by department or region.

Conclusion

The Gaviria government had a consistent, clear policy for these groups, and the policy had some notable success—at least for a time. However, even in the case of the definition of *paramilitary* or *self-defense* groups there is confusion in Colombia. Guerrilla groups, such as

FARC, have "self-defense" groups that, even though not active guerrillas, form a network near the camps of "Bolivarian militias" to inform them of outsiders.[34] But in addition, the army has established networks of peasants to inform them, and various landowners and peasant groups keep their self-defense groups simply because the government still does not guarantee life, honor, and property in rural areas of Colombia. Members of the disbanded paramilitary groups in the Magdalena Medio area have suggested the creation of "national militias" to oppose the guerrilla "Bolivarian militias." They argue that such national militias should be under the direct control of the government and the army in order "to avoid problems" and so that the organized delinquency of the drug dealers does not influence them.[35]

Further, it is clear that as long as there are guerrillas, some private individuals in Colombia will exercise their right to defend themselves and perceive their role to be that of defeating the insurgents. In mid-1992, for example, the Bogotá newspapers reported that guerrilla groups were heading for Casanare, as new petroleum exploration began. Also reported was that paramilitary groups, especially from Magdalena Medio, were also going to that region—as a reaction to the guerrilla presence.

Like members of guerrilla groups and drug bands, many paramilitary members enjoy, because of their illegal activities, better lifestyles than they would in legitimate occupations. So, although it seems clear that private justice will continue in Colombia, at least so long as the government does not extend effective police control to the country, two qualifications need to be made to that conclusion.

First, there is little evidence that anyone in the Gaviria government had given much thought to that matter. In July 1992, when I asked an official in the presidency who was charged with studying the paramilitary groups about the cost of such effective police service for the entire country, he replied, "I should have an answer to that, and I have thought about it. But I do not know."[36] Two years later another high-level executive branch official described the current policy: sixteen members of the national police in every municipality in 1994 and a total of 114,000 police by the year 2000. Yet it is not completely clear that such a number of police will be sufficient. This topic is considered in greater depth in chapter 10.

Second, for the members of paramilitary groups, like the guerrillas, some sort of government policy might be necessary to reintegrate them into the legitimate economy. Given the scarcity of resources for the guerrilla reinsertion, one might ask where the funds for paramilitary reinsertion would come from.

Writing in the penultimate year of the Gaviria government, the Inter-American Commission on Human Rights—an institute of the Organization of American States—showed the continued weakness of the Colombian government when it concluded:

> The Government's credibility on the human rights issue depends in large measure on its ability to control these [paramilitary] groups. The excesses committed by paramilitary groups and the State's inability to control them are doubtless a major source of human rights violations in which the Colombian Government is responsible: 1) because it is not providing the citizenry with the protection to which it is entitled; 2) because many of the paramilitaries' actions have some kind of support from members of the Armed Forces, and 3) because almost 90% of the murders and atrocities committed by paramilitary groups have never been punished and the facts will never be brought to light. The latter not only damages the international image of the justice system in Colombia but also tarnishes the images of recent administrations, despite their obvious and genuine efforts to control the violence rampant in Colombia.[37]

9

Changing the Colombian State

Constitutional and Judicial Reforms

In this chapter, I consider more general policies than I did in the previous chapters. Here, the topic is the Barco and Gaviria policies that were designed to change the Colombian state through constitutional and judicial reform. In previous chapters, I considered the idea that a more open, democratic system would remove the cause for the guerrilla conflict. Here, I also examine the idea that a state with a stronger justice system would have less conflict because citizens and groups such as drug dealers and paramilitary squads would be more likely to fear punishment for wrongdoing. The chapter begins with a consideration of the "democratic" aspects of the 1991 constitution; I follow with a discussion of the Barco attempts to change the judicial system and conclude with the Gaviria judicial reforms that came after the new constitution.

Increased Democracy through the Constitution of 1991

Although it did not accomplish "redemocratization," the new constitution was an effort to make Colombia more democratic as one way to resolve the conflicts so prevalent in the country, especially in the 1980s. Guerrilla leaders, as well as others, had long argued that Colombia needed to be much more democratic. By the late 1980s some political leaders concluded that the problem might be in the political system. This was not the first time in Colombian history that changing the constitution was seen as a manner of conflict resolution. The Bogotá daily, *El Tiempo*, stated: "In Colombian history when crises have become so bad that the society seems to be breaking up, when civil wars get extremely serious, or impunity overcomes the institutions, when public order becomes lack of order, and when the governmental branches are powerless to do anything, Colombians begin the clamor for a constituent assembly."[1]

This had been seen five times: (1) in 1827 when the Congress of Gran Colombia, overcome by the complete anarchy of the six-year-old country, called for a constituent assembly; (2) in 1885 when the ruling Conservative Party sought out Liberals to help with a constituent assembly; (3) in 1905 when Rafael Reyes convoked another; (4) in 1952 when Roberto Urdaneta, acting president, made the Conservative-dominated Congress assemble one that ironically first legitimated the power of military dictator Gustavo Rojas Pinilla; and (5) in 1957 when a plebiscite created the National Front.[2]

There could be no doubt that by the end of the 1980s, Colombia was once again in a crisis situation. As previous chapters have shown, guerrilla groups existed throughout the decade, albeit with occasional cease-fires. Also, drug dealers were responsible for the death of some fifteen hundred people between August 1989 and August 1990, including the three presidential candidates who were assassinated in the 1990 presidential election. And paramilitary groups functioned in many rural parts of the country, at times assisted by drug dealers and at others by the armed forces. "Clean-up squads" appeared in Cali, Bogotá, and other major cities, ridding them of "throw-away people" (*"desechables"*), who commonly included the homeless, drug addicts, and homosexuals. Common crime was rampant, with the government itself stating that 80 percent of the crimes were not reported and of those reported, 90 percent did not lead to indictment and conviction. During the 1980s, murder became the most common cause of death in the country, with more than twice the number of murders in Colombia than in the United States (despite its 33 million citizens as compared to 250 million). In short, the country did seem to be breaking up.

Constituent or constitutional conventions do not come about easily in any country with a reigning constitution, especially one like the Colombian constitution of 1886. It stated that constitutional reform could only take place if the National Congress passed changes in two consecutive sessions.

Before following the constitutional process, however, another method was considered. On January 30, 1988, President Barco wrote to the newspaper *El Espectador*, stating his intention to have the voters vote on the abrogation of Article 13 of the plebiscite of 1957 that prohibited constitutional change through referendum. After conversations with political leaders over the following week, the Barco administration developed its position that the following should occur: a plebiscite on March 13 (the day of local and regional elections) to allow the constitution to be changed other than by Congress in two consecutive sessions; a convocation of a constituent assembly or special session of Congress to act as such; and a referendum to approve the reforms recommended by the constituent assembly. Although this was agreed to by Conservative Party leader Misael Pastrana, the council of state found this arrangement to be unconstitutional.[3]

In May 1988 President Barco and Liberal leaders Hernando Durán Dussán and Luis Carlos Galán presented a program of constitutional reform to be considered in the ordinary sessions of Congress. Among its numerous articles, this proposal included sections strengthening the justice system, affording better protection for human rights, creating a prime minister who was removable by vote of Congress, strengthening the Congress, and reforming the state of siege.[4] This proposal was sent to the Congress at its next session.

The Congress began work on the constitutional reform, including the idea of having a referendum in January 1990 on the following issues: a special national electoral district for demobilized guerrillas, to get seats with fewer votes than would be necessary if they ran in the normal way; obligatory voting; the popular election of a vice president beginning in 1994; the possible division of *departamentos* into *provincias* (provinces); and, should there be procedural irregularities, the product of the constitutional reform being considered.

In November 1989 President Barco let it be known that he was against three parts of the constitutional reform being considered by the Congress: the censure of ministers, the naming of a vice president, and the process for choosing members of the *Consejo Superior de la Administración de Justicia* (Superior Council for the Administration of Justice). Former president Carlos Lleras Restrepo, writing in his journal *Nueva Frontera*, denounced "obscure interests" in the Congress and called for a constituent assembly. This came right after the first commission of the lower house, which by a vote of 19 to 14 added a vote on extradition to the referendum called for January 21. Minister of Government Carlos Lemos Simmonds warned, "You would be calling the Colombians not to a referendum but to a carnage, because it would provoke a tremendous violence, deaths, intimidation." The supporters of the idea in the Cámara protested that they were not allied with the drug dealers and that they only wanted to end the war that the country was experiencing.[5] Carlos Lleras Restrepo stated his opinion that it was naive to believe that there was no connection between the narcos and the congressmen calling for a yes-or-no vote on extradition.[6]

President Barco and Liberal Party leader Julio César Turbay tried to save the constitutional reform in the Congress, even when only six days remained in the session. They argued that the referendum should include only two questions—one regarding the establishment of a national electoral district for guerrilla groups in truces and the other regarding the call for a constituent assembly.[7]

The congressional reform did not pass during the congressional sessions. As a result, party leaders Julio César Turbay and Misael Pastrana quit as heads of their respective parties. The former was quickly asked to return by the Liberal national leaders, and he did so. President Barco said at the closing of Congress: "During two years the nation has carried out an intense process of reflection about its institutions and about that which is useful and that which is not. This experience will help us, once again, to find with greater serenity the definition of the institutional transformations that the country urgently needs. The efforts made should be taken advantage of in the future. We should search for new paths, this time on firmer foundations, especially in the matter of constitutional reform."[8] So two years had been wasted; the question became again one of whether or not to have a constituent assembly.

The call for such an assembly had first been made by former president Carlos Lleras Restrepo on July 5, 1987, for the purpose of adopting measures to reestablish the rule of law. Although two weeks later, former president Alfonso López Michelsen argued that a constituent assembly was unconstitutional, on October 20 the national directorate of the Liberal Party called for the government to explore the paths to call such an extraordinary meeting, a move that was supported the next day by J. Emilio Valderrama, member of the Social Conservative directorate. On October 24, Procurator Carlos Mauro Hoyos insisted that President Virgilio Barco create a commission to talk about a constituent assembly. And on October 26, Minister of Justice Enrique Low Mutra said that the government was ready to hear proposals about convoking a constitutional assembly.[9] Despite additional statements of support from both workers and businesspeople, the government did nothing until September 30, 1988, when it sent a proposal for constitutional amendments to the National Congress.

After the failure of this proposal at the end of 1989, on February 9,

1990, a student movement calling itself We Can Still Save Colombia delivered a letter to President Barco in which they and the thirty thousand people who signed it supported the proposal of a plebiscite to
reform the country's institutions.[10] Afterward the students' position
became a "seventh ballot" at the time of the congressional elections on
March 11, a proposal that was soon supported by the newspaper *El
Tiempo*, by former president López, and four Liberal candidates for the
presidency. One of them, César Gaviria, proposed an agreement between the parties, through which an extraconstitutional way of reforming the constitution would be found.[11] By March 1 there was political consensus in favor of the seventh ballot.

More than a million such ballots were deposited. After the Supreme
Court ruled that this was an acceptable way of changing the 1889 constitution, on May 27, 1990 (the day of the presidential election), Colombian voters voted yes or no on this question: "In order to fortify participatory democracy, do you vote for the convocation of a Constituent
Assembly with representation of social, political, and regional forces,
integrated democratically and popularly, to reform the Constitution of
Colombia?" There were 4,991,887 affirmative votes and 226,451 negative.[12]

By late July 1990, president-elect Gaviria presented a formal proposal of the following ten topics to be considered by the constituent
assembly:

1. Congressional reform, including different functions for the two
   houses, a new system of elections, and a national electoral district
   for guerrilla groups observing truces
2. Changes in the justice system, including plea bargaining, pardon
   by judges, the use of plural judges in some cases, and the protection of the identity of the judges and witnesses
3. Democratization of the public administration system so that interested parties could make their opinions known before administrative decisions were made
4. More express enumeration and protection of human rights
5. Statutes to regulate political parties and opposition, including
   financial control
6. Redistribution of governmental rights to legislative and executive
   leaders at the departmental and municipal levels
7. Mechanisms to give citizens more rights to participate in the political, social, economic, administrative, and cultural aspects of
   the nation, including the referendum

8. Changes of the state of siege, with more precise parameters for the transitory, abnormal situation and with various stages according to the nature of the disruption of public order
9. Involvement of the National Congress increasingly in the economic planning process and in investment programs
10. Power for the Congress to carry out investigations in its oversight control of the executive

The president-elect, however, made it clear that the reforms were only a means to a solution, not a solution per se. "Obviously it would be simplistic to pretend that with reforms the violence and terrorism would disappear immediately. It [constitutional reform] deals with finding more efficacious instruments to face them."[13]

The Supreme Court later ruled that although the election of a constituent assembly was constitutional, limiting the assembly to the consideration of Gaviria's ten points was not. This, in effect, meant that this would be a constituent assembly with no obvious leader unless a disciplined party got an absolute majority. Because that did not happen, all proposals had some possibility of adoption, leading some to call the final product a "patch-work quilt" or a "stew" ("*sancocho*").

Elections for the constituent assembly were held on December 6, 1990, with a proportional representation system with a national constituency to elect seventy members. Two additional members were to be chosen by indigenous groups and two by demobilized guerrilla groups. The results of the election gave twenty-five seats to the Liberal Party (although they came from various lists), nineteen to the *Alianza Democrática M-19* (AD-M19 [Democratic Alliance M-19], based on the guerrilla group M-19, which had demobilized in 1989), eleven to the *Movimiento de Salvación Nacional* (MSN, Movement of National Salvation, a splinter group of the Conservative Party led by Alvaro Gómez), five to the *Partido Social Conservador* (PSC, Social Conservative Party), four to Independent Conservatives, and eight to Independents.

Before the assembly convened, "working tables" were established throughout the country. In addition ten preparatory "commissions" were established. Within a month, 150 proposals had been received by the following commissions: 1, Congress; 2, justice and public ministry; 3, public administration; 4, human rights; 5, political parties and opposition; 6, departmental, district, and municipal system; 7, participation mechanisms; 8, state of siege; 9, economic issues; and 10, fiscal control.[14] The assembly began its sessions of 150 days on February 5, 1991, and the new constitution was promulgated on July 4, 1991. As a transitory measure, the Congress elected in 1990 was dissolved, with a special commission of eighteen to serve as the legislative body until a new Congress was elected. This *"Congresito"* was appointed by the constituent assembly, in the same partisan proportions as the assembly. Half of the members could come from the constituent assembly.

Demonstrating the consensual nature of the assembly, three co-presidents were chosen from the major parties: Horacio Serpa Uribe from the Liberal Party, Alvaro Gómez Hurtado from the Movement of National Salvation, and Antonio Navarro Wolff from the AD-M19. The assembly members were divided into five commissions, with each member choosing the commission on which he or she wished to serve.[15] As table 9.1 demonstrates, no division tried to be proportional to the total membership of the assembly. The five commissions were as follows:

1. Fundamental principles, rights, duties, guarantees, and liberties, mechanisms and institutions of protection, democratic participation, electoral system, political parties, opposition rights, constitutional reform mechanisms
2. Territorial ordering of the state, and local and regional autonomy
3. Reforms of the executive, the Congress, law enforcement and military, state of siege, international relations
4. Reforms of the justice system
5. Economic, social, and ecological affairs, finance, fiscal control[16]

The task for the five commissions was considerable, as 150,000 recommendations had come through the "working tables," along with 131 proposals from the executive branch, the judicial system, and the members of the assembly, as well as another 26 proposals from economic interest groups and more than 100 from private citizens.[17] These included 50 proposals from Liberal Party members, 33 from the Movement of National Salvation, 21 from the AD-M19, 3 from the Conservative Party, 3 from the Christian movement, 4 from the Patriotic Union, and 2 from the Indigenous movement.[18]

The internal operation of the constituent assembly had a first debate before full plenary sessions, a second debate at the commission level, and a final debate once again at the plenary level. The commissions quite often split into subcommissions. For example, the third commission divided into legislative branch, executive branch, branches of public power, armed forces, state of siege, and international relations,[19] whereas the fourth commission had subgroups concerned with principles of judicial organization and the organs of judicial administra-

Table 9-1. Membership in the Five Commissions of the Constituent
Assembly, by Political Party

| Party | Commission | | | | | Total |
	I	II	III	IV	V	
Liberal	3	7	4	3	8	25
AD-M19	5	3	5	2	4	19
MSN	3	1	2	2	3	11
PSC	2	1	1	—	1	5
Independent Conservative	—	—	1	1	1	3
Others	3	2	3	1	—	9
Total	16	14	16	9	17	72

Source: Data Bank, Departamento de Ciencia Política, Universidad de los Andes, 1991.
AD-M19, Alianza Democrática M-19 (M-19 Democratic Alliance); *MSN, Movimiento de Salvación Nacional* (Movement of National Salvation); *PSC,* Partido Social Conservador (Social Conservative Party).

tion—the Supreme Court, council of state, and constitutional court.
They were concerned with public ministry and human rights, as well
as prosecutors and the system of indictment.[20] Not surprisingly, at
times it was not clear which commission should be considering proposals, and at times ad hoc commissions were set up to resolve jurisdictional disputes.

The Results of the Constituent Assembly

The first major research question to be addressed in this chapter is
whether conflict resolution resulted from the Colombian constituent
assembly of 1991. The analysis to follow develops eight major themes
related to that question, as those themes were debated in the assembly
and the media. They are first presented in arguments that had to do
with process; then themes having to do with product are presented.
The product arguments are subdivided into the argument that more
democracy was the solution to conflict and the argument that more
efficient law enforcement was more important.[21]

Peace Because of the Democratic Process in the Assembly

The constituent assembly itself was a model of democracy, some
constituents emphasized. As one stated, "The assembly gave an example of how *guerrilleros* could participate peacefully in the political pro-

cess. It was a scene of persons who had been kidnapped sitting beside those who kidnapped them."[22] And another added: "The assembly showed all Colombians that things could be accomplished through dialogue, consultation, and negotiation. The most important thing about the assembly was that it was done by representatives of all parts of the country. No one was excluded. In this sense the assembly was a school of toleration for the entire country. It left those who continue violent acts without justification."[23]

This same argument was expressed in the media by Enrique Santos Calderón: "The democratic spectacle of the Constituent Assembly has no precedent in the recent history of the country. Never before had such a heterogeneous group of Colombians gathered—expresidents, exministers, exguerrilleros, labor union members, indigenous ones, journalists, judges—to discuss and write a new Constitution. It was in this sense an emotional scene of national reconciliation, the spirit of which will no doubt be radiated over the entire community."[24]

Peace Because of Increased Democracy

Members of the constituent assembly argued that six different changes they included in the new constitution would increase democracy in Colombia. They all, at least tacitly, assumed that if the country could be more democratic, there would be less reason for violence. Clearly, it was the guerrilla violence being considered in this case, although many assumed that if the *subversivos* disappeared, the paramilitary groups would also.

Peace because of changes in the presidency

The tendency in Colombia, culminating in the 1968 constitutional reform, had been for the president to have increasing power. Participants in the assembly made three changes in the constitution of 1991.

The first revision to make Colombia more democratic was to require that an absolute majority choose the president. Previously, a plurality had been sufficient, and at times when there were three or more candidates (1982 and 1990, most recently), presidents had been elected with less than 50 percent of the vote.

The subcommission on the executive branch of the third commission, when making this proposal, first quoted the three parts of "Duverger's Law" (concerning the relationship between electoral systems and political parties) and then stated as follows:

With the desire of fortifying multiparty democracy, it is advisable to maintain the system of proportional representation for the election of congress, assemblies, and town councils; in the same way, [it is advisable] to modify the current system of presidential election by establishing one of absolute majority or two-round, encouraging in that way multipartyism, the political participation of diverse sectors, and a coalitionist atmosphere in government. . . . The system of two rounds, we have said, stimulates multipartyism and third forces, fortifying democracy and the diversity of options, thus enriching the political future of a people.[25]

A second "democratic" change in the presidency was the stipulation of one term. Under the constitution of 1886, an individual could not be elected for consecutive periods as president. He could, however, be elected for nonconsecutive terms. Although this was most recently the case fifty years ago (Alfonso López Pumarejo, 1934–1938, 1942–1945), other presidents had tried for reelection, including Alfonso López Michelsen (1974–1978), who was the Liberal candidate in 1982.

The constitution of 1991 made it impossible for an individual ever to be president a second time. The reason for this, according to the third commission, was that, although an open system with the possibility of reelection might encourage the free play of political forces and improve the quality of the alternatives for the electorate, "The prohibition of reelection . . . tries to avoid the participation of the president in the election to that post and the installation of personalist dictatorships or the inadvisable prolongation of the democratic mandate; in addition, it permits more rotation of persons in the office of president, facilitating greater participation of different political forces; finally, it tries to keep the cancer of clientelism from continuing to corrupt the country through permanent expectations of reelection."[26]

The third change of the presidency was the replacement of the *designado* (designate), chosen by the Congress for a two-year term, with an elective vice president. Although the candidate for the second position did not have to come from the same political party as the presidential candidate, the same ticket would have to be presented for both electoral rounds.

The third commission had such an even split between the continuation of the designate and the new vice president that two reports were sent to the assembly. In arguing the latter, Antonio Navarro Wolf and two other members of the AD-M19 stated: "The creation of the vice presidency to replace the designate constitutes one of the various reforms that the country insists on in order to advance in the democratization of the conformation of public power and the reestablishment of popular sovereignty."[27]

The Liberal Party failed in its attempt to require that the vice president come from the same party as the president.[28] Their basic argument, as expressed by Minister of Government Humberto de la Calle, was that having the vice president from a different party was a blow to the strength of party organizations.[29] A constituent assembly member from the *Unión Patriótica*, however, argued that this was beneficial because it would give more power to smaller parties. "No candidate will be able to win the 1994 presidential election without being in coalition with the AD M-19 or the National Salvation Movement."[30]

Changes in the Congress

If there was one part of the Colombian political system that was "broken" and needed fixing, consensus had it that it was the National Congress. Members of Congress in recent years had seemed to be more concerned with their individual well-being than with that of the nation. Absenteeism was high, in part because members could also be elected to departmental assemblies and town councils; "principal" members left the Congress, to be replaced by their "alternates"; foreign trips at the expense of the taxpayers were common; and "pork barrel" legislation (not for projects but for the congressional members to funnel to their supporters directly) was passed each session.

A Conservative Party proposal stated:

> For the Conservative Party the congress is the essential part of democracy and it has to be defended.... Prevent parliamentary absenteeism ...; removal from office for entering into conflicts of interest ...; elimination of pork barrel legislation ...; prohibition of more than one legislative seat and the carrying out of other governmental duties; and ending of the alternate system with the end that legislative activity be carried out fully. In addition we propose the elimination of all possibilities of nepotism.[31]

AD M-19 delegates Alvaro Echeverry Uruburo y Rosemberg Pabón Pabón, in a very similar fashion, stated:

> The congress cannot be blamed for all the bad things of the nation, but neither can it be ignored that its lack of prestige, incapacity, and weakness are a dangerous Achilles heel of the Colombian state. Our reality is so tempestuous and chaotic that only a profoundly legitimate state—a renovated and powerful democracy—can guide us to a future of dignity and development. We need a Parliament that is active and respectable, technical and rational, a control and counterweight of the Executive....
>
> More than any other political factor, the lack of an organ capable of bringing together, expressing, and being politically able to express, in a pacific and rational way, the representation of the different sectors

and interests of national life, which is the raison d'être of the parliamentary institution, has been in our homeland the source of violence and civil wars.[32]

So both extremes of the partisan continuum argued to reform the Congress. Although there were some disagreements (AD M-19 calling for a unicameral congress, for example), the consensus was, to the end of making the Congress a more effective branch of government, that two changes were needed in the new constitution.

First, the power of Congress was increased by allowing it to have votes of censure against ministers. It was believed that this characteristic of parliamentary regimes would make it more likely that the president would consult with the Congress.[33] Additionally, the Congress was to have more power because the Senate would have to approve any extension of the state of exception (which replaced the state of siege) beyond the first ninety days. And Congress was given more initiative in the budgetary process than it had before.[34]

Second, to avoid some of the difficulties of previous legislatures, additional controls were placed on members. To professionalize the Congress, members could no longer hold other public posts. Nor would there be alternative members of the body. To raise the ethics of the body, the new constitution banned unjustified foreign trips, nepotism, and, most important, pork barrel legislation. To avoid the continuing problem of absenteeism, the new constitution stated that members of Congress who missed six votes in plenary sessions would lose their positions.[35]

Change of states of exception

Another "democratic" change was in the states of exception. Under the constitution of 1886, in cases of foreign wars or internal disturbances the president had the right to declare a state of siege. There were no time limits on states of siege, and since the 1940s, Colombia had been governed through them more often than not. As Liberal constituent Iván Marulanda Gómez stated: "The almost permanent application of the state of siege in Colombia, throughout recent years, has taken credibility and effectiveness from the mechanisms of exception, and at the same time has put the system of individual and political liberties in danger, the very ones that we have wanted to consecrate in society in accordance with the democratic vocation and will of Colombians."[36]

Conservative delegate Cornelio Reyes disagreed with this, arguing that at least in recent decades, a state of siege had not implied the suspension of political liberties: "The liberty of opinion, of expression, of press, of association, of public meetings, of opposition to the government have been fully exercised. Many elections have been held under the state of siege, without the state of exception having impeded the free mobilization of political groups or having created obstacles for voting."[37]

Despite Reyes's logic, the final solution was a "state of exception" that constrained the president much more than the previous "state of siege" did. Human rights and liberties could not be denied. None of the branches of government would be suspended during that time. As soon as the causes for calling the exceptional state were ended, so must the exceptional powers be ended. Most important, the president could declare the state of exception for only ninety days during a calendar year, after which it could be extended for another ninety days by a vote of the Senate.[38] So in the end the state of exception could be in force only for 180 days of a calendar year.

New electoral rights

Another set of constitutional changes gave Colombians the opportunity to make more choices through elections than ever before. These included the election of governors, recall votes, a national electoral district for the upper house of Congress, clear rights for the opposition, a "programmatic vote," and a separate electoral board to supervise all elections. One member of the assembly summarized as follows: "There is more democracy ... from popular consultation, referendums, the possibility of new constituent assemblies, the possibility of direct consultation with the people, the programmatic vote, the election of governors, the two-round election of the president, the election of the vice president. A long list of rights, needed in a country like Colombia. Democracy was extended and made more profound, representative democracy as well as direct democracy."[39] Another member of the assembly, concentrating on Colombians who felt underrepresented because they were members of neither the Liberal nor the Conservative Party, added, "Because of the vice president, two rounds [for presidential election], and the national district for Senate, smaller parties will have more power than before."[40]

Under the constitution of 1886 all governors were named by the president. Perhaps the clearest statement of the reason for change was made by Jaime Castro, although he voted against it for other reasons: "Those who defend the popular election of governors sustain that it's simply about a form—authentic and genuine—of participatory democracy, through which the presence of the citizens in the selection of one of its closest authorities will be assured."[41] The argument for this change was summarized by Minister of Government Humberto de la Calle Lombana when he stated:

> To our way of thinking this is a healthier mechanism than the one currently used, in that it strengthens the authority of the governors and gives them independence to face inevitable political pressures. But, in addition, as additional arguments in favor of this change, we could add that it accentuates the process of local and regional autonomy; that it invigorates the role of the departments and the assemblies, thrusting them forward as favorable scenarios of regional democracy; and that it provides the basis to liquidate the old system that, in reality, has been exhibiting increasing difficulties.[42]

The idea of the programmatic vote was that, should an elected official not comply with the promises made during the campaign, the voters would have the right to recall him or her. As explained by constituent Carlos Holmes Trujillo, it

> would create in addition, the incorporation of a new factor of independence for the elector and would give place to the existence of another area of participation since the citizen would be capable of taking positions on specific points of a proposal that is considered of interest for the development of his own locality. It would require, in the same way, the development of campaigns which are based on reality. . . . The criteria which orient this proposal are the independence of the elector, the commitment of the elected, the stimulus to participation, the recall election, and the maturity of the electoral process.[43]

Opposition rights

Horacio Serpa Uribe, Liberal co-president of the assembly, made the most eloquent defense of opposition rights that ended up in various parts of the constitution. He believed that, given the importance in a true democracy of groups being able to criticize the government, the constitution should include the following: access to the means of communication of the state, proportional to the representation won for the legislative body; access to official information, with the exception of that prohibited by law; the right to reply to inexact and injurious statements made by high-level officials of the state, in a form equivalent to that which produced the same; and equality of opportunities for all citizens, without distinction of political affiliation or lack thereof, of access to public posts.[44]

Finally, to oversee all the new electoral rights, an independent electoral branch was established. This was proposed by consensus by the commissions that considered it and was, according to Horacio Serpa, an indispensable element for the democratic system. It has its own functions and budgetary autonomy.[45]

Decentralization of government

Another strategy for resolving conflict was to shift more decision making to the regional, departmental, and local areas. Some considered these reforms to be a "mortal blow to the centenary Colombian centralism,"[46] but it is clear that it was the desired goal of the majority of the assembly. As stated by constituent Orlando Fals Borda, one of the proponents of the change of local governments: "Above all, this recognizes that which we Colombians have created in our development. The new entities exist, so that what the constitution does is recognize them and thus bring the norm into harmony with reality. . . . Since we were in school we have learned that Colombia is a country of regions. All right. It's time to recognize social and economic development policies that benefit the regional communities and the provinces."[47] Carlos Holmes Trujillo added, "Our duty was to fortify participatory democracy. Planning should have its origin in the municipality so that the process begins from the base and goes to higher levels."[48]

More individual rights

The general theme of peace through new rights was expressed clearly by a member of the *Unión Patriótica:* "Now there is no reason to go to the mountains [as guerrillas] because the Indians are protected, the disadvantaged have their social protection."[49] Indeed, the rights went beyond political ones to include health and environmental safety, good housing, and a social security system. The rights of workers included the following, as outlined by a constituent from the *Alianza Democrática M-19*, Angelino Garzón:

> The first is the right to work and the special protection that the state should give to it. The second aspect concerns the obligatory activity of the state for the training, professional and technical education, and placement of people of working age. A third theme is a Statute of Work, that the congress should pass, with a series of labor, social, and union guarantees for workers. The right of union organization has also been improved, stating the autonomy of the unions and the prohibition of the suspension of the juridical personality of the unions

by administrative means. Another new right is that of collective bargaining. . . . And there are two new aspects that seem extremely important: first, the existence of a tripartite organism of prior consultation, composed of representatives of workers, employers, and the
government, that has the objective of developing labor relations, con-
tributing to the solution of labor conflict, and defining salary and labor policies; and second, the participation of workers in the manage-
ment of enterprises.[50]

Reforms of the Judicial System

The constitutional reform of 1991 was the fourth step in the efforts
of the Barco and Gaviria administrations to strengthen the Colombian
judicial system. Preceding it were a new code of criminal procedure
of 1987, a new justice law of the same year, and the organization of the
Specialized Jurisdiction of Public Order in 1990. In all the theme was
the same: conflict can be ended (if not "resolved") through having a
stronger legal system that makes potential delinquents fear the consequences.

The Barco Reforms

The code of criminal procedure of 1987

The first initiative to build up the legal system during the Barco
years was the new code of criminal procedure of 1987. It contained
four basic changes in Colombian criminal guidelines: (1) the establishment of a technical corps of the judicial police; (2) the beginning of
judicial processes only when a defendant could be named; (3) the
granting of the ability to classify cases to investigative judges; and
(4) the establishment of shorter legal processes.

At first look, statistics seemed to indicate that these changes led to a
more "efficient" legal system. The percentage of cases completed went
from 39 percent in 1987, to 84 percent in 1988, to 106 percent in 1989,
to 96 percent in 1990.[51] The figure in 1989 simply meant that part of
the backlog of cases was being taken care of. Yet a closer look at the
statistics gives two good reasons to doubt that this was indeed a more
efficient judicial system. First, the number of legal processes (preliminary hearings and trials) went down in a country in which violence
was increasing. And second, the number of indictments stayed just
about the same over the four years.

This problem was attributed to the new duty of the investigative
judges who "issued indictments only when they had gathered the evi-

dence necessary to be certain of the responsibility of the accused. This interpretation, which clearly was not the spirit of the regulation and was due, without doubt, to the defective training of the judges who taught the new procedure, led to less work for the trial judges who, upon receiving cases that had been so thoroughly studied, could easily render a verdict."[52]

Law 30 of 1987

Law 30 gave the president the right to reform the judicial system through the creation, elimination, or fusion of judicial offices; through the modification of their responsibilities; and through the simplification of certain processes. Using those powers, in 1989 President Barco modified the code of criminal procedure of 1987, eliminating jury trials, which before had been necessary only in homicide cases. The law also permitted the creation of new courts and the hiring of new personnel for the judicial system. Incredibly enough, a commission charged with studying where to place those new personnel concluded that there was justification for only one-third of the 9,600 positions made possible by the law.[53]

The specialized jurisdiction of public order

Using the state of siege powers of the 1886 constitution, President Barco tried to make the judicial process more efficient through modified regulations for the judgment of civilians by military courts, the establishment of special courts, a special tribunal of investigation, and the creation of a tribunal of public order.

Having civilians tried by military courts was a procedure that many Colombian governments had used, arguing that it was quicker and more efficient. The Supreme Court, however, in March 1987 declared this practice to be unconstitutional.

A 1984 law had set up two hundred courts to try cases of terrorism and drug trafficking. These courts, which had special procedures, were to last for only six years, and because the problems clearly had not been solved, the Barco government decided to prolong their existence.

Barco also attempted to set up a special tribunal of investigation. As President Betancur had established such a tribunal for the investigation of the Palacio de Justicia incident, President Barco created one to investigate acts "against the life and personal integrity that were caused by the 'special social commotion.' "[54] The Supreme Court found this tribunal to be unconstitutional in June of 1987.

The tribunal of public order was the subsequent attempt of the Barco government to combat the growing crime wave. It consisted of ninety courts throughout the national territory, with special procedures for the trial of crimes "with terrorist goals" against the national order. A study done of these courts at the beginning of 1990 concluded that 553 cases, out of 3,339 begun, led to verdicts. That 17 percent completion rate compared with 13 percent in the ordinary courts, not considered sufficient improvement by the Barco government.[55]

Changes to the Judicial System during the Gaviria Years

It was clear that the Barco changes to the judicial system were far from sufficient to meet the challenge. As a result, the Gaviria government participated in making three major changes to the legal system, which were (1) continuation of the Barco modifications of the public order jurisdiction; (2) the new constitution, and (3) a reform of the national police.

The tribunal of public order

President Gaviria changed the tribunal of public order again through decrees of late 1990 and early 1991 "with the goal of creating efficient and efficacious ways to investigate and adjudicate cases committed by criminal organizations that try to destabilize the institutional order."[56] To reach that goal, President Gaviria reorganized the public order jurisdiction and the special courts as follows:

— To avoid conflict, special judges and public order judges were joined together.
— To end the insular nature of the judicial offices, five sectional directorates were established in Bogotá, Medellín, Cali, Barranquilla, and Cúcuta, with each organized into four functional sections.
— To begin the approach to the accusatory system, a large part of the responsibility for the investigative function was assigned to the judicial police.
— To protect the judges better, new mechanisms were put in place to ensure their safety in their places of work, homes, and travel.
— To modernize the processes, new technology, such as computers and fax capability, were introduced.

In January 1991 ninety-six judges began work in this new jurisdiction of public order. Statistics the following year indicated that it might have been more efficient: 80 percent of the cases tried the first

year led to convictions, as compared to 30 percent in the previous jurisdiction.[57]

Judicial changes in the constitution of 1991

In addition to increased democratization, another major objective of
the constitution of 1991 was to strengthen the judicial system. The tacit
assumption was that many people broke the law because they had no
fear of punishment. Although this was certainly the case for common
crime, the same argument could be made for the paramilitary groups,
the drug dealers, and the guerrillas.

There was no doubt that the Colombian judicial system was in complete paralysis as the constituent assembly met. To rectify that situation, the new constitution brought several major changes. It created a
new constitutional court to be the guardian of the constitution and a
new superior council of the judicature to direct the administration of
the judicial system, including the recruitment, promotion, and disci-
plining of judges, as well as the resolution of jurisdictional conflicts
among judges. The constitution continued the council of state (to control all those decrees issued by the executive) and the Supreme Court
(as court of last appeal).

The constitution also made certain changes at the lower levels of
the judicial system. Within indigenous areas, indigenous judges were
chosen; they were to function within the traditional norms so long as
they did not conflict with the constitution. Justices of the peace were
elected in each municipality to resolve individual and communal
problems.[58]

Without doubt the most important change to the judicial system
was the establishment of the Office of the General Prosecutor. The
office, within the judicial branch, would have all the functions previously held by the National Directorate of Criminal Instruction and
the six hundred judges under it. Unlike the previous system, however,
the national prosecutor (elected by the Supreme Court from three candidates sent by the president) would direct and coordinate the technical bodies of the judicial police.[59]

The constituents felt that the new prosecutor system would lead to
better conflict resolution in the country. One predicted: "Violence that
comes from common crime is going to have a powerful enemy in the
new justice system."[60] And Horacio Serpa argued: "The criminal investigation system in Colombia has failed and has failed unceasingly
in spite of constant reforms and of the efforts of all the presidents, and
it needs a radical restructuring. The Office of the General Prosecutor

is that. It has not been possible to identify criminals, to indict them, or to judge them. Rampant violence is permanent and includes the factors of drug traffickers, guerrillas, paramilitary groups, and all because of impunity."[61]

Along the same lines, Minister of Justice Jaime Giraldo Angel pointed out that the Direction of Criminal Instruction was a branch of the fourth category, having to deal with more powerful branches such as the national police. Further, the Direction had no hierarchical relationship with the judges who tried cases. Therefore it was an advantage to have created the national prosecutor who would direct the entire accusatory system.[62]

Reforms to the judicial system (most notably the "anonymous judges") had begun before the new constitution. At about the time the new constitution was promulgated, the minister of justice reported that since the "anonymous judges" system had begun in mid-January, 230 cases had been completed, with 187 found guilty and 43 found innocent.[63] Although Giraldo Angel placed much faith in the new prosecutor's office, he also thought, "The so-called anonymous judge cannot disappear."[64]

Evidence shows that the national prosecutor's office has increased the efficiency of law enforcement in Colombia. The Inter-American Commission on Human Rights, hardly a fan of any recent Colombian government, concluded: "During its first year, the Office of the Prosecutor General managed to handle 186,000 of the 325,000 cases it received when it started the function, which made the system 50% more efficient than it had been."[65]

Although that progress is notable, the establishment of the office of the prosecutor general also had its difficulties. Many of the lower-level officials in the regional offices had been *jueces de instrucción* (judges of preliminary investigation) who continued to perform in the new structure as they had in the older one. As one high-level official in Bogotá concluded, "There is no doubt that the general prosecutor and his assistant have done well. They are men of high prestige, doing a good job. But below them, especially in the regions, the quality of personnel is very uneven."[66]

That conclusion demonstrates several key problems of institution building. Often a short-term solution (to hire people with experience in the previous structure) slows or even impedes the new institution. And the personalistic nature (naming illustrious leaders to the new organizations) runs the same risk that all personalistic structures do: the eminent leader someday will disappear. In the case of Colombia's office of the prosecutor general, Alejandro de Greiff had to step down in 1994 because he had reached the age of mandatory retirement.

Reform of the national police

Although strengthening the judicial system through prosecutors' offices was of great importance, many other characteristics of the law enforcement system needed to be reformed. All aspects called for new funds and for structural change.

In early 1992 the national police had the following characteristics. First, members did not live in barracks (unlike the armed forces) and patrolled alone on many occasions. Second, new members had a salary of COL$90,000 monthly (about US$125). Third, service requirements included the following: to become a second lieutenant, three years of service were necessary; to become a lieutenant, another four; a captain, another four; a major, five more; lieutenant colonel, five; and colonel, five. Finally, members' misbehavior was not tolerated; in 1990 and 1991 more than two thousand police personnel were dismissed for different kinds of irregularities.[67]

In 1993 the national police had 90,885 members, of which 4.3 percent were upper-level officers, 6.4 percent lower-level officers, 76.4 percent agents, and 13 percent auxiliary troops and students in academies. In the preceding twelve years, the number of police had increased by 57 percent. According to one source the number of inhabitants per police member was 315—an acceptable level for a developing country—at least according to the chief of the justice and security unit of the national planning department.[68] The magazine *Semana*, however, reported that Colombia had one police officer for each 537 inhabitants, as compared to some European countries in which the proportion is 1 to 100.[69]

During 1992 and 1993, after the young daughter of a police officer was raped and killed in a Bogotá police station, the government called for a complete study of the national police. Committees within the police, as well as within the National Congress, made recommendations, with the final result that Law 62 of 1993 controlled the structure. Under Law 62, the national police remained under the ministry of defense, although the police had the responsibility to keep mayors and governors informed of their activities. There are three kinds of police (urban, rural, judicial), with the first two distinguished not only by size of location but also by the preventive nature of the first and the punitive character of the second. Put in other words, in areas where more than fifty thousand people lived, the police would emphasize common crime, whereas in the smaller areas they would take action against the guerrillas and drug dealers.[70]

The law also changed educational requirements for entry into the police force and paths of advancement within it. A sociologist reported: "Now a high school diploma is needed for entry (although that doesn't mean a heck of a lot, if it is from some high schools). Perhaps more importantly, before a person who entered at the lowest level had no way to become an officer; after a few years he was at the highest rank he could ever make and hence there was no incentive to be a good policeman. Now he can, if he shows merit, become an officer."[71]

Law 62 also created a national commission to receive citizen complaints and to oversee the discipline of the police. However, the commission lacked sufficient authority either to develop communication structures with the public or to do internal investigations of the police. The growth of private security services in Colombia led the new law to create a superintendency, independent of the national police, to control such organizations.[72]

This reform, carried out in a very democratic fashion, probably is but the first step in police reform. Similar studies are needed of the armed forces. And no policies of the government in Bogotá can be effective for the entire country until there is efficacious law enforcement coverage of all its parts. It is not surprising that, from time to time, there are debates in Colombia about whether the resources dedicated to the police and military are sufficient to bring law enforcement to the entire country.

Conclusion

On July 4, 1991, there was a rush of euphoria as the constituent assembly proclaimed the new constitution. After the signing, as the national orchestra played Handel's "Hallelujah Chorus," television viewers saw members of the assembly—men and women, former guerrillas and people previously kidnapped by them, indigenous citizens and citizens from the *oligarquía* (people of great wealth and power), Roman Catholics and representatives of the Evangelical movement—embracing each other. A group of some seventy Colombians of different backgrounds had learned to get along with each other, something sorely missing in Colombian history.

What should one conclude about the Colombian constitution of

1991? This section evaluates first the immediate effects of the new constitution and second, the Colombian regime as developed by the constituent assembly.

Immediate Effects

A Latin American tradition, going back to colonial times, is to have formal laws that informally are not carried out. Colombia surely has participated in that tradition. That has also been the case with constitutions. Through the constitutions of 1853, 1858, and 1863, Colombia became one of the most federalist systems of the world; indeed, perhaps a better term would be *confederal*. According to the Rionegro constitution (1863), the federated states had sovereignty, with the central government having only the powers of foreign relations and some powers in the case of foreign wars. There were no limits to individual liberties; each state had its own army. It has been reported that Victor Hugo (considered by the Colombians to be the intellectual author of the Rionegro constitution) remarked, when Colombians delivered him a copy, "This must be a country of angels."[73] There was, under the Rionegro constitution, complete freedom in arms production and traffic. Civil wars and violence were rampant. Between 1863 and 1885 there were more than fifty insurrections, as well as forty-two different constitutions in the nine states.[74]

Thinking that once again the country might experience a gap between the formal document and the real world, Enrique Santos Calderón wrote in *El Tiempo* of his fear that it was another "constitution for angels":

> Everything is contemplated, from the rights of children, touching on the congestion of businesses, and even to "the free development of personality." In this country of laws, it is already known that these usually are on paper only. As Kundera would say, "Human rights are one thing and human desires another."
>
> Colombia has, at last, a new constitution. More ample, more participatory, and more democratic. How it is converted into the motor for a more solid and modern country, instead of a source of new crises and frustrations, is the great challenge that we all have before us.[75]

Perhaps it is too soon for a definitive evaluation of the new constitution. However, three happenings might be mentioned because they demonstrate that increased democratization did not automatically lead to peace.

Continuation of violence

First, in July 1991, Colombian newspapers reported another "clean-up squad" in Pereira, hometown of President Gaviria, killing "throw-away people"—homosexuals, drug users, the homeless. During the year that followed, kidnappings, homicides, and thefts continued at levels at least as high as before. This will be considered more in chapter 10.

Electoral fragmentation

Second, the elections of October 1991, March 1994, and May–June 1994 under the new constitution were not such that one can clearly say that the country had changed, despite new electoral rules. In the first election, the Liberal Party remained as the majority party, winning 58 of the 100 senatorial posts, more than half of the lower house of Congress, and 20 of the 27 governorships. However, the Liberal Party, led by Alfonso López Michelsen, used a "Wasp Swarm Operation" *(Operación avispa)* strategy. This tactic of getting regional leaders to head a senatorial list in the proportional representation system resulted in a majority party with little ideological agreement. The Conservative Party was split, with Andrés Pastrana's *Nueva Fuerza Democrática* winning nine senatorial posts; Alvaro Gómez Hurtado's *Movimiento de Salvación Nacional* won only five. Other Conservatives won an additional 15 percent of the vote. The *Alianza Democrática M-19* won nine seats in the Senate, much below the 27 percent of the vote of the constituent assembly a year before.[76]

In interpreting all of this, the weekly magazine *Semana* asked, "What New Country?" and concluded as follows:

> The problem before was the lack of ideological boundaries between the two parties. The problem now is that there are no parties. Now the electoral map of the country seems to be one of a majority party without electoral unity or ideological consistency and of a series of multiparty forces even less coherent, despite electoral unity. The intent of the reformers of ending the two-party system was achieved, but at the reverse of that which was proposed. Instead of three or more comparable forces remaining and ending the primary place of Liberalism, that which was achieved was to elevate the latter almost to the category of the only party, through the breaking up of the former second party.[77]

The Colombian system is clearly much more open than before—perhaps too much so, causing confusion for the elector. The 1994 election for the Senate shows this, with the following number of senators elected: Liberals, 53; Conservatives (including the NFP [*Nueva Fuerza Política,* New Social Force]), 22; MSN, 2; Indians, 2; M-19, 1; Christians, 1; and other movements, 19. The AD M-19 elected no senators, in large part because they also adopted a "wasp swarm" strategy. Thirty-six political parties offered lists of candidates; there were 251 lists of candidates (with 1,978 aspirants) for the 100 Senate seats (not including the two indigenous senators). There were 674 lists (with 3,355 hopefuls) for the 163 lower house positions. Only two of the lists for the Senate elected more than one candidate (two each); in effect, that meant that ninety-eight lists were represented in the new Senate.

In the presidential elections, although a second round was necessary (Samper led Pastana by only 0.3 percent in the first round), in the end the two major presidential candidates were from the traditional political parties, with candidates for vice president coming from the same parties. This led some to wonder why a second round was really needed.

Continuation of guerrilla and drug violence

Third, as discussed in chapter 6, although negotiations with the two remaining guerrilla groups took place in Caracas, Venezuela, in late 1991 and in Tlaxcala, Mexico, in early 1992, no progress was made. In October 1992 the government announced that the next round, scheduled to begin at the end of that month, would not be held because the guerrillas were continuing all of their violent activities. And Pablo Escobar had escaped in July 1992. Although extradition was no longer a problem for him and the other drug leaders, their power seemed little diminished from what it had been in the Barco years.

Of course one might argue that it was too soon for the new democratic measures to take root. Yet the cynic might want to see some change in that time. Little was apparent.

Clearly, the members of the constituent assembly did not intend for the government to be weaker. Rather than calling for an end of checks and balances as a way of strengthening government, the 1991 constitutional authors placed their hope of a rejuvenated Congress in a new set of rules that would make the members full-time, that would require attendance (at least for votes), and that would make nepotism and partisan payoffs impossible. Yet over half of the members of the first Congress that met in 1992 had been in Congress before; attendance for nonvoting sessions was very poor, and through semantic slight of hand the partisan payoffs, now unconstitutional, were made anyway in 1992. The first attempt of a vote of censure (against the minister of defense for the Pablo Escobar escape) failed. Ironically, that seems to have been the case because President Gaviria managed to convince the members of the Liberal Party to back his minister.

This leads to the question of what the country would be likely to do if the president had less power and the Congress failed to increase its own power proportionately. Another aspect of this new relationship had to do with the states of exception. Clearly, Colombia would not be governed consistently under state-of-siege circumstances. But again the executive had been weakened, and even with the agreement of the Congress the exceptional states would not last more than half of each calendar year. Because there was no indication that the *Fuerzas Armadas de la Revolución Colombiana* or the *Ejército de Liberación Nacional* would stop their guerrilla violence and because Pablo Escobar was once again a fugitive from justice (with some incidents of narcoterrorism), was this a sign of a potentially serious power vacuum?

Political parties might have been expected to fill this power vacuum. Yet, as shown, the first results of the new electoral rights were a dominant but very divided Liberal Party, along with other, very small parties. The "wasp swarm" strategy reflected the regional basis of Colombian politics. Congress had never functioned well before the reform because members had more loyalty to local leaders than to national ones. The first election of the new constitution suggests that, national electoral district for Senate or not, this had not changed. It was dubious, regardless of Gaviria's success in defeating the vote of censure, whether the Liberal Party would have the discipline to be powerful in the Congress.

It is still too soon to tell whether laws guaranteeing other electoral rights, such as that of referendum, will have an effect or not. The first law passed under the new initiative of granting rights of the Colombian people was one dealing with kidnapping, making the prison sentences longer for committing the crime, and, as in the case of Italy, making it formally impossible for anyone to pay a ransom to the kidnappers.

The decentralization of government, along with the democratic election of governors, places government closer to the people. In some localities, however, the "people" having voting blocks are paramilitary groups, insurgent bands, and drug dealers. One can question whether decentralization is likely to be effective, as departmental and municipal governments have few independent sources of tax revenue. The solution to this problem is for increasingly larger proportions of national tax revenues to be redistributed to the departmental and municipal levels (at the same time they receive new functions, in education for example). Yet, given the centralist tradition of the country, Colombian leaders have not yet made clear distinctions about what local and departmental functions are, as compared to the national ones.

Although there is no doubt that increasing the individual rights of Colombians should lead to a more peaceful country, there are some concerns about this. One is whether, in a country in which even the right to life is not guaranteed, these other rights can be put into practice. Another is the cost of these rights. The ministry of the treasury estimated that in the first year, the costs of the constitutional reforms would be COL$254 billion and, when they are in full effect, COL$3.4 trillion. The ministry had already begun planning a tax reform to make the legal reforms possible. A comparison of the costs for 1992 and 2002 for some of the new reforms is shown in table 9.2. In all, ten years into the new constitution the spending will be COL$1.6 trillion. When the country reaches the full effect of the constitution, the new expenditures will represent 1.73 percent of the gross domestic product and 15.8 percent of governmental income.[78] One can be seriously concerned as to whether any underdeveloped country can afford such expenses, especially one that pretends to be undergoing a neo-Liberal change, with more privatization of services and lower government budgets.

The Failures of the Constituent Assembly

Not all members of the assembly or national leaders were content with the contents of the new constitution, nor did they think it would resolve conflicts in Colombia. These arguments can be divided into two major groups: that more fundamental issues were not addressed and that the *"sancocho"* ("stew") had internal contradictions and/or mistakes.

Lack of basic societal changes

One member of the assembly said that the constituent assembly did not bring peace and perhaps even was not capable of doing so. The argument was quite simple. It made reference to the fact that the two major guerrilla groups (the *Ejército de Liberación Nacional* and the *Fuerzas Armadas de la Revolución Colombiana*) were not part of the assembly: "We will not have peace while there is hunger in this country. The Constituent Assembly was arrogant in the matter of peace. They didn't want the guerrillas to be there. Especially the M-19 was arro-

Table 9-2. Costs of 1991 Constitution Reforms (in COL$ billion)

Provision	Cost	
	1992	2002
Free medical treatment for children under one year of age (40 percent within "poverty" level of family income)	$ 47	$ 156
Rights of older population (will total 640,000 by beginning of next century)	91	339
Help for disabled	79	256
Protection of environment	15	766
Reforms of justice system	21	80
Total Costs	$254[a]	$3,400[a]

Source: Alberto Martínez M., "La nueva Constitución económica," *El Espectador,* June 30, 1991, p. 1B.
[a]Includes other costs not itemized above.

gant. This country will not be in shape even if the guerrillas hand in their arms. If there is no self-examination on the part of those who have always had everything, how can it be hoped that there will be on the part of those who have never had anything?"[79]

Internal contradictions and mistakes in the new constitution

The other set of arguments from the constituents came from those who thought that the *"sancocho"* was internally inconsistent. This was stated forcefully by Jaime Castro, in relation to the national district for the senate:

> The election of all of the Senate in a national district takes away representativeness and, therefore, political legitimacy from the highest legislative body of the country. It institutionalizes, in addition, a regressive centralist tendency that is exactly against one of the purposes of the process under way: the fortifying of participatory democracy through decentralization and the affirmation of our nationality in the richness of its human, geographical, and cultural diversity. . . .
>
> The national district, in addition, distances the elector from the elected and eliminates the responsibility of the latter to his electors because it makes the viability of the recall election impossible.[80]

Alberto Zalamea, the only member of the assembly who did not attend the signing ceremony of the new constitution on July 4, argued that it was mistaken in taking power away from the president, leaving him with protocol functions and placing him in fear of a vote of censure of his ministers. "It will be a hybrid that tries to give many responsibilities to the state, while taking them away from the executive, which is very curious."[81] The Bogotá daily, *El Espectador*, particularly concerned that the constitution did away with extradition, mentioned not only the vote of censure but the popular election of governors and decentralization as faults.[82]

The Roman Catholic Church, however, saw grave problems with the new constitution (no doubt in large part because divorce was made possible, even for marriages within the church). The president of the Colombian Bishops' Conference, Pedro Rubiano Sáenz, deplored the attitude about the concordat between the Colombian government and the Vatican and the approval of divorce and lamented that the country had fallen into the "abyss of permissiveness and of moral decay."

> It worries us how the moral sensitivity of the conscience of the country is weakened and how the clear distinction between good and evil is lost. Not only are they complacent about the practice of abortion, of contraception, and of biogenetic manipulation, but also they propose them as an expression of a badly understood liberty. . . . No matter how much they say that the Constitution approves divorce for Catholic matrimonies, we affirm and we will always teach that according to Catholic faith and doctrine valid marriage is indissoluble and that the annulment of some civil effects of sacramental marriages cannot destroy the relationship.[83]

The president of the Senate, Aurelio Iragorri Hormaza, with reference to the ending of the Congress elected in 1990 and its replacement in the interim with an appointive commission, complained that "our state of law has been diluted and broken while simultaneously the powers of the legislative branch are given to the president." He criticized the dissolution of the Congress and stated that it represented "a mortal institutional step whose only objective is to satisfy the electoral ambitions of some constituents with the sacrifice of the state of law."[84]

Others criticized the new constitution for being merely platonic aspirations,[85] for destroying the power of the president at the worst possible time,[86] for bankrupting the national government by redistributing tax revenues to the departmental and municipal levels,[87] and for spelling out so many human rights for a country "in which human rights are violated in a thousand ways and criminals continue with impunity."[88]

The constituent assembly of 1991 was called at a desperate time in Colombian history, one in which the entire country seemed to be coming apart. Clearly, the new constitution will take years to put into effect and will have to overcome both tradition and the lack of funds that come with underdevelopment. It is based on the assumption that the lack of democracy was a more important problem than the lack of authority, differentiating Colombia from Peru, in which President Fugimori arrived at the opposite conclusion.

It is beyond the scope of this book to compare the Colombian case with Peru in which, with less democracy, President Fugimori's government was able to end much of the guerrilla violence.[89] Clearly, Abimael Guzmán had much more power in the *Sendero Luminoso* of Peru than any Colombian guerrilla leader did. We have already mentioned the death of one FARC leader, which in the end had little effect. Second, both the FARC and the ELN had importance in Colombia, making it more of a multiguerrilla country than Peru, even with the presence of the *Movimiento Revolucionario Tupac Amarú* in Peru. Finally, the role of the military was always quite different in Peru.

Nonetheless, I hope that in the next century the Colombian constitution of 1991 will be judged as having been helpful in bringing the country out of its difficulties. I hope it was not simply another constitution written for angels—worth only the paper it was written on.

10

Conclusion

Assessment of Success

In the terminology of public policy analysis, the previous chapters have described "policy output," that is, the Barco and Gaviria governments' deliberate actions to affect policy. In this chapter, I begin with the question, How well was the Colombian government able to implement its policies? Or, to use the policy terminology again, How good was its policy outcome?[1] I examine trends in crime statistics, including homicides, kidnapping, disappearances, and other human rights abuses. In this way it is possible to compare the amount of violence in Colombia *before* the attempts to lessen it, to the amount *during* the Barco and the Gaviria governments. That analysis should reveal whether the policies described had any effect on the level of violence in Colombia. I have limited the analysis to one set of policies—those having to do with crime—which is justified because in a sense this entire book has been about "crime," whether it was instigated by the guerrilla groups, narcoterrorists, or military squads.

I first consider crime in Colombia, emphasizing the most serious crime (homicide) but also considering kidnappings and disappearances, as well as other human rights violations such as tortures, arrests, and threats. I then conclude the book by analyzing the reasons that the records of the two presidents were not better.

Violence in Colombia in 1994 Compared to 1986

I have described at length the conflict-resolution efforts of two presidents. In trying to evaluate whether there was less or more violence as a result of those efforts, various factors complicate the analysis. One is the reliability of data. I give several sets, as no data set is completely reliable. Another complication is policy lag. It is unlikely that any new policy would have had immediate effects, especially on a conundrum as complex as Colombian violence.

Time-series data do allow us to reach certain conclusions in the comparisons of the Barco and Gaviria administrations. However, we should always be cautious—and always open to conflicting interpretations.[2]

The first set of data comes from the Inter-American Commission on Human Rights, a commission that over the years has been quite critical of the Colombian government's handling of human rights violations. Table 10.1 shows the commission's accounting of violence levels from 1981 to 1991. The first obvious conclusion is that turbulence is greater at the end of the period than at the beginning, with political assassinations increasing by nearly 700 percent, deaths in combat by 1,400 percent, and kidnapping by 1,500 percent. Although total numbers of murders increased less dramatically (264 percent), the total number for a nation of 35 million people is very large. Indeed, it has been estimated that in 1993, Colombia had a full 10 percent of the murders in the world.[3]

The second major conclusion, shown in table 10.2, is that all indicators of violence were higher in the Barco years than in the Betancur ones. This clearly shows three things: (1) the effect of the combination of a reinitiation of guerrilla violence; (2) the appearance of death squads, with the tacit approval if not active support of the Colombian armed forces; and (3) the "drug wars." These statistics tempt one to conclude, in keeping with the title of a recent Colombian book, that it was the Barco years when Colombia became screwed up.[4] Yet every leader governs in a context that has been created by both his immediate and distant predecessors. The situation Virgilio Barco faced was the result of the entire history of violence as a part of the Colombian political model.

The third major conclusion, also shown in table 10.2, is that, with the exception of political assassinations, there was more violence during the first Gaviria year than during the Barco ones. This is one definite limitation to the data of the Inter-American Commission.

As indicators of trends over time, the data shown in table 10.1 were converted to ratios of the number of violations in one year to the number of the same violations the previous year (see table 10.3). Using the "decision rule" that an increase of .50 (indicating an increase of 50 percent over the previous year) is worthy of mention, the first conclusion

Table 10.1. Human Rights Violations in Colombia, 1981–1991

Year	Political assassina-tions	Disappear-ances	Social cleansings[a]	Deaths in combat	Kidnap-pings	Total murders	Political violence (%)[b]
1981	269	101	—	95	99	10,713	4.34
1982	525	130	—	69	136	10,580	6.84
1983	594	109	—	173	167	9,721	9.01
1984	542	122	—	225	299	10,694	8.31
1985	630	82	—	386	286	12,899	8.51
1986	1,387	191	—	362	180	15,672	12.38
1987	1,651	109	—	313	259	17,419	11.90
1988	2,738	210	273	1,083	718	21,100	20.40
1989	1,978	137	364	732	781	23,312	13.77
1990	2,007	217	267	1,229	1,282	24,267	15.33
1991	1,829	180	389	1,364	1,550	28,284	13.30

Source: Inter-American Commission on Human Rights, *Second Report on the Situation of Human Rights in Colombia* (Washington, D.C.: General Secretariat, Organization of American States, 1993), 123, 183.
[a]No data available for some years.
[b]Political crimes divided by total crimes.

Table 10.2. Average Number of Human Rights Violations in Colombia, 1983–1993

President	Political assassina-tions	Disappear-ances	Deaths in combat	Kidnap-pings	Total murders	Political violence (%)[a]
Betancur	788.25	126.00	286.50	233.00	12264.50	9.55
Barco	2093.50	168.25	839.25	760.00	21524.50	15.35
Gaviria[b]	1829.00	180.00	1364.00	1550.00	28284.00	15.33
Average	1484.00	150.77	651.88	613.56	18160.00	12.54

Source: Calculations compiled from Inter-American Commission on Human Rights, *Second Report on the Situation of Human Rights in Colombia* (Washington, D.C.: General Secretariat, Organization of American States, 1993), 123, 183.
[a]Political crimes divided by total crimes.
[b]One year only.

is that the number of political assassinations took dramatic jumps in 1986 (a year in which Belisario Betancur was president until August 7) and in 1988 (a Barco year). The most striking increase in disappearances also occurred in 1986, even though there were two others in the Barco years of 1988 and 1990. Although the most extraordinary rise in

Table 10.3. Increase in Human Rights Violations in Colombia, 1981–1991

Year	Political assassina- tions	Disappear- ances	Social cleansings[a]	Deaths in combat	Kidnap- pings	Total murders	Political violence (%)[b]
1982	1.95[c]	1.29	—	0.73	1.37	0.99	1.58
1983	1.13	0.84	—	2.51[c]	1.23	0.92	1.32
1984	0.91	1.12	—	1.30	1.79[c]	1.10	0.92
1985	1.16	0.67	—	1.71[c]	0.96	1.21	1.02
1986	2.20[c]	2.33[c]	—	0.94	0.62	1.21	1.45
1987	1.19	0.57	—	0.86	1.44	1.11	0.96
1988	1.66[c]	1.92[c]	—	3.46[c]	2.77[c]	1.21	1.71[c]
1989	0.72	0.65	1.33	0.68	1.09	1.10	0.68
1990	1.01	1.58[c]	0.73	1.67[c]	1.64[c]	1.04	1.11
1991	0.91	0.82	1.46	1.11	1.21	1.17	0.86

Source: Calculations compiled from Inter-American Commission on Human Rights, *Second Report on the Situation of Human Rights in Colombia* (Washington, D.C.: General Secretariat, Organization of American States, 1993), 123, 183.
[a]No data available for some years.
[b]Political crimes divided by total crimes.
[c]Increase at least 50 percent higher than previous year.

"deaths in combat" came in 1988, also a Barco year, there were others in 1983 (a Betancur year) and 1988 and 1990 (both Barco years). As for crimes that were in part nonpolitical, the number of kidnappings increased most of all in 1988 and 1990, both Barco years, as well as in 1984. Total murders never increased 50 percent in one year, although the trend was always upward, but they did increase most during 1985 and 1986 (Betancur years) and 1988 (a Barco year). Only one time did the ratio of political violence go up by more than 50 percent—the Barco year of 1988.

Two things in table 10.3 are most notable. The first is that 1988 was the year in that decade when violence most increased. This is contrary to the idea that the August 1989–August 1990 period of total war between Pablo Escobar and the Barco government was the worst of recent Colombian history. Although that might have been true in the major cities and hence for the *gente decente* ("decent people," a common term for the well-to-do) who were being murdered, the figures suggest that the year of the dramatic quantum leap of violence in Colombia was 1988. This was the year that most characterized the Barco presidency. There were increases of violence because of guerrilla activity, paramilitary actions, and drug dealer operations, all of which exacerbated the general breakdown of law enforcement, making nonpolitical

Table 10.4. Human Rights Violations in Colombia, 1988–1994

Violation	1988[a]	1989	1990[b]	1991	1992	1993[b]	1994[b]
			Year				
Political assassinations	952	464	313	560	1,242	957	692
Presumed political assassinations	1,856	1,505	1,694	1,269	1,073	1,467	931
Social cleansing	224	365	267	389	528	198	253
Deaths in combat	1,304	734	—	1,385	1,638	1,150	1,098
Obscure assassinations	2,853	4,035	4,585	5,909	5,171	5,121	4,437
Disappearances	193	132	—	180	237	173	161
Kidnappings	174	204	—	366	241	—	—
Wounded	763	970	—	1,386	1,313	1,030	1,410
Tortures	32	28	—	290	97	185	94
Arrests (for political reasons)	1,093	732	—	1,392	261	1,781	2,076
Death threats	132	109	—	208	147	317	231

Source: Justicia y Paz, volumes 1 through 7.
[a]First quarter incomplete.
[b]No data available for some categories.

violence even more likely to enjoy impunity and hence even more likely to occur.

Tables 10.4, 10.5, and 10.6 present similar data sets from another source—the Roman Catholic Church's Intercongregational Commission of Justice and Peace. This clerical group reports human rights violations from both personal testimonies and from the media. The important point is not whether their data are more reliable; rather, it is a question of trends. Further, there are human rights violations in the church's report that do not appear in that of the Inter-American Commission on Human Rights. Finally, the church's data allow us to analyze César Gaviria's presidency more completely.

Table 10.5 shows that, with one possible exception, human rights violations were more numerous in the Gaviria years than in the Barco ones. The one possible exception is in "presumed political assassinations," although if that category is added to "political assassinations," the Barco administration averaged 2,261.3, whereas the average during

Table 10.5. Comparison of Human Rights Violations in Colombia during Barco and Gaviria Years (averages)

Violation	Barco	Gaviria
Political assassinations	576.3	860.2
Presumed political assassinations	1685.0	1185.0
Social cleansing	285.3	342.0
Deaths in combat	1020.5	1317.8
Obscure assassinations	3824.3	5159.5
Disappearances	162.5	187.8
Wounded	866.5	1284.8
Tortures	30.0	166.5
Arrests (for political reasons)	912.5	1102.0
Death threats	120.5	225.8

Source: Calculations compiled from *Justicia y Paz*, volumes 1 through 7.

Table 10.6. Comparison of Human Rights Violations in Colombia in 1994, by Quarter

Violation	Quarter			
	First	Second	Third	Fourth
Political assassinations	219	129	164	180
Presumed political assassinations	281	189	245	216
Social cleansing	68	104	22	59
Deaths in combat	302	258	365	173
Obscure assassinations	859	1,190	1,191	1,197
Disappearances	32	24	56	49
Wounded	395	236	361	275
Tortures	53	14	14	13
Arrests (for political reasons)	622	265	771	418
Death threats	47	42	99	43

Source: Justicia y Paz, volumes 1 through 7.

the Gaviria years was 2,045.2. With a slight bit of rounding, that means 216 fewer people were killed for "political" and "presumed political" reasons each year during the Gaviria years.

Table 10.6 presents the same data set for 1994, divided by quarter. This analysis is relevant because the violations were generally fewer in number in 1994 than in the previous three years. The table does show that in many cases the fourth-quarter figures were lower than those for the first quarter, which clearly was not the case for "obscure assassinations" or disappearances. Further, one should ask if a decline from

Table 10.7. Human Rights Violations, 1990–1992

	Year		
Violation	1990	1991	1992
Serious			
Massacres	15	12	34
Disappearances	109	153	186
Tortures	116	191	341
Serious wounds	68	98	198
Total Serious	308	454	759
Minor			
Minor wounds	251	527	596
Arrests	191	446	394
Searches	89	194	177
Threats	78	174	208
Other minor	98	222	243
Total minor	707	1,563	1,618[a]
Grand Total	1,015	2,017	2,377[a]

Source: Procuraduría General de la Nación, Cuadro 11.
[a]Rounding in the source.

219 political assassinations to 180 is significant. This analysis is justified because of individuals, both within the Gaviria government and
outside it, who by 1994 had concluded that the corner had been turned
in violence in Colombia.

A final set of data, drawn from human rights violations reported to
the Colombian government itself, is shown in table 10.7. By ignoring
the fact that it is only for three years[5] and averaging the two Gaviria
years, the conclusion is, once again, that there were more human rights
violations during the Gaviria years than during the Barco ones.

Homicide rates in Colombia would ultimately reach astronomical
levels. The homicide rate was not only the highest in the world in a
recent five-year period (77.5 per 100,000 inhabitants), but it was three
times higher than in the second country (Brazil, 24.6 per 100,000) and
over nine times higher than in the United States (8.0 per 100,000).[6]

Other sources conclude that "political homicides," which include
"presumably" political homicides and those in battles with guerrilla
groups as well as "clearly" political ones, varied between 11 and 18
percent of the total homicides between 1988 and 1990.[7] If the fifteen
hundred deaths from the drug war in 1989 and 1990 are added in, po-

litical homicides make up 24.6 percent in 1990, clearly the worst of recent years.

Good empirical studies of violence at the local level in Colombia have been few. One, which was carried out by Colombian sociologist Alvaro Camacho, concluded that 75 to 80 percent of the violence in Cali was "private," that is, having nothing to do with political issues but with the private settling of accounts on such matters as debt, property, sexual and marital issues, robberies, barroom brawls, and family violence. As a result homicides in 1986 averaged between 2.17 and 6.46 per day in Cali and between 5.77 and 9.70 in Medellín.[8] This is precisely what we mean when we say that the Colombian government was in one of its most inefficient periods.

Reasons that Conflict Resolution Was Not More Successful

The study of conflict resolution in this book has shown that both the Barco and Gaviria governments had failures as well as successes as they tried to convince various groups working outside the law to stop doing so. Barco "succeeded" with the M-19, Gaviria with the Medellín drug terrorism and with some paramilitary groups. But the data presented have demonstrated that those policies were not sufficient to end or even diminish significantly the violence in Colombia. In the final part of this book, I offer a multivariate explanation of this "scorecard" of failures and successes. My explanation will be more general than the specific conclusions that have ended each preceding chapter.

Throughout this study, it has been obvious that the three kinds of violence being considered are different, but interrelated. The oldest—guerrilla violence—was originally inspired by ideology when the Colombian political system was closed due to the National Front. The paramilitary violence was originally a way for individuals and groups to defend themselves against the guerrillas because the Colombian government was either not willing or not capable of doing so. The drug phenomenon appeared because of the development of a market, and at least some of the drug groups used violence from the beginning; the Medellín directed it against the government when they perceived that the rules of the game had been changed on them.

Later on, drug groups cooperated with guerrillas, and drug groups took over paramilitary groups. Nevertheless, there was never a case when a unified drug group took over all paramilitary groups or cooperated with all guerrilla groups against the government. Indeed, Colombian reality was never a two- or even a three-actor reality. Rather it was an n-actor reality in which the "n" was quite large. As a result, both governments had at least two policies (for guerrillas and narcos) and sometimes a third for paramilitary groups. Some would also suggest that possibly the Gaviria government had a different policy for the Cali drug group than for the Medellín one. Meanwhile, common violence (measured in this study through homicides) became even more prevalent than before, although Colombia had long had one of the most crime-filled societies in the world.

Basic human rights were not respected in Colombia before 1986, and between that date and 1994 there was no apparent progress in approaching that goal. The most difficult problem with the Colombian government during the period studied had to do with the deaths and disappearances during the dirty war, clearly a violation of rights. After a dirty war of the magnitude that Colombia suffered, one should not have anticipated immediate changes. In keeping with this, even a year after the approval of the new constitution, Juan E. Méndez, executive director of Americas Watch, stated: "Despite the good intentions of the government and its willingness to introduce reforms, the human rights situation has not improved. The continuity of predominance of violence threatens the Colombian change toward political pluralism. As never before, the guerrillas initiated attacks against civilians and unacceptable targets. Counterinsurgency operations of the armed forces and the self-defense groups, with the badly disguised assistance of army officers, illustrate dirty war tactics that violate the internationally recognized standards."[9] Méndez recommended that the government start its campaign against impunity by suppressing the assistance of military officers to paramilitary groups.

This study began with the statement that, in Colombia, policies could not be applied throughout the entire nation because of the power of guerrilla groups, drug dealers, and paramilitary organizations. In this case, by the end of the Gaviria presidency, Colombia had a slightly stronger government than before the Barco presidency: the M-19, much of the EPL, and the CRS no longer existed as guerrilla groups; many of the paramilitary organizations (at least in theory) had demobilized; and the power of the Medellín drug group had declined. Optimists both outside[10] and within[11] the Colombian government argued that the number of deaths from guerrilla warfare, drug conflict, and paramilitary activities had decreased by 1994.

Of course the Colombian government is not as strong as it would have been if the conversations in Caracas and Tlaxcala had led to the demobilization of the FARC, the ELN, and the dissident EPL groups; if all paramilitary groups had demobilized; if Pablo Escobar and the Medellín drug group, as well as the Cali group, had settled their problems through plea bargaining; and if the Colombian government, for the first time in its history, had devised a national constabulary force, effectively covering the country with well-paid troops.

There were key decisions in Colombian history that led to a political regime that worked fairly well in some conflict resolutions but had weaknesses for other kinds.[12] They were the following—not necessarily in chronological order:

1. The decision not to construct a strong law enforcement branch of government for fear it would threaten civilian government (1830 to the present)
2. The decision to allow private groups to take the place of official law enforcement (from the landowners of the nineteenth century to the paramilitary groups, assisted by the military, to fight the guerrillas in the 1980s)
3. The decision that violence was justified in the name of political party (beginning in 1838 and continuing until at least 1965)
4. The decision that religion was part of the partisan conflict, even though nearly all were Catholic (beginning in 1853 and continuing through *La Violencia*)
5. The decision of elite sectors of the Liberal and Conservative parties to enter into coalitions, despite the partisan violence that also existed (beginning in the nineteenth century and going until the constitution of 1991)
6. The decision that partisan violence might be amnestied (various times, most recently in 1953 and 1958)
7. The decision that, given the relatively closed nature of the political regime during the National Front, guerrilla violence was justified (late 1950s to the present)
8. The decision to amnesty guerrilla violence (all presidents between Turbay and Gaviria)
9. The decision of the Barco and Gaviria governments to talk to people who were talking to the drug lords in order to end the terrorism of the latter

Colombian scholars, in their writings and interviews, mention variations of these arguments when discussing the current violence in their homeland. Using their variations, it seems to me that the explanation of why the scorecards of the Barco and Gaviria administrations were not better is a multivariate one, with three major parts. The first, which summarizes the nine points listed, is that conflict resolution was not more successful because of the decisions made in the previous 160 years of national independence. It simply will take time to change structures that have existed for such a long time.

Second, conflict resolution was not more successful because of the great amount of money that the drug trade brought into Colombia. Nothing will be possible until that money flow stops. And third, conflict resolution was not more successful because of the changes in Colombian society. A political regime that might have worked for a rural society simply will not perform efficiently in an urban one.

For short-hand purposes I shall call these arguments Sins of the Fathers, Money Talks, and Modernization, respectively. As will be obvious, the three are not mutually exclusive and can be interwoven.

Sins of the Fathers

Given the "decisions" of Colombian history just referred to, the government cannot impose control over the national territory today because it never developed that ability in the past. Although there are other causes, here I stress the weakness of the state, the tradition of violence, and the intensity of the conflict because of its religious aspect.

One of the policies was to avoid constructing a large police force that would allow the national government to apply its decisions in all parts of the country. Therefore, it is said, this pattern is just being continued. Former president López believed that the paramilitary groups were the logical extension of the pattern set by the large landowners of the previous century. It should also be remembered that the Colombian government, during the presidency of Guillermo León Valencia, called for all private citizens to assist the military in its struggle against the guerrillas.

So, Fernán E. González González concludes that

in spite of the formal centralism and presidentialism of the constitution, it has been impossible to construct a modern state over the areas of traditional and interest group power, but neither does the state identify completely with those private powers. In that way, a kind of political short circuit is produced by the clash of two logics, one modernizing and the other traditional, that tend to neutralize each other: An inefficacious omnipresence of the state is the result, with sufficient power to make local and regional initiates difficult but without the capacity to impose modernizing reforms in the national peripheries.[13]

Into that institutional vacuum, González González continues, new actors entered to perform the functions that the state might have performed, but never did.[14] And because of the power of those new actors (guerrillas, drug dealers, paramilitary squads), "Are we not witnessing today the onset of a greater collapse of the institutions of the state?"[15]

Clearly then, Colombia lacked a strong state at the beginning of the time span this study covers. It might have been slightly stronger at the end of the Gaviria government, depending on the results of the reform of the national police. However, the state was not then, and still is not, strong enough to meet its challenges.

Added to this weak state is the long history of violence in Colombia. Political competition was not limited to peaceful means; there were eight civil wars during the nineteenth century, six of which pitted all (or part) of one party against the other party. As a result of these civil wars (which, in total, lasted eleven of the sixty-three years between 1839 and 1902), the peasant masses "participated" in national politics and knew of the national political system. Of course this did not mean that the masses had influence on the policies of the elites. Most of the mass participation was originally because of their ascription to a patron, who instructed them to fight. In those civil wars thousands of poor *campesinos* died.

The tradition continued in the twentieth century, with a short period of partisan violence in 1932 and *La Violencia* from roughly 1946 to 1964. The Colombian historian Fabio Zambrano Pantoja interprets this historical trend as follows: "The *real* people, that is to say, the majority of the population, learned politics through the use of arms before they did through the exercise of the suffrage. First one learned to fight and later to vote. This caused the exercise of politics to be conceptualized as a conflict before it was conceptualized as a place of concord, in this way applying the generalized idea that *war is the continuation of politics by other means*."[16] This same pattern continued into this century, and Zambrano Pantoja concludes: "In practice the advance of universal suffrage was accompanied with the fortifying of the local bosses and the regional ones, who continued exercising politics at the level of confrontation, in a relationship of friend-enemy with adversaries."[17]

The frequency and intensity of violence in the nineteenth century had effects that lasted at least until the end of *La Violencia*. The numerous civil wars and the widespread participation of the *campesinos* in them led to a strict and intense partisan socialization of the masses. Many (if not most) *campesino* families had "martyrs," that is, family members who had been killed, disabled, or raped by members of the other political party. Whereas original party identification of *campesinos* came from those of their *patrones*, at some point this identification developed a life of its own, based on the past. Eduardo Santa, a Colombian sociologist, said that Colombians began to be born "with party identifications attached to their umbilical cords."[18] As a result, other cleavages (such as social class and regionalism) became secondary to that of the primary party. Third parties were notably unsuccessful until the 1990s.

Violence became the normal way to handle things. As a Colombian sociologist said in an interview, "We have no ways to channel conflicts. Probably because of the traditional, oligarchic set up of the Liberal and Conservative parties, we never developed peaceful ways to resolve conflict. If we have disagreements we only think of violence as the way to solve them."[19]

It is more difficult to map the direct connection between the partisan and the current violence. Some studies suggest a clear connection. Eduardo Pizarro, for example, shows how the FARC guerrilla group developed in areas where there was a "persistence of the forms of the earlier political violence, especially the 'political banditry,' which survived until at least 1965."[20] The research of Alfonso Salazar shows that young people in Medellín who were participating in the drug and common crime violence of the 1980s came from families who had been forced to that city by the partisan violence of the 1950s and 1960s.[21]

Others are more skeptical of the connection. Perhaps one should be very careful with automatic explanations such as "the culture of violence" or "violence causes violence."

Yet there is another aspect that we must not overlook, more as a result of the violence than a cause of it. As pointed out by one sociologist, two new structures for mobility developed in Colombia: one from the violent groups—guerrillas, paramilitary squads, and drug dealers—and another from groups to defend other citizens from those lawbreakers.[22] Alvaro Camacho's research on Cali found that there were "4,500 private policemen registered with local authorities," while the local police force had 2,800 men.[23] This raises two questions: How many "private" policemen did Cali have who were not registered with the local authorities, and how many people in Colombia have employment in private security agencies? Whatever the answers to those questions are, they clearly indicate the difficulties in solving such a perplex conundrum.

Modernization

Chronologically, the first complication in the transition from the traditional system that did not work very well to the current one, which functions even worse, was the process of modernization in Colombia. In the past fifty years, the country has changed. Its people are no longer illiterate and rural; they are more literate and urban. Gonzalo Sánchez points out that at the end of World War II, "Almost three fourths of the population was composed of peasants; more than half was illiterate; and 3 percent of the landowners monopolized half the land."[24]

This modernization caused several kinds of complications. The first was simply having people in closer contact with each other than before. As a Colombian historian stated, "Urbanization brought many problems of conflict from the countryside to the cities. People are closer together in the cities, have more conflicts, and use violence in those conflicts."[25]

A second complication of modernization is the lessening of the spiritual power of the Roman Catholic Church. One must remember that the church was part of the problem in the nineteenth century, as argued earlier, and that Colombia had mass carnage in the name of political party when the power of that religious institution was at its apogee. Nevertheless, the church did try to teach a moral code; with urbanization, however, the power of the Roman Catholic Church decreased in Colombia. One of the most dramatic indications of this weakening is the proportion of Colombian women who began using artificial birth-control methods, recently reported to be nearly two-thirds—the highest in the world.[26] Although that statistic per se is not important for a study of violence in Colombia, it does suggest that other things taught by the church (such as "Thou shall not kill") probably came to have less importance than they did in the more rural past.

Two caveats seem warranted, however. First, the church was never especially successful in Colombia with its message, "Thou shall not kill." Indeed, I have just argued that violence, including violent deaths for political reasons, was part of the Colombian tradition. Second, it should be stressed that disobeying the church's position on artificial birth control is meant as only a rough indication of the diminishing power of that institution.

Finally, modernization means mass media, and that means more information about the violence that is taking place. Although the Colombian government has tried to restrict publicity about the violence, at times it clearly is impossible to avoid knowing about the most recent guerrilla attack, the latest car bomb, the massacres of the paramilitary groups, the hijacking of buses, the murder of soccer players.

Money Talks

The second complication in the transition from the traditional system that did not work very well to the current one that functions even worse has to do with the vast amount of money that came to Colombia with the drug trade. The Colombian economist Francisco Thoumi states: "Several authors have tackled the difficult task of estimating the size of the Colombian illegal PSAD industry's income. . . . Although subject to great uncertainty these estimates that Colombian industry profits have fluctuated between U.S. $2 and $5 billion per year."[27]

Although the exact amount of wealth repatriated is unknown, there is no doubt that a considerable amount of it was returned through arms shipments. Further, the demand for arms went up, as organized crime (from drugs, guerrillas, death squads) wanted additional weapons and private citizens needed defense equipment to protect themselves.[28] There are no figures for total number of light fire arms in Colombia, but over thirty thousand were sold legally in each year between 1991 and 1993.[29]

The effect of drug wealth has been seen throughout this study. Chapters 5 and 8 showed how paramilitary groups changed from being groups of private farmers and ranchers, producing legal products, to groups dominated by the *narcotraficantes*. The chapters on guerrilla groups, especially chapter 6, argued that one of the major reasons that the Colombian governments failed in their negotiations was that the guerrilla groups had such wealth from cocaine and poppies that there was little the government could offer that interested them. Reports in chapters on guerrilla groups, paramilitary squads, and drug dealers indicated that each of these groups was better armed than the government.

Whereas the lawbreaking groups seem to have had unlimited funds, that surely has not been true for the Colombian government. At various points in this study, I have shown that a higher percentage of the government's budget was being placed into the armed forces and the police. This has, logically, meant that a lower proportion is being used in other areas. An analysis of the government's budget between

1980 and 1990 showed that expenditures on social matters (education, health, housing, social security) had fallen from 41 to 34 percent of the budget, although that meant a relatively constant 7.5 percent of the gross domestic product.[30] If one believes the logic of former president Belisario Betancur that subjective and objective factors cause violence, it seems illogical to leave funding for social programs at such a low level.

General Conclusions

The first part of this chapter leads to the conclusion, in almost all cases, that there was more violence during the Gaviria government than the Barco government and more in the Barco government than in the Betancur period. What is one to infer? One explanation is that the process, begun even before the Betancur administration, resulted in violence that increased in the Barco and Gaviria years because of the force of momentum. Another argument is that the reforms of the Gaviria years (especially those of the system of justice—the establishment of the office of the general prosecutor, the end of narcoterrorism because of the mistakes made by Pablo Escobar after his plea bargain, and the partial demobilization of the death squads)—simply did not have time to take effect. But perhaps they will some day.

A final explanation of this dilemma is that something more profound continued happening in Colombia during the Gaviria years, originally called the "partial breakdown of the state" in the case of *La Violencia*. In his study of that period of partisan violence in the 1940s through the 1960s, political scientist Paul Oquist argues: "Intense partisan rivalry led to an extreme decrease in state power, which was manifested by: (1) the breakdown of the nation's political institutions; (2) the loss of legitimacy of the state for significant parts of the population; (3) contradictions within the armed apparatus of the state; and (4) the physical absence of the state in certain areas of the country."[31] That a similar process occurred in Colombia in the 1980s has been suggested by several scholars, including Fernán E. González González, who writes: "For many we live in an almost apocalyptic situation: it is thought that we are watching the wreckage of our democratic institutions, the destruction of all the values, and the breakdown of order in the nation."[32]

González, however, quickly points out that this conclusion is based on a mythology of Colombian history, not the reality: "It is conjectured in this way that a golden age existed in the past when everything went well, moral principles were respected, and harmony reigned between human beings."[33] Colombian history demonstrates that "partial collapses" did not occur to a government structure that was effective throughout the entire country. That has never existed. And hence it would be preferable to conceive *La Violencia* of the 1940s through the 1960s and the violence of the 1980s and 1990s as low points in the effectiveness of the Colombian national government, which at no point in its history has applied its laws successfully in the entire country.[34]

No one, to my knowledge, has attempted a precise measurement of this in Colombia. Yet it seems certain, at least intuitively, that the concentration of the government on the violence coming from guerrilla groups, drug dealers, and death squads left it neither time nor financial resources for adequate efforts to prevent "common" crime. So if a man has an argument with his neighbor, and if the man thinks it is very unlikely that he will be arrested, indicted, tried, or punished, why not solve the problem personally? Or if, late one night in Medellín, a group of inebriated men meet a soccer player whom they incorrectly blame for Colombia's failure in the World Cup competition, why not just kill him? That is what happened in the case of Andrés Escobar.

Hence the description of the current "partial collapse" of the Colombian state seems well captured by political scientists Luis Javier Orjuela and Cristina Barrera P.:

> Geographic marginality, the scarce social and transportation infrastructure, the difficulties of police control, administrative corruption, party incapacity—all are conditions which are favorable to the cultivation and processing of the coca leaf and in which the space left by the State is filled by the drug dealers, the armed opposition groups, the civil movements and the vigilante groups, whether they are called "self-defense" or "paramilitary" ones. . . . We find ourselves, then, facing a fragmented State that has lost the monopoly of the legitimate use of force; a State that lost its capacity to represent and integrate new social forces and, therefore, the possibility to channel social tensions and regulate conflicts.[35]

The State, Violence, and the Future of Colombia

One obvious conclusion from this study is that a modern state has never existed in Colombia. As defined by Charles Tilly, the state is an organization that controls the means of coercion within a given territory, which is differentiated from other organizations operating in the same territory, autonomous, centralized, and formally coordinated.[36] This simply means that the Colombian government has never been willing, or able, to extend "the power and range of a more or less autonomous political unit by conquest, alliance, bargaining, chicanery, argument, and administrative encroachment."[37]

If one could measure this over time (not that anyone has), no doubt the conclusions would be that the high points of state penetration were right after the beginning of the National Front, with that power decreasing, first, with the emergence of the guerrilla groups, second with the appearance of the paramilitary squads, and finally with the beginning of the drug trade and terrorism. This study suggests that the lowest point of Colombian government power in recent years was at the end of the Virgilio Barco presidency and that perhaps in some ways the power increased during the Gaviria years.

Another related and obvious conclusion of this study is that the contemporary violence in Colombia is so complex that there is no easy solution to it. Some people are more optimistic than others about the possible solutions, arguing that the Gaviria administration had turned the corner in the nation's history. Indeed there were a number of successes, albeit small ones, in Gaviria's final year. The first was the demobilization of part of the ELN. The second was the demobilization of three militia groups of Medellín. The third was the demobilization of part of the FARC—the Francisco Gárnica Front. The other important successes had to do with the capture or death of guerrilla leaders. One was Alfonso Cano, captured in Bucaramanga in 1993; another was Francisco Caraballo, killed in 1994.

Because of all of these successes, some high-level officials had the attitude that Colombia had turned the corner. This was seen clearly in an interview with a high-level member of the executive branch:

> This year every *municipio* [municipality] in Colombia will have at least a contingency of sixteen police. The goal is to have 114,000 police by the year 2000, and with the very important police reform, the country will have an effective constabulary for the first time.
>
> Meanwhile violence is decreasing. Guerrilla violence is diminishing. The actions that they are carrying out are more small-scale than before. Paramilitary violence has become more small-scale also. There never was a national coordination of paramilitary groups, but now the groups are smaller.
>
> The army is also patrolling in more, but smaller groups. They

are hence covering more of the country. . . . The *fiscalia* [National Prosecutor's Office] is making progress, but it has had a lot of difficulties. The fiscal and the vice fiscal are first rate, but below that there is diminishing quality. The problem is not lack of resources; they have enough. . . . The number of homicides did not increase in 1993, but stayed at about the same number as 1992.

The CRS and the Medellín militia turning themselves in was very important. For one thing, there are other, small guerrilla groups within the FARC that might do the same. For another, other militias in other cities have been very impressed with what Jorge Orlando Melo was able to do in Medellín. There has even been progress in Urabá, with a presidential counsellor.[38]

The assumptions of this individual were that this would be enough police for effective law enforcement, that narcoterrorism would not re-emerge, and that the tide was turning against the guerrilla groups.

Francisco Leal Buitrago, writing just before the Gaviria administration began, was much less optimistic about the state of his homeland:

There is no doubt that the social cost of the recent national political process has been immense. Added to the lack of governmental political capacity has been the indolence of the dominant organizations of civil society. . . . The tradition of terror of the waning ruling class to any form of social mobilization continues weighing excessively on private and official decisions related to an active public opinion as a mechanism of organized political pressure. It is a fact that both the State and civil society are politically weak and unorganized; as a result they are helpless in face of unfavorable circumstances.[39]

Although Leal Buitrago went on to state that the new government had possibilities of correcting these problems, there is no indication that it did so.

As one looks to Colombia's future, clearly many concerns must be kept in mind. Charles Berquist argues, for example, in the introduction to *Violence in Colombia: The Contemporary Crisis in Historical Perspective:* "It would be nice to believe that the current violence in Colombia could be resolved by the elimination of the drug trade, remote as that possibility may be. The authors of these essays argue, however, that no such quick fix, even were it possible, would address the heart of the problem. Only a basic democratization of Colombian society—informed by an understanding of past conflicts and aimed at fundamental social and political reform—will create the conditions for future peace."[40]

At this point there is no indication that the drug trade is being eliminated. Although the original reason for drug terrorism (the use of extradition) had been removed, why should we be so naive as to surmise that drug terrorism might not emerge again for some other reason? Although small guerrilla groups and fronts have recently demobilized, the news each week includes yet another subversive attack, with deaths and property damage. If the constitution of 1991, both in process and product, did not satisfy the guerrillas (who after all had been in the mountains because of the closed political system), and if their wealth is so considerable because of drugs, kidnapping, and extortion, exactly what will it take to convince them? And if the guerrilla groups do not disappear, would it not be disingenuous to think that paramilitary groups will?

More democracy (perhaps too much) did come with the constitution of 1991, at least formally. Fundamental social reform, which seems unlikely at this point, is more plausible if, after the time for learning the new constitution is over, a political party system should emerge that is based on democratic competition around different ideas of how to solve the economic and social problems of Colombia. It is not clear whether or not that is likely in the world after the "end of history," when ideology has been left in the past.

Thus it seems most reasonable for Colombians to wait patiently as they learn new patterns—both political and personal conduct patterns. As a "new democracy," it might take several four-year cycles of elections before political party leaders realize that the *"operación avispa"* strategy (operating various party lists, with local notables heading them) does not make long-term sense, despite its putative benefits in the short term. As for personal conduct, it will take a long time for all to understand (should the general prosecutor's office and the reformed national police undertake it) that breaking the law leads to possible arrest, trial, conviction, and time in jail.

This would be a complete departure from Colombia's history and will not happen in days, weeks, or even a few years. Rather, it will happen only as time passes and as many individual Colombians know people who have suffered the consequences of breaking the law, as today individual Colombians know people who have suffered from guerrilla groups, narcoterrorism, and death squads. A great moral revolution seems as unlikely in Colombia as it does in the rest of the world, so the country must hope that behavioral changes come from these structural ones. It seems quite possible that, twenty or so years from now, analysts will see the César Gaviria presidency as the time not when the future arrived in Colombia but when the past started to end.

Final Words

In May 1994 a bus was hijacked in Bogotá one evening by a half-dozen men and two women. This *"bus ejecutivo"* (executive bus, meaning that it costs more than ordinary buses and does not allow more people than seats) was driven around town for two hours, with no lights on, while over forty occupants were robbed. On several occasions the bus pulled over to dark places and some of the women passengers were raped. In the public outcry that followed, individuals reported similar incidents in taxis and even in other buses.

In June 1994 Andrés Escobar, middle defender for the Colombian national soccer team, was killed outside a bar in Medellín. Escobar had been responsible for an *autogol* (term used when a player accidentally scores a goal for the other team) in the national team's loss against the United States in the World Cup competition.

In the executive bus hijacking the large rewards offered led to the apprehension of the robbers within a week. Similarly, the alleged assassins of Andrés Escobar were captured in Medellín, only a few days after their killing of the soccer star. So in some cases Colombian justice seemed to be working. But those were exceptional cases, either because they were important people or there was much publicity. After all, it was no ordinary bus, but an executive bus, and the young man killed in Medellín was a star of the national soccer team.

The conclusion I offer, however, is that in the majority of cases the Colombian judicial system is not working. Of the crimes reported in 1983, only 10 percent led to verdicts, according to the Colombian government; the Inter-American Commission on Human Rights put the figure at 4 percent. The same commission reported that the *fiscalía* set up by the 1991 constitution had increased the number of cases processed by 50 percent by 1993, indicating that perhaps data will show that the Gaviria reforms led to a turnaround in the system. The current data do not yet lead to that definitive conclusion, although information that permits us to conclude that the judicial system has really changed will not be available until years from now.

In the meantime we can only conclude, as the Intercongregational Commission of Justice and Peace did in its founding document of March 1988: "For various years Colombia has lived in a progressively depreciated situation of the denial of and attempts against the elemental rights of human beings. The fundamental right to life has been violated, every day in a more alarming way, by assassination and forced disappearance."[41]

Epilogue

At this writing, more than three years have passed since the end of the Gaviria government. Unfortunately, nothing in the government of Ernesto Samper allows us to be more optimistic about the changes brought by the eight years of the Barco and Gaviria governments. Indeed, one might conclude that things are even worse, which suggests another book. I reach that conclusion because of the following events since August 7, 1994, listed in no particular order:

— *Drug monies seemed, even more than before, to have completely infiltrated the Colombian political system.* The lower house of the National Congress considered the accusation that Ernesto Samper had received as much as US$6 million from the Cali drug leaders in the 1994 campaign. Although the legislative body refused to impeach Samper, many (including the U.S. government) considered him to have been guilty, not adequately judged by a Congress in which many members had also received drug money.

— *Drugs continued to be exported from Colombia in roughly the same amount,* with new leaders and new "cartels" appearing. Although the key leaders of the Cali group were now in jail and narcoterrorism did seem to be a thing of the past, one report suggested that the imprisoned Cali leaders—the Rodríguez Orejuela brothers—were plotting the deaths of Samper, the national prosecutor, the U.S. ambassador, and others.[42]

— *Guerrilla groups continued to be active in ambushes, bombings, and kidnapping,* in August 1996 capturing sixty members of the army in the Amazon jungle region and proposing that they would be released only when the Colombian government agreed to remove all troops from the area. In May 1997 journalist Jorge Enrique Botero interviewed FARC leader Alfonso Cano and concluded that the guerrilla group had no interest in demobilization or turning in their arms, unless the government agreed to a social and economic program "of a communist party in power."[43]

— *Paramilitary groups continued to flourish,* even when leaders such as Fidel Castaño disappeared and were replaced by others, such as

Fidel's brother Carlos. According to Human Rights Watch, Castaño's group killed three hundred noncombatants between July and December 1996.[44] The combination of higher guerrilla and paramilitary activity led the newsweekly *Semana* to the conclusion that the 1998 presidential election is likely to be the bloodiest of Colombian history.[45] Given the sad history of Colombian democracy, one can only hope that the newsmagazine misses its prediction.

— *In 1997 there was repeated information in the press that seemed to indicate that, for the first time, the paramilitary groups were going to have a national organization.* One of their goals, surely not new, was to have the same status as guerrilla groups.

— *Finally, the U.S. government refused to certify, in both 1996 and 1997, that the Colombian government was cooperating in antidrug activities.* This "decertification" could have effects on legal Colombian exports, as well as the amount of resources the country receives for its antidrug activities.

In the first paragraph of this book I stated that both President Virgilio Barco Vargas and President César Gaviria Trujillo felt they had to do something to end the use of violence by leftist guerrillas, drug dealers, and paramilitary groups. Those groups were using violence against the government and the people and were controlling vast areas of the country. In reaction the government itself was at times violating the human rights of Colombians. The chapters that followed went into great detail about their activities, but in chapter 10 I argued that the empirical indices showed little or no improvement.

I fear I must conclude this book by hypothesizing that all kinds of violence worsened during the Samper years. I have two hopes: first that I am wrong and second that I will have the opportunity to return to Colombia to research the book that will show that.

Notes

1. Introduction: Attempts at Conflict Resolution in Colombia, 1986–1994

1. Charles Tilly, "Reflections on the History of European State-Making," in *The Formation of National States in Western Europe,* ed. Charles Tilly (Princeton: Princeton University Press, 1975), 6.

2. Charles Tilly, "War Making and State Making as Organized Crime," in *Bringing the State Back In,* eds. Peter Evans, Dietrich Reuschemeyer, and Theda Skocpol (Cambridge: Cambridge University Press, 1985), 169.

3. Ibid.

4. Philippe C. Schmitter and Terry Lynn Karl, "What Democracy Is . . . And Is Not," *Journal of Democracy* 2 (summer 1991): 78.

5. Samuel P. Huntington, *The Third Wave: Democratization in the Late Twentieth Century* (Norman: University of Oklahoma Press, 1991), 10.

6. Edward C. Banfield, *Civility and Citizenship in Liberal Democratic Societies* (New York: Paragon House, 1992), xi.

7. Gabriel A. Almond, *Comparative Politics: System, Process, and Policy* (Boston: Little, Brown, 1978). This is but one example of the structural functionalist concepts.

8. Theda Skocpol, "Bringing the State Back In: Strategies of Analysis in Current Research," in *Bringing the State Back In,* eds. Peter Evans, Dietrich Reuschemeyer, and Theda Skocpol (Cambridge: Cambridge University Press, 1985), 28.

9. John D. Martz, *The Politics of Clientelism: Democracy and the State in Colombia* (New Brunswick: Transaction Publishers, 1997), 15.

10. Ibid., 25–31.

11. Ibid., 30.

12. Barbara Geddes, *Politician's Dilemma: Building State Capacity in Latin America* (Berkeley: University of California Press, 1994), 18.

13. Francisco Leal Buitrago and Andrés Dávila Ladrón de Guevara, *Clientelismo: El sistema político y su expresión regional* (Bogotá: Tercer Mundo Editores, 1990), 36–37.

14. Peter Evans, Dietrich Reuschemeyer, and Theda Skocpol, "On the Road toward a More Adequate Understanding of the State," in *Bringing the State Back In,* eds. Peter Evans, Dietrich Reuschemeyer, and Theda Skocpol (Cambridge: Cambridge University Press, 1985), 348.

15. I know of no expert who has attempted to state what portion of the country is controlled by the three groups, although, as chapter 6 shows, there was great disagreement between the government and the guerrillas over that question in one case.

16. Dr. John Swain, a colleague of mine at the University of Alabama, kindly suggested this way of looking at it to avoid tautological reasoning.

17. Peter Hakim and Abraham F. Lowenthal, "Latin America's Fragile Democracies," *Journal of Democracy* 2 (summer 1991): 26.

18. Confidential interview, Colombian historian, Bogotá, May 25, 1994.

2. The Historical Context for Bargaining: The Weak Colombian State and the Emergence of Opposition

1. Perhaps most notably, this argument was made by Louis Hartz in *The Founding of New Societies* (New York: Harcourt, Brace & World, 1964).

2. John Leddy Plelan, "Authority and Flexibility in the Spanish Bureaucracy," *Administrative Science Quarterly* (June 1960): 51.

3. Ibid., 60.

4. John Leddy Phelan, *The Kingdom of Quito in the Seventeenth Century: Bureaucratic Politics in the Spanish Empire* (Madison: The University of Wisconsin Press, 1967), 3.

5. Ibid., 22.

6. Ibid., 26.

7. David Busnell, *The Making of Modern Colombia: A Nation In Spite of Itself* (Berkeley: University of California Press, 1993), 12.

8. Ibid., 36–37.

9. Alfonso López Michelsen, "Del origen de la violencia en Colombia," *El Tiempo* (Bogotá), July 14, 1991.

10. Charles Tilly, "War Making and State Making as Organized Crime," in *Bringing the State Back In*, eds. Peter Evans, Dietrich Reuschemeyer, and Theda Skocpol (Cambridge: Cambridge University Press, 1985), 173.

11. Francisco Leal Buitrago, "Defensa y seguridad nacional en Colombia, 1958–1993," in *Orden mundial y seguridad: Nuevos desafíos para Colombia y América Latina,* eds. Francisco Leal Buitrago and Juan Gabriel Tokatian (Bogotá: Editorial Tercer Mundo, 1994), 132.

12. Geddes, 7.

13. Confidential interview, former minister of mines and petroleum, May 26, 1981.

14. Confidential interview, former minister of the treasury, April 20, 1981.

15. Miguel Urrutia, "Diversidad ideológica e integración andina," *Coyuntura Ecónomica* 10 (1980): 197.

16. Jonathan Hartlyn, "Interest Groups and Political Conflict in Colombia: A Retrospective and Prospective View" (paper presented at the U.S. State Department Conference on Colombia, Washington, D.C., November 9, 1981).

17. Quoted in Daniel L. Premo, "The Armed Forces and Colombian Politics: In Search of a Mission." Chestertown, Md.: Washington College, 1981, mimeographed.

18. J. Mark Ruhl, "An Alternative to the Bureaucratic-Authoritarian Regime: The Case of Colombia," *Inter-American Economic Affairs* 35 (1981).

19. The first was the estimate given in Premo, "The Armed Forces and Co-

lombian Politics." The second was stated by John Agudelo Rios, president of Betancur's Peace Commission. See *El Espectador* (Bogotá), October 14, 1986. The third was given in a confidential interview, member of the executive branch, July 21, 1992.

20. Eduardo Pizarro Leongómez, "Revolutionary Guerrilla Groups in Colombia," in *Violence in Colombia: The Contemporary Crisis in Historical Perspective*, eds. Charles Berquist, Ricardo Peñaranda, and Gonzalo Sánchez (Wilmington, Del.: Scholarly Resources, Inc., 1992), 177.

21. Ibid., 180–81.

22. Ibid., 179.

23. Ibid., 182–83.

24. Ibid., 185.

25. *El Tiempo*, Mar. 24, 1981.

26. *El Espectador*, May 23, 1982.

27. For a discussion of the Security Statute see Harvey F. Kline, *Colombia: Democracy under Assault* (Boulder, Colo.: Westview Press, 1995), 86–87.

28. *El Espectador*, Nov. 21, 1982.

29. Ibid., May 27, 1984.

30. *Cromos*, July 19, 1985.

31. Bruce Bagley, "Colombia and the War on Drugs, *Foreign Affairs* 67 (1988): 73–74.

32. Ibid., 75–76.

33. Richard B. Craig, "Domestic Implications of Illicit Drug Cultivation, Processing, and Trafficking in Colombia" (paper presented at the U.S. State Department Conference on Colombia, November 9, 1981), 4–5.

34. Ibid.

35. Luis Javier Orjuela and Cristina Barrera P., "Narcotráfico y política en la década de los ochenta: Entre la represión y el diálogo," in *Narcotráfico en Colombia: Dimensiones políticas, económicas, jurídicas e internacionales*, eds. Carlos G. Arrieta, Luis J. Orjuela, Eduardo Sarmiento, and Juan G. Tokatlian (Bogotá: Tercer Mundo Editores, 1989), 209.

36. Ibid.

37. Ibid., 215.

38. The Colombian economist Francisco E. Thoumi argues that these are not "cartels" in the sense of his discipline because there is more than one, they are loosely organized, and they do not cooperate to set prices. See Francisco E. Thoumi, *Political Economy and Illegal Drugs in Colombia* (Boulder, Colo.: Lynne Rienner Publishers, 1995), 142–43.

39. *Latin America Weekly Report*, Jan. 8, 1982.

40. *El Espectador*, Dec. 28, 1984.

41. *Semana*, Oct. 17, 1989, p. 23.

42. Orjuela and Barrera P., 239, quoting *El Tiempo*, July 19, 1984, pp. 1A, 8A.

43. Orjuela and Barrera P., 236.

44. *Semana*, Aug. 7, 1990.

45. Ibid., Apr. 16, 1991.

46. Confidential interview, Bogotá, July 21, 1991.

47. *Semana*, May 17, 1988, p. 26.

48. Ibid.

49. Ibid.

50. Gonzalo Sánchez, "La Violencia in Colombia: New Research, New Questions," *Hispanic American Historical Review* 65 (1985): 790; emphasis in the original.

51. *El Espectador*, Feb. 19, 1989.

52. Orjuela and Barrera P., 225–26, quoting Comisión de Estudios sobre la Violencia, *Colombia, violencia y democracia* (Bogotá: Universidad Nacional, n.d.), 88.

53. Gustavo Gorriti, "Latin America's Internal Wars," *Journal of Democracy* 2 (winter 1991): 86–87.

54. Peter Hakim and Abraham F. Lowenthal, "Latin America's Fragile Democracies," *Journal of Democracy* 2 (summer 1991): 18–19.

The Virgilio Barco Government, 1986–1990

1. *El Espectador*, May 27, 1986.

2. Ibid., Aug. 24, 1986.

3. Barco's Guerrilla Policy

1. It should be noted that the composition of this group, a small guerrilla group centered in the Cauca department and primarily composed of indigenous people, was to change with the addition of the FARC to the coordinating alliance.

2. *El Tiempo*, Aug. 10, 1986.

3. *El Espectador*, Oct. 14, 1986.

4. *El Mundo*, Nov. 14, 1986.

5. Ibid.

6. *El Tiempo*, Sept. 23, 1986.

7. *El Espectador*, Jan. 30, 1987.

8. Ibid., June 22, 1986.

9. Ibid.

10. Ibid.

11. *El Colombiano*, June 26, 1986.

12. *El Espectador*, Oct. 4, 1987.

13. Ibid., June 12, 1987.

14. Ibid., June 5, 1988.

15. Ibid., July 31, 1988.

16. Ibid., Aug. 21, 1988.

17. Ibid., Aug. 28, 1988.

18. Ibid., Oct. 9, 1988.

19. Ibid., Aug. 7, 1988.

20. Ibid., July 2, 1989.

21. Ibid., Nov. 20, 1988.

22. Interview, Colombian sociologist, July 27, 1992.

23. Ana María Bejarano, "Estrategias de paz y apertura democrática: Un

balance de las administraciones Betancur and Barco," in *Al filo del caos: Crisis política en la Colombia de los años 80,* eds. Francisco Leal Buitrago and León Zamosc (Bogotá: Tercer Mundo Editores, 1990), 93–96.

24. *El Espectador,* Mar. 19, 1989.
25. Ibid., July 23, 1989.
26. Ibid., Dec. 24, 1989.
27. Ibid.

4. Barco's Drug Policy

1. Orjuela and Barrera P., 247–48, quoting "Realizaciones del programa de cambio: El gobierno cumple con Colombia" (report of the presidency to the National Congress, December 16, 1989, 139–40).
2. Ibid., 248.
3. *El Tiempo,* Jan. 15, 1987.
4. Alan Riding, "Cocaine Billionaires: The Men Who Hold Colombia Hostage," *New York Times Magazine,* Mar. 8, 1987.
5. *New York Times,* Jan. 26, 1988, p. 1.
6. *El Espectador,* Feb. 7, 1988.
7. Ibid., Jan. 3, 1988.
8. *Semana,* Aug. 28, 1989.
9. *New York Times,* Aug. 25, 1989.
10. *Semana,* Oct. 9, 1989.
11. *El Espectador,* Aug. 20, 1989.
12. *Semana,* Aug. 28, 1989.
13. *New York Times,* Aug. 29, 1989.
14. *Cromos,* Aug. 29, 1989.
15. *New York Times,* Aug. 23, 1989.
16. Ibid., Aug. 31, 1989.
17. *Semana,* Sept. 12, 1989, p. 35.
18. *New York Times,* Aug. 25, 1989.
19. *Semana,* Nov. 7, 1989, p. 28.
20. Ibid., Dec. 12, 1989, p. 52.
21. *Christian Science Monitor,* Dec. 19, 1989.
22. *Semana,* Dec. 19, 1989, p. 28.
23. Ibid.
24. Ibid.
25. Ibid.
26. Ibid., Oct. 10, 1989, pp. 24–29.
27. *New York Times,* Aug. 30, 1989.
28. Ibid.
29. *Semana,* Apr. 3, 1990, p. 22.
30. *New York Times,* Mar. 30, 1990.
31. Orjuela and Barrera P., 272.
32. Ibid.
33. *Semana,* Jan. 23, 1990, p. 24.
34. Ibid., p. 25.

35. Ibid., p. 26.
36. Ibid., p. 27.
37. Ibid., p. 25.
38. Ibid., Feb. 20, 1990, p. 23.
39. *New York Times,* Mar. 30, 1990.
40. *El Espectador,* May 17, 1989.
41. *Semana,* Feb. 20, 1990, p. 23.
42. Ibid., p. 25.
43. Confidential interview, Colombian political scientist, Bogotá, May 19, 1994.
44. *Semana,* Feb. 20, 1990, p. 25.
45. Ibid., Apr. 3, 1990, p. 28.
46. Ibid., Sept. 19, 1989, pp. 26–28.
47. Ibid., July 10, 1990, p. 40.
48. Ibid., p. 41.
49. Ibid., July 31–Aug. 7, 1990.
50. Ibid.
51. Ibid.
52. Ibid., Aug. 28, 1990, p. 35.
53. Ibid.
54. Ibid., Sept. 4, 1990, p. 34.
55. Orjuela and Barrera P., 253.

5. Self-Defense, Private Justice, and Paramilitary Groups: The Final Piece of the Jigsaw Puzzle

1. *El Espectador,* May 11, 1986.
2. Enrique Santos Calderón, "Procurador habemus," *El Tiempo,* May 18, 1986.
3. *El Mundo,* Sept. 26, 1986.
4. *El Espectador,* Feb. 20, 1987.
5. Ibid., Aug. 2, 1987.
6. Ibid., Nov. 15, 1987.
7. *Semana,* Dec. 13, 1988, p. 36.
8. Ibid.
9. Ibid.
10. Ibid., Nov. 22, 1988, p. 34.
11. Eduardo Pizarro Leongómez, "Revolutionary Guerrilla Groups in Colombia," in *Violence in Colombia: The Contemporary Crisis in Historical Perspective,* eds. Charles Berquist, Ricardo Peñaranda, and Gonzalo Sánchez, (Wilmington, Del.: Scholarly Resources, 1992), 189–90.
12. *Semana,* Jan. 24, 1989, p. 23.
13. Ibid., p. 25.
14. Ibid., Mar. 7, 1989, p. 23.
15. Ibid., p. 25.
16. Ibid., Mar. 14, 1989, p. 44.
17. Ibid., p. 24.

18. Ibid., p. 25.

19. Ibid., May 17, 1988, p. 28.

20. Ibid., p. 30.

21. Ibid., p. 32.

22. Ibid., p. 33.

23. Ibid., Jan. 31, 1989, p. 28.

24. Ibid., p. 33.

25. Ibid., p. 33.

26. Ibid., Oct. 25, 1988, p. 42.

27. Ibid.

28. Ibid., Jan. 24, 1989, p. 25.

29. Ibid., Apr. 11, 1989, p. 28.

30. Ibid., May 2, 1989, p. 34.

31. Ibid., p. 35.

32. Ibid.

33. Ibid., Dec. 13, 1988, p. 32.

34. Ibid., May 17, 1988, p. 35.

35. Ibid., Jan. 24, 1989, p. 24.

36. Ibid., Apr. 11, 1989, p. 25.

37. Ibid., p. 26.

38. Ibid., p. 27.

39. Ibid., p. 34.

40. Ibid.

41. *El Espectador*, June 4, 1989.

42. Republic of Colombia, *The Struggle against Violence and Impunity: A Democratic Commitment* (Bogotá: Office of the President, 1988), 11–12, 18–19.

43. *Semana*, May 17, 1988, p. 33.

44. Ibid., Jan. 24, 1989, p. 26.

45. Ibid., p. 27.

46. Ibid., p. 28.

47. Ibid., Apr. 11, 1989, p. 23.

48. Ibid.

49. Ibid., May 2, 1989, p. 36.

50. *El Espectador*, July 22, 1990.

51. Ibid., Jan. 14, 1990.

52. Ibid., Dec. 24, 1989.

53. *Semana*, Oct. 2, 1990.

54. Ibid., July 3, 1990.

55. Ibid., Aug. 15, 1989, p. 24.

56. Ibid., p. 25.

57. Ibid., p. 26.

58. Ibid., Aug. 3, 1990.

59. Ibid.

60. Orjuela and Barrera P., 266.

61. *El Espectador*, Sept. 2, 1984.

62. Human Rights Watch, *Colombia's Killer Networks: The Military-Paramilitary Partnership and the United States,* summary, pp. 1, 2 (http://www.hrw.org/summaries/s.colombia9611.html).

The César Gaviria Government, 1990–1994

1. *El Tiempo,* Aug. 8, 1990.
2. Ibid.
3. *Semana,* Aug. 14, 1990, p. 39.

6. Negotiations between the Government and the Guerrilla Groups

1. *El Tiempo,* Aug. 8, 1990.
2. *Semana,* Aug. 28, 1990, p. 30.
3. Ibid., Jan. 19, 1991, p. 20.
4. Ibid.
5. Ibid.
6. *El Espectador,* May 12, 1991.
7. *Semana,* May 21–28, 1991, p. 28.
8. "Palabras del señor ministro de gobierno, Humberto de la Calle Lombana, en la instalación de las conversaciones de Caracas," in Presidencia de la República, *Propósitos para ponerle fin al conficto armado* (Bogotá: Presidencia de la República, 1992), 32–33, *El Espectador* (Bogotá), June 6, 1991.
9. *El Espectador,* June 6, 1991.
10. *El País,* June 6, 1991.
11. Ibid., June 7, 1991.
12. *El Tiempo,* June 11, 1991.
13. *La Prensa,* June 12, 1991.
14. Ibid., June 13, 1991.
15. *El Tiempo,* June 16, 1991.
16. Ibid., June 25, 1991.
17. *El Espectador,* June 24, 1991.
18. Ibid., June 26, 1991.
19. Ibid., June 27, 1991.
20. *El Tiempo,* June 28, 1991.
21. *El Espectador,* June 28, 1991.
22. *El Tiempo,* July 2, 1991; July 3, 1991.
23. *El Espectador,* July 4, 1991.
24. *El Tiempo,* July 6, 1991, p. 6C.
25. *El Espectador,* July 6, 1991.
26. *El Tiempo,* July 8, 1991.
27. Ibid., July 11, 1991.
28. *El Tiempo,* July 12, 1991; *El Espectador,* July 13, 1991.
29. Ibid., July 14, 1991.
30. *Semana,* July 30, 1991, p. 24.
31. *El Tiempo,* Sept. 2, 1991.
32. *El Nuevo Siglo,* Sept. 3, 1991.
33. *El País,* Sept. 12, 1992.
34. *El Espectador,* Sept. 11, 1991, p. 10A.
35. *El País,* Sept. 12, 1991, p. 9.
36. *El Espectador,* Sept. 12, 1991.
37. Ibid.

38. Ibid.
39. *La Prensa,* Sept. 11, 1991.
40. *El Espectador,* Sept. 16, 1991.
41. *La Prensa,* Sept. 18, 1991.
42. *El Espectador,* Sept. 20, 1991.
43. Ibid., Oct. 1, 1991.
44. Ibid., Sept. 17, 1991.
45. Ibid., Sept. 30, 1991.
46. Ibid.
47. *El Nuevo Siglo,* Oct. 1, 1991.
48. Confidential interview, Colombian historian, July 22, 1992.
49. *El País,* Oct. 4, 1991.
50. Ibid., Nov. 4, 1991.
51. *El Espectador,* Oct. 31, 1991.
52. *El Tiempo,* Nov. 1, 1991.
53. *El Nuevo Siglo,* Nov. 11, 1991.
54. *El Espectador,* Nov. 6, 1991.
55. *El Nuevo Siglo,* Nov. 11, 1991.
56. *El Tiempo,* Nov. 20, 1991.
57. *Semana,* Mar. 3, 1992, p. 26.
58. Ibid., p. 27.
59. *El Nuevo Siglo,* Feb. 3, 1992.
60. Ibid.
61. William Ramírez Tobón, "¿Alguien quiere volver a Tlaxcala?" *Análisis Político* 16 (May–Aug. 1992): 60.
62. *El Tiempo,* Feb. 26, 1992.
63. Ibid., Mar. 1, 1992.
64. Ibid.
65. Ibid., Mar. 8, 1992.
66. *El Espectador,* Mar. 11, 1992.
67. *El Tiempo,* Mar. 12, 1992.
68. Ibid.
69. *La Prensa,* Mar. 13, 1992.
70. Ibid.
71. *El Tiempo,* Mar. 15, 1992.
72. Ibid., Mar. 16, 1992.
73. *El Espectador,* Mar. 18, 1992.
74. Ibid., Mar. 21, 1992.
75. *La Prensa,* Mar. 23, 1992.
76. *El Tiempo,* Mar. 23, 1992.
77. Ibid., Mar. 25, 1992.
78. *El País,* Apr. 2, 1992.
79. *La Prensa,* Apr. 2, 1992.
80. *El País,* Apr. 9, 1992.
81. *El Nuevo Siglo,* Apr. 12, 1992.
82. Confidential interview, Colombian sociologist, Bogotá, July 17, 1992.
83. *El Tiempo,* May 5, 1992.
84. *El Espectador,* May 10, 1992.
85. Ibid., June 7, 1992.

86. Ibid., July 10, 1992.
87. Ibid., Apr. 9, 1994.
88. Ibid., Mar. 21, 1993.
89. Confidential interview, Colombian sociologist, Bogotá, May 22, 1994.
90. *El Tiempo*, May 27, 1994.
91. Ibid., July 16, 1994.
92. *El Espectador*, June 7, 1992.
93. Confidential interview, Colombian historian, Bogotá, July 22, 1992.
94. Confidential interview, Colombian sociologist, Bogotá, July 17, 1992.
95. *La Prensa*, May 10, 1992, p. 3.
96. Ibid., May 17, 1992, p. 4.
97. Fernando Cortés and Manuel Vicente Peña, "Vientos de guerra," *El País*, Apr. 5, 1992, pp. 2–3.
98. *Semana*, Feb. 19, 1991, p. 17.
99. Ibid., pp. 18–19.
100. *El Tiempo*, June 7, 1992, p. 1B.
101. Ibid.
102. *El Espectador*, Sept. 20, 1992, p. 6A.
103. Confidential interview, executive branch member, Bogotá, July 21, 1992.
104. Confidential interview, Colombian historian, Bogotá, July 22, 1992.
105. Confidential interview, Colombian sociologist, Bogotá, July 17, 1992.
106. Confidential interview, Colombian political scientist, Bogotá, July 27, 1992.
107. Ibid.
108. Confidential interview, Colombian historian, Bogotá, July 22, 1992.
109. Confidential interview, Colombian political scientist, Bogotá, July 27, 1992.
110. Confidential interview, Colombian historian, Bogotá, July 22, 1992.

7. Gaviria's Drug Policy

1. *El Tiempo*, Aug. 8, 1990.
2. Ibid.
3. Ibid.
4. *Semana*, Aug. 28, 1990, pp. 30–31.
5. *New York Times*, Aug. 27, 1990.
6. *Semana*, Feb. 5, 1991, p. 14.
7. Ibid., Sept. 11, 1990, p. 19.
8. Ibid.
9. Ibid., Feb. 5, 1991, p. 15.
10. Ibid.
11. Ibid., Nov. 6, 1990, p. 38.
12. Ibid.
13. Ibid.
14. Ibid., Nov. 27, 1990, p. 25.
15. Ibid.
16. Ibid., p. 26.

17. Ibid., p. 27.
18. Ibid., p. 25.
19. Ibid., Dec. 25, 1990, p. 25.
20. Ibid., p. 27.
21. Ibid., p. 28.
22. Ibid.
23. Ibid.
24. Ibid., Jan. 22, 1991, p. 20.
25. Ibid., p. 21.
26. Ibid., Feb. 5, 1991, p. 15.
27. Ibid., p. 16.
28. Ibid.
29. Ibid., p. 24.
30. Ibid., p. 25.
31. Ibid., May 21, 1991, p. 16.
32. Ibid., pp. 27–28.
33. Ibid., p. 17.
34. Ibid., June 11, 1991, p. 35.
35. Ibid., June 25, 1991, p. 36.
36. *El Espectador,* July 4, 1991.
37. *El Tiempo,* July 4, 1991.
38. *El Espectador,* June 25, 1991, p. 9A; June 27, 1991, p. 7A.
39. Ibid., July 5, 1991.
40. *Semana,* June 9, 1992, p. 31.
41. *El Tiempo,* July 18, 1991.
42. *Semana,* June 9, 1992, pp. 32–33.
43. *El Espectador,* June 30, 1991.
44. *Semana,* July 14, 1992, p. 42.
45. Ibid., Aug. 11, 1992, p. 30.
46. Ibid., p. 31.
47. Ibid., July 28, 1992, p. 22.
48. Ibid., p. 24.
49. Ibid., p. 25.
50. Ibid., pp. 26–27.
51. Ibid., p. 28.
52. Ibid., p. 33.
53. Ibid., Aug. 18, 1992, p. 26.
54. Ibid., p. 28.
55. Ibid., Oct. 13, 1992, pp. 34–35.
56. Ibid., p. 36.
57. Ibid., p. 37.
58. Ibid., Oct. 20, 1992, p. 43.
59. Ibid., Dec. 15, 1992, pp. 44–45.
60. Ibid., Dec. 1, 1992, p. 40.
61. Ibid., Jan. 12, 1993, p. 22.
62. Ibid., Jan. 26, 1993, p. 18.
63. Ibid., p. 19.
64. Ibid., Feb. 9, 1993, p. 30.
65. Ibid., Feb. 23, 1993, pp. 30, 32.

66. Ibid., p. 23.
67. Ibid., Feb. 16, 1993, p. 35.
68. Ibid., Mar. 2, 1993, p. 22.
69. Ibid., Mar. 30, 1993, p. 36.
70. Ibid., Apr. 20, 1993, p. 41.
71. Ibid., p. 42.
72. Ibid., pp. 43–44.
73. Ibid., May 28, 1991, p. 25.
74. Ibid., Feb. 5, 1991, p. 17.
75. Ibid., June 25, 1991, p. 30.
76. Ibid., June 25, 1991, p. 34.
77. Ibid., June 9, 1992, p. 38.
78. *El Espectador,* July 12, 1991.
79. Ibid., July 17, 1991.
80. Ibid., July 18, 1991.

8. The Gaviria Policy for Paramilitary Groups

1. Confidential interview, member of the executive branch, July 21, 1992.

2. Sources were less available in the case of paramilitary groups, both in the public media and in the data bank of the political science department at the Universidad de los Andes. I am not certain if this means that there was less going on than in the cases of the guerrillas and drug dealers or if it was simply perceived as less important.

3. Inter-American Commission on Human Rights, *Second Report on the Situation of Human Rights in Colombia* (Washington, D.C.: General Secretariat, Organization of American States, 1993), 225.

4. Confidential interview, member of the executive branch, July 21, 1992.

5. *Semana,* Sept. 18, 1990, p. 27.

6. Ibid., Apr. 16, 1991, p. 14.

7. Ibid., Dec. 10, 1991, p. 42.

8. Ibid., Apr. 14, 1992, p. 43.

9. Fernando Cortés, "La jugada," *La Prensa,* Mar. 29, 1992, pp. 14–15.

10. *Semana,* Apr. 16, 1991, pp. 14, 16.

11. Cortés, "La jugada," pp. 14–15.

12. *Semana,* Apr. 16, 1991, p. 18.

13. Ibid., Apr. 16, 1991, p. 18.

14. Ibid., Dec. 10, 1991, p. 42.

15. *El Tiempo,* July 10, 1991, p. 8A.

16. Ibid., July 22, 1991, p. 1A.

17. *El Espectador,* July 22, 1991, p. 10A.

18. *El Tiempo,* July 22, 1991, p. 12A.

19. *El Espectador,* July 23, 1991, p. 10A.

20. *El Tiempo,* July 25, 1991, p. 11C.

21. Ibid., July 31, 1991, p. 7C.

22. Ibid., July 26, 1991, p. 12B.

23. *El Espectador,* July 25, 1991, p. 12A.

24. Confidential interview, Colombian member of the executive branch, May 29, 1994.

25. Confidential interview, Colombian sociologist, July 18, 1991.

26. *Semana,* Apr. 14, 1992, pp. 30–31.

27. Confidential interview, Colombian member of the executive branch, July 21, 1992.

28. Confidential interview, Colombian sociologist, July 17, 1992.

29. Fernando Cortés, "La paz, qué Caracas," *La Prensa,* Oct. 6, 1991, pp. 2–3.

30. Confidential interview, political science professor, July 27, 1992.

31. Confidential interview, Colombian member of the executive branch, July 21, 1992.

32. Confidential interview, Colombian member of the executive branch, July 21, 22, 1992.

33. Inter-American Commission on Human Rights, *Second Report,* 36.

34. Eduardo Pizarro Leongómez, *Las FARC: De la autodefensa a la combinación de todas las formas de lucha* (Bogotá: Tercer Mundo Editores, 1991), especially pp. 167–86; also Fernando Cortés and María Claudia Peña, "Así va la guerra," *La Prensa,* June 7, 1992, p. 8.

35. Cortés and Peña, p. 9.

36. Confidential interview, Colombian member of the executive branch, July 21, 22, 1992.

37. Inter-American Commission on Human Rights, *Second Report,* 36.

9. Changing the Colombian State: Constitutional and Judicial Reforms

1. *El Tiempo,* Apr. 24, 1990.

2. Ibid.

3. *El Espectador,* Feb. 21, 1988.

4. Ibid., May 22, 1988.

5. Ibid., Dec. 3, 1989.

6. Ibid., Dec. 10, 1989.

7. Ibid.

8. Ibid., Dec. 17, 1989.

9. *El Tiempo,* May 25, 1990.

10. *El Espectador,* Feb. 9, 1990.

11. *El Tiempo,* Mar. 4, 1990.

12. *El Espectador,* May 28, 1990.

13. Ibid., July 29, 1990.

14. Ibid., Sept. 17, 1990.

15. Interview, Colombian university professor studying the constituent assembly, Bogotá, July 1991.

16. Data bank, Departamento de Ciencia Política, Universidad de los Andes.

17. *El Tiempo,* Mar. 10, 1991.

18. Ibid., Mar. 9, 1991.

19. Ibid., Feb. 26, 1991.

20. Ibid., Mar. 9, 1991.

21. There was no attempt to obtain a random sample of the assembly. Hence the analysis indicates the kind of thoughts expressed about conflict resolution but is not intended to order them in relation to which were considered more important to the assembly as a whole or to any one of the political parties.

22. Interview, member of the constituent assembly, Liberal Party.

23. Interview, member of the constituent assembly, National Salvation movement.

24. Enrique Santos Calderón, "La nueva carta: Un reto," *El Tiempo*, July 4, 1991.

25. *Gaceta Constitucional*, Apr. 9, 1991, p. 20.

26. Ibid., p. 21.

27. Ibid., Apr. 8, 1991, p. 18.

28. *El Tiempo*, June 21, 1991.

29. *El Espectador*, July 7, 1991.

30. Interview, member of the constituent assembly, Unión Patriótrica. Ironically, de la Calle was elected vice president in 1994, running as a Liberal with Liberal Ernesto Samper. The UP constituent was clearly wrong. See chapter 10 for a discussion of some of the surprises of the new constitution.

31. *Gaceta Constitucional*, Mar. 19, 1991, p. 39.

32. Ibid., Apr. 17, 1991, p. 2.

33. Ricardo Santamaría and José Hernández, "El nuevo país ya tiene marco político," *El Tiempo*, June 30, p. 1991.

34. Ibid.

35. Ibid.

36. *Gaceta Constitucional*, June 20, 1991, p. 26.

37. Ibid., June 23, 1992, p. 3.

38. *El Espectador*, July 1, 1991.

39. Interview, member of the constituent assembly, Liberal Party.

40. Interview, member of the constituent assembly, Unión Patriótica.

41. *Gaceta Constitucional*, June 15, 1991, pp. 6–7.

42. *El Espectador*, June 22, 1991.

43. *Gaceta Constitucional*, Apr. 15, 1991, p. 11.

44. Ibid., June 4, 1991, p. 3.

45. Ibid.

46. *El Tiempo*, May 16, 1991.

47. Ibid., May 24, 1991.

48. *Gaceta Constitucional*, Apr. 15, 1991, p. 11.

49. Interview, member of the constituent assembly, Unión Patriótica.

50. *El Espectador*, June 30, 1991.

51. "Justicia y violencia," *Coyuntura Social* 6 (June 1992): 39.

52. Ibid., 40.

53. Ibid., 41.

54. Ibid., 43.

55. Ibid.

56. Ibid.

57. Ibid., 44–45.

58. *El Tiempo,* July 1, 1991.

59. Ibid.

60. Interview, member of the constituent assembly, Liberal Party.

61. *El Tiempo,* June 6, 1991.

62. Ibid.

63. *El Espectador,* July 3, 1991.

64. *El Tiempo,* July 10, 1991.

65. Inter-American Commission on Human Rights, *Second Report,* 56.

66. Confidential interview, member of the executive branch, Bogotá, May 29, 1994.

67. Ibid.

68. Javier Torres Velasco, "La ciudadanía pacta con su policía: El proceso de modernización de la policía nacional de Colombia," in *Orden mundial y seguridad: Nuevos desafíos para Colombia y América Latina,* eds. Francisco Leal Buitrago and Juan Gabriel Tokatian (Bogotá: Editorial Tercer Mundo, 1994), 188.

69. *Semana,* Feb. 25, 1992, pp. 27–29.

70. Torres Velasco, 199.

71. Confidential interview, Colombian sociologist, Bogotá, May 21, 1994.

72. Torres Velasco, 200–201.

73. Jaime Jaramillo Uribe, "Etapas y sentido de la historia de Colombia," in Mario Arrubla and others, *Colombia hoy* (Bogotá: Siglo Veintiuno Editores, 1980), 46.

74. Francisco Leal Buitrago, "Social Classes, International Trade and Foreign Capital in Colombia: An Attempt at Historical Interpretation of the Formation of the State, 1819–1935," Ph.D. diss., University of Wisconsin, 1974, 112.

75. Santos Calderón, "La nueva carta."

76. *El Espectador,* Nov. 3, 1991.

77. *Semana,* Oct. 29–Nov. 5, 1991.

78. Alberto Martínez M., "La nueva constitución económica," *El Espectador,* June 30, 1991.

79. Interview, member of the constituent assembly, Unión Patriótrica.

80. *Gaceta Constitucional,* June 13, 1991, p. 3.

81. *El Tiempo,* May 26, 1991.

82. "La réplica del orangután," *El Espectador,* June 20, 1991.

83. *El Espectador,* July 5, 1991.

84. *El Tiempo,* July 5, 1991.

85. Enrique Caballero, "Cambio de clima," *El Espectador,* July 7, 1991.

86. Juan Diego Jaramillo, "La contra reforma," *El Tiempo,* July 13, 1991.

87. Vladimiro Narango, "Primer vistazo a la nueva constitución (II)," *El Espectador,* July 15, 1991.

88. Jorge Child, "¿Cuál consenso?" *El Espectador,* July 20, 1991.

89. The comparison that should be done has been started in Harvey F. Kline and Charity Bennett, "Colombia and Peru: Were the Political Responses to Guerrillas and Drugs Different Because the Problems Were Different or Because the Countries Were?" (paper delivered at the annual meeting of the Southeast Council of Latin American Studies, San José, Costa Rica, Feb. 1997).

10. Conclusion: Assessment of Success

1. This terminology comes from Philippe C. Schmitter, "Military Intervention, Political Competitiveness, and Public Policy in Latin America," in *Armies and Politics in Latin America*, ed. Abraham Lowenthal (New York: Holmes & Meier, 1976), 120.

2. For purposes of analysis (especially given the "policy lag" difficulty just mentioned), all of 1990 is considered part of the Barco government, just as all of 1994 is considered to be in the Gaviria government.

3. Confidential interview, Colombian sociologist, May 24, 1994; confidential interview, Colombian historian, May 25, 1994; confidential interview, Colombian member of the executive branch, May 30, 1994.

4. The book, which did not conclude what I do here, is *En que momento se jodió Colombia* (Bogotá: Editorial Oveja Negra, 1990).

5. This was the second of two reports by the general procurator's office. Unfortunately, the first was not available.

6. Armando Montenegro Trujillo, *Justicia y desarrollo* (Bogotá: Departamento Nacional de Planeación), April 20, 1994.

7. "Justicia y violencia," 49.

8. Alvaro Camacho, "Public and Private Dimensions of Urban Violence in Cali," in *Violence in Colombia: The Contemporary Crisis in Historical Perspective*, eds. Charles Berquist, Ricardo Peñaranda, and Gonzalo Sánchez, (Wilmington, Del.: Scholarly Resources, Inc., 1992), 241–42.

9. *El Espectador*, July 15, 1992.

10. Confidential interview, Colombian historian, Bogotá, May 25, 1994.

11. Confidential interview, member of the executive branch, Bogotá, May 30, 1994.

12. Kline, *Colombia: Democracy under Assault*, 132–33. The historical circumstances leading to these "decisions" are described in that book.

13. Fernán E. González González, "¿Hacia un 'nuevo colapso parcial del estado'? Precariedad del estado y violencia en Colombia," *Análisis Conflicto Social y Violencia en Colombia* 50 (Sept. 1988): 8.

14. Ibid., 11.

15. Ibid., 12.

16. Fabio Zambrano Pantoja, "Contradicciones del sistema político Colombiano," *Análisis Conflicto Social y Violencia en Colombia* 50 (Sept. 1988): 23; emphasis in the original.

17. Ibid., 26.

18. Eduardo Santa, *Sociología política de Colombia* (Bogotá: Ediciones Tercer Mundo, 1964), 44–48.

19. Confidential interview, Colombian sociologist, Bogotá, May 24, 1994.

20. Pizarro Leongómez, "Revolutionary Guerrilla Groups in Colombia," 174.

21. Alfonso Salazar J., *No nacimos pa'semilla* (Bogotá: CINEP, 1990), passim.

22. Confidential interview, Colombian sociologist, Bogotá, June 21, 1991.

23. Camacho, "Public and Private Dimensions of Urban Violence," 259.

24. Gonzalo Sánchez, "The Violence: An Interpretive Synthesis," in *Violence in Colombia: The Contemporary Crisis in Historical Perspective*, eds. Charles

Berquist, Ricardo Peñaranda, and Gonzalo Sánchez (Wilmington, Del.: Scholarly Books, 1992), 77.

25. Confidential interview, Colombian historian, Bogotá, May 25, 1994.

26. *New York Times,* July 15, 1994, p. A6.

27. Thoumi, 199.

28. Andrés José Soto Velasco, "El control de las armas ligeras," in *Orden mundial y seguridad: Nuevos desafíos para Colombia y América Latina,* eds. Francisco Leal Buitrago and Juan Gabriel Tokatian (Bogotá: Ediciones Tercer Mundo, 1994), 124.

29. Ibid., 126.

30. "Gasto Social," *Coyuntura Social* 6 (June 1992): 13.

31. Paul Oquist, *Violence, Conflict, and Politics in Colombia* (New York: Academic Press, 1980), 177.

32. González González, 5.

33. Ibid.

34. In addition to the González González article and an interview cited elsewhere, this point was made to me by Vanessa Gray, a former student of mine at the University of Massachusetts and currently a Ph.D. student at the University of Miami, in a conversation on May 25, 1994.

35. Orjuela and Barrera P., 212–13.

36. Charles Tilly, "Western State-Building and Theories of Political Transformation," in *The Formation of National States in Western Europe,* ed. Charles Tilly (Princeton: Princeton University Press, 1975), 638.

37. Ibid., 636.

38. Confidential interview, member of the executive branch, Bogotá, May 30, 1994.

39. Francisco Leal Buitrago, "Estructura y coyuntura de la crisis política," in *Al filo del caos: Crisis política en la Colombia de los años 80,* eds. Francisco Leal Buitrago and León Zamosc (Bogotá: Tercer Mundo Editoriales, 1990), 54–55.

40. Charles Berquist, "Introduction: Colombian Violence in Historical Perspective," in *Violence in Colombia: The Contemporary Crisis in Historical Perspective,* eds. Charles Berquist, Ricardo Peñaranda, and Gonzalo Sánchez (Wilmington, Del.: Scholarly Books, 1992), 7–8.

41. "Comisión Intercongregacional de Justicia y Paz: Acta de fundación," *Justicia y Paz* 1 (1988): 1.

42. *El Tiempo,* May 19, 1997.

43. *Semana,* May 26, 1997, p. 16.

44. Joshua Hammer, "Colombia: 'Head Cutters' at War," *Newsweek,* June 2, 1997, p. 42.

45. *Semana,* Mar. 31, 1997.

Bibliography

Interviews

Interviews of Constituent Assembly Members Conducted by the Universidad de los Andes

Alianza Democrática M-19 (five)

Liberal Party (four)

Movimiento de Salvación Nacional (five)

Presidential advisor (one)

Social Conservative Party (two)

Unión Patriótica (one)

Other Interviews

Executive branch member, July 16, 1992

Executive branch member, July 21, 1992

Executive branch member, July 21 and 22, 1992

Executive branch member, May 29, 1994

Executive branch member, May 30, 1994

Executive branch member, July 30, 1995

Former minister of mines and petroleum, May 26, 1981

Former minister of the treasury, April 20, 1981

Historian, July 22, 1992

Historian, May 25, 1994

Member of Constituent Assembly *(Unión Patriótica),* July 11, 1991

Political scientist (non-Colombian) studying constituent assembly, July 1991 (various times)

Political scientist, July 27, 1992

Political scientist, May 19, 1994

Sociologist, June 21, 1991

Sociologist, July 18, 1991

Sociologist, July 17, 1992

Sociologist, July 27, 1992

Sociologist, May 22, 1994
Sociologist, May 24, 1994

Books, Articles, and Other Publications

Almond, Gabriel A. *Comparative Politics: System, Process, and Policy.* Boston: Little, Brown, 1978.

Bagley, Bruce. "Colombia and the War on Drugs." *Foreign Affairs* 67 (1988): 70–92.

Banfield, Edward C. *Civility and Citizenship in Liberal Democratic Societies.* New York: Paragon House, 1992.

Bejarano, Ana María. "Estrategias de paz y apertura democrática: Un balance de las administraciones Betancur and Barco." In *Al filo del caos: Crisis política en la Colombia de los años 80,* edited by Francisco Leal Buitrago and León Zamosc. Bogotá: Tercer Mundo Editores, 1990.

Bejarano, Jesús Antonio. *Una agenda para la paz: Aproximaciones desde la teoría de la resolución de conflictos.* Bogotá: Tercer Mundo, 1995.

Berquist, Charles. "Introduction: Colombian Violence in Historical Perspective." In *Violence in Colombia: The Contemporary Crisis in Historical Perspective,* edited by Charles Berquist, Ricardo Peñaranda, and Gonzalo Sánchez. Wilmington, Del.: Scholarly Books, 1992.

Busnell, David. *The Making of Modern Colombia: A Nation In Spite of Itself.* Berkeley: University of California Press, 1993.

Caballero, Enrique. "Cambio de clima." *El Espectador,* July 7, 1991, p. 3A.

Camacho, Alvaro. "Public and Private Dimensions of Urban Violence in Cali." In *Violence in Colombia: The Contemporary Crisis in Historical Perspective,* edited by Charles Berquist, Ricardo Peñaranda, and Gonzalo Sánchez. Wilmington, Del.: Scholarly Books, 1992.

Child, Jorge. "¿Cuál consenso?" *El Espectador,* July 20, 1991, p. 3A.

Colmenares, Germán. *Partidos políticos y clases sociales.* Bogotá: Ediciones Universidad de los Andes, 1968.

Comisión de Estudios sobre la Violencia. *Colombia, violencia y democracia.* Bogotá: Universidad Nacional, n.d.

"Comisión intercongregacional de justicia y paz: Acta de fundación." *Justicia y Paz* 1 (1988): 1.

Cortés, Fernando. "La jugada." *La Prensa,* March 29, 1992, pp. 14–15.

———. "La paz, qué Caracas." *La Prensa,* October 6, 1991, pp. 2–3.

Cortés, Fernando, and Manuel Vicente Peña. "Vientos de guerra." *El País,* April 5, 1992, pp. 2–3.

Cortés, Fernando, and María Claudia Peña. "Así va la guerra." *La Prensa,* June 7, 1992, p. 8.

Craig, Richard B. "Domestic Implications of Illicit Drug Cultivation, Processing, and Trafficking in Colombia." Paper presented at the U.S. State Department Conference on Colombia, November 9, 1981.

Dahl, Robert. *Dilemmas of Pluralist Democracy.* New Haven: Yale University Press, 1982.

de Soto, Hernando, and Deborah Orsini. "Overcoming Under-development." *Journal of Democracy* 2 (spring 1991): 105–13.

Diamond, Larry. "Three Paradoxes of Democracy." *Journal of Democracy* 1 (summer 1990): 48–60.

Duzán, María Jimena. "Colombia's Bloody War of Words." *Journal of Democracy* 2 (winter 1991): 99–106.

En que momento se jodió Colombia. Bogotá: Editorial Oveja Negra, 1990.

Evans, Peter, Dietrich Reuschemeyer, and Theda Skocpol. "On the Road toward a More Adequate Understanding of the State." In *Bringing the State Back In,* edited by Peter Evans, Dietrich Reuschemeyer, and Theda Skocpol, 347–66. Cambridge: Cambridge University Press, 1985.

Fals Borda, Orlando. *Subversión y cambio social.* Bogotá: Ediciones Tercer Mundo, 1968.

García Durán, Mauricio. *Proceso de paz: De la Uribe a Tlaxcala.* Bogotá: CINEP, 1992.

"Gasto Social." *Coyuntura Social* 6 (June 1992): 13–20.

Geddes, Barbara. *Politician's Dilemma: Building State Capacity in Latin America.* Berkeley: University of California Press, 1994.

González González, Fernán E. "¿Hacia un 'nuevo colapso parcial del estado'? Precariedad del estado y violencia en Colombia." *Análisis Conflicto Social y Violencia en Colombia* 50 (September 1988): 5–12.

Gorriti, Gustavo. "Latin America's Internal Wars." *Journal of Democracy* 2 (winter 1991): 85–98.

Guzmán, Germán, Orlando Fals Borda, and Eduardo Umaña Luna. *La Violencia en Colombia.* Vol. 1. Bogotá: Ediciones Tercer Mundo, 1962.

Hakim, Peter, and Abraham F. Lowenthal. "Latin America's Fragile Democracies." *Journal of Democracy* 2 (summer 1991): 16–29.

Hammer, Joshua. "Colombia: 'Head Cutters' at War," *Newsweek,* June 2, 1997, pp. 42, 43.

Hartlyn, Jonathan. "Drug Trafficking and Democracy in Colombia in the 1980s." Working Paper, Institut de Ciències Polítiques i Socials, Barcelona, 1993.

———. "Interest Groups and Political Conflict in Colombia: A Retrospective and Prospective View." Paper presented at the U.S. State Department Conference on Colombia, Washington, D.C., November 9, 1981.

Hartz, Louis. *The Founding of New Societies.* New York: Harcourt, Brace & World, 1964.

Henao, José María, and Gerardo Arrubla. *Historia de Colombia.* 8th ed. Bogotá: Talleres Editoriales de la Librería Voluntad, 1967.

Huntington, Samuel P. "The Modest Meaning of Democracy." In *Democracy in the Americas: Stopping the Pendulum,* edited by Robert A. Pastor, 11–28. New York: Holmes & Meier, 1989.

———. *The Third Wave: Democraticization in the Late Twentieth Century.* Norman: University of Oklahoma Press, 1991.

Inter-American Commission on Human Rights. *Second Report on the Situation of Human Rights in Colombia.* Washington, D.C.: General Secretariat, Organization of American States, 1993.

Jaramillo, Juan Diego. "La contra reforma." *El Tiempo,* July 13, 1991, p. 5A.

Jaramillo Uribe, Jaime. "Etapas y sentido de la historia de Colombia." In *Colombia hoy,* edited by Mario Arrubla and others, 15–51. Bogotá: Siglo Veintiuno Editores, 1980.

"Justicia y violencia." *Coyuntura Social* 6 (June 1992): 38–54.

Kline, Harvey F. *Colombia: Democracy under Assault.* Boulder, Colo.: Westview Press, 1995.

———. "From Rural to Urban Society: The Transformation of Colombian Democracy." In *Democracy in Latin America: Colombia and Venezuela,* edited by Donald L. Herman, 17–46. New York: Praeger, 1988.

Kline, Harvey F., and Charity Bennett. "Colombia and Peru: Were the Political Responses to Guerrillas and Drugs Different Because the Problems Were Different or Because the Countries Were?" Paper presented at the annual meeting of the Southeast Council of Latin American Studies, San José, Costa Rica, February 1997.

Leal Buitrago, Francisco. "Defensa y seguridad nacional en Colombia, 1958–1993." In *Orden mundial y seguridad: Nuevos desafíos para Colombia y América Latina,* edited by Francisco Leal Buitrago and Juan Gabriel Tokatian, 131–72. Bogotá: Editorial Tercer Mundo, 1994.

———. *Estado y política en Colombia.* Bogotá: Siglo Veintuno, 1984.

———. Estructura y coyuntura de la crisis política. In *Al filo del caso: Crisis política en la Colombia de los años 80,* edited by Francisco Leal Buitrago and León Zamosc, 27–56. Bogotá: Tercer Mundo Editoriales, 1990.

———. "Social Classes, International Trade and Foreign Capital in Colombia: An Attempt at Historical Interpretation of the Formation of the State, 1819–1935." Ph.D. diss., University of Wisconsin, 1974.

Leal Buitrago, Francisco, and Andrés Dávila Ladrón de Guevara. *Clientelismo: El sistema político y su expresión regional.* Bogotá: Tercer Mundo Editores, 1991.

López Michelsen, Alfonso. "Del origen de la violencia en Colombia." *El Tiempo,* July 14, 1991, p. 5A.

Martínez M., Alberto. "La nueva constitución económica." *El Espectador,* June 30, 1991, p. 1B.

Martz, John D. *The Politics of Clientelism: Democracy and the State in Colombia.* New Brunswick: Transaction Publishers, 1997.

Millett, Richard L. "Is Latin American Democracy Sustainable?" *North-South Issues* 23 (1993): 1–6.

Narango, Vladimiro. "Primer vistazo a la nueva constitución (II)." *El Espectador,* July 15, 1991, p. 3A.

Needler, Martin C. *The Problem of Democracy in Latin America.* Lexington, Mass.: D.C. Heath, 1987.

Office of the Presidency, Republic of Colombia. *Realizaciones del programa de cambio: El gobierno cumple con Colombia.* Report to the National Congress, December 16, 1989.

Oquist, Paul. *Violence, Conflict, and Politics in Colombia.* New York: Academic Press, 1980.

Orjuela, Luis Javier, and Cristina Barrera P. "Narcotráfico y política en la década de los ochenta: Entre la represión y el diálogo." In *Narcotráfico en Colombia: Dimensiones políticas, económicas, jurídicas e internacionales,* edited by Carlos G. Arrieta, Luis J. Orjuela, Eduardo Sarmiento, and Juan G. Tokatlian, 203–76. Bogotá: Tercer Mundo Editores, 1989.

Phelan, John Leddy. "Authority and Flexibility in the Spanish Bureaucracy." *Administrative Science Quarterly* (June 1960): 47–65.

———. *The Kingdom of Quito in the Seventeenth Century: Bureaucratic Politics in the Spanish Empire.* Madison: The University of Wisconsin Press, 1967.

Pizarro Leongómez, Eduardo. *Las FARC: De la autodefensa a la combinación de todas las formas de lucha.* Bogotá: Tercer Mundo Editores, 1991.

———. "Revolutionary Guerrilla Groups in Colombia." In *Violence in Colombia: The Contemporary Crisis in Historical Perspective,* edited by Charles Berquist, Ricardo Peñaranda, and Gonzalo Sánchez, 169–94. Wilmington, Del.: Scholarly Resources, Inc., 1992.

Premo, Daniel L. "The Armed Forces and Colombian Politics: In Search of a Mission." Chestertown, Md.: Washington College, 1981. Mimeograph.

Presidencia de la República. *Propósitos para ponerle fin al conficto armado.* Bogotá: Presidencia de la República, 1992.

Ramírez Tobón, William. "¿Alguien quiere volver a Tlaxcala?" *Análisis Político* 16 (May–August 1992): 55–68.

"La réplica del orangután." *El Espectador,* June 20, 1991, p. 2A.

Republic of Colombia. *The Struggle against Violence and Impunity: A Democratic Commitment.* Bogotá: Office of the President, 1988.

Riding, Alan. "Cocaine Billionaires: The Men Who Hold Colombia Hostage." *New York Times Magazine,* March 8, 1987, p. 27.

Ruhl, J. Mark. "An Alternative to the Bureaucratic-Authoritarian Regime: The Case of Colombia." *Inter-American Economic Affairs* 35 (1981): 43–69.

Salazar J., Alfonso. *No nacimos pa'semilla.* Bogotá: CINEP, 1990.

Sánchez, Gonzalo. "The Violence: An Interpretive Synthesis." In *Violence in Colombia: The Contemporary Crisis in Historical Perspective,* edited by Charles Berquist, Ricardo Peñaranda, and Gonzalo Sánchez, 75–124. Wilmington, Del.: Scholarly Books, 1992.

———. "La Violencia in Colombia: New Research, New Questions." *Hispanic American Historical Review* 65 (1985).

Santa, Eduardo. *Sociología política de Colombia.* Bogotá: Ediciones Tercer Mundo, 1964.

Santamaría, Ricardo, and José Hernández. "El nuevo país ya tiene marco político." *El Tiempo,* June 30, 1991, p. 1B.

Santos Calderón, Enrique. "La nueva carta: Un reto." *El Tiempo,* July 4, 1991, p. 4A.

———. "Procurador habemus." *El Tiempo,* May 18, 1986, p. 4A.

Schmitter, Philippe C. "Military Intervention, Political Competitiveness, and Public Policy in Latin America." In *Armies and Politics in Latin America,* edited by Abraham Lowenthal, 113–69. New York: Holmes & Meier, 1976.

Schmitter, Philippe C., and Terry Lynn Karl. "What Democracy Is . . . And Is Not." *Journal of Democracy* 2 (summer 1991): 75–88.

Skocpol, Theda. "Bringing the State Back In: Strategies of Analysis in Current Research." In *Bringing the State Back In,* edited by Peter Evans, Dietrich Reuschemeyer, and Theda Skocpol, 3–37. Cambridge: Cambridge University Press, 1985.

Soto Velasco, Andrés José. "El control de las armas ligeras." In *Orden mundial y seguridad: Nuevos desafíos para Colombia y América Latina,* edited by Francisco Leal Buitrago and Juan Gabriel Tokatian, 119–30. Bogotá: Ediciones Tercer Mundo, 1994.

Thoumi, Francisco E. *Political Economy and Illegal Drugs in Colombia.* Boulder, Colo.: Lynne Rienner Publishers, 1995.

Tilly, Charles. "Reflections on the History of European State-Making." In *The Formation of National States in Western Europe,* edited by Charles Tilly, 3–83. Princeton: Princeton University Press, 1975.

———. "War Making and State Making as Organized Crime." In *Bringing the State Back In,* edited by Peter Evans, Dietrich Reuschemeyer, and

Theda Skocpol, 169–91. Cambridge: Cambridge University Press, 1985.

———. "Western State-Building and Theories of Political Transformation." In *The Formation of National States in Western Europe,* edited by Charles Tilly, 601–38. Princeton: Princeton University Press, 1975.

Torres Velasco, Javier. "La ciudadanía pacta con su policía: El proceso de modernización de la policía nacional de Colombia." In *Orden mundial y seguridad: Nuevos desafíos para Colombia y América Latina,* edited by Francisco Leal Buitrago and Juan Gabriel Tokatian, 173–205. Bogotá: Editorial Tercer Mundo, 1994.

Urrutia, Miguel. "Diversidad ideológica e integración andina." *Coyuntura Ecónomica* 10 (1980): 187–203.

Zambrano Pantoja, Fabio. "Contradicciones del sistema político Colombiano." *Análisis Conflicto Social y Violencia en Colombia* 50 (September 1988): 19–26.

Index

About the Author

Harvey F. Kline is a professor of political science and director of the Latin American Studies program at the University of Alabama. He has published four other books on Colombia politics.